US Foreign Policy in Context

This work blends strategic analysis of contemporary US foreign policy with long-term historical discussion, producing an important argument relevant to the debates surrounding both the merits of contemporary US foreign policy and the long-term trends at work in American political culture.

Rather than providing a detailed historical study of the Bush administration itself, the book seeks to locate Bush within the historical context of the US foreign policy tradition. It makes the case for nationally specific ideological factors as a driver of foreign policy and for the importance of interaction between the domestic and the international in the emergence of national strategy.

The contemporary element focuses on critiquing the George W. Bush administration's National Security Strategy, perceived by many as a radical and unwelcome ideological departure from past policy, and its broader foreign policy, concentrating especially on its embrace of liberal universalism and rejection of realism. This critique is supported by an argument, based upon historical cases, seeking to explain American leaders' persistent resistance to the prescriptions of realism. Quinn argues for some causal connection between historically evolved ideological constructions and the character of the nation's more recent international strategy.

Providing a valuable addition to the field, this book will be of great interest to scholars in American politics, US foreign policy and US history.

Adam Quinn is a Lecturer in the Department of Political Science and International Studies at the University of Birmingham. He has previously published articles in *International Studies Perspectives*, *Politics & Policy* and *Global Society*.

Routledge Studies in US Foreign Policy
Edited by: Inderjeet Parmar, University of Manchester and John Dumbrell, University of Durham

This new series sets out to publish high quality works by leading and emerging scholars critically engaging with United States Foreign Policy. The series welcomes a variety of approaches to the subject and draws on scholarship from international relations, security studies, international political economy, foreign policy analysis and contemporary international history.

Subjects covered include the role of administrations and institutions, the media, think tanks, ideologues and intellectuals, elites, transnational corporations, public opinion, and pressure groups in shaping foreign policy, US relations with individual nations, with global regions and global institutions and America's evolving strategic and military policies.

The series aims to provide a range of books – from individual research monographs and edited collections to textbooks and supplemental reading for scholars, researchers, policy analysts, and students.

United States Foreign Policy and National Identity in the 21st Century
Edited by Kenneth Christie

New Directions in US Foreign Policy
Edited by Inderjeet Parmar, Linda B. Miller and Mark Ledwidge

America's 'Special Relationships'
Foreign and domestic aspects of the politics of alliance
Edited by John Dumbrell and Axel R. Schäfer

US Foreign Policy in Context
National ideology from the Founders to the Bush Doctrine
Adam Quinn

US Foreign Policy in Context
National ideology from the Founders to the Bush Doctrine

Adam Quinn

LONDON AND NEW YORK

First published 2010
by Routledge
2 Park Square, Milton Park, Abingdon, Oxfordshire OX14 4RN

Simultaneously published in the USA and Canada
by Routledge
711 Third Avenue, New York, NY 10017

Routledge is an imprint of the Taylor & Francis Group, an informa business

First issued in paperback 2011

© 2010 Adam Quinn

Typeset in Times New Roman by Taylor & Francis Books

All rights reserved. No part of this book may be reprinted or reproduced or utilized in any form or by any electronic, mechanical, or other means, now known or hereafter invented, including photocopying and recording, or in any information storage or retrieval system, without permission in writing from the publishers.

British Library Cataloguing in Publication Data
A catalogue record for this book is available from the British Library

Library of Congress Cataloging in Publication Data
Quinn, Adam.
  US foreign policy in context : national ideology from the founders to the Bush doctrine / Adam Quinn.
    p. cm. – (Routledge studies in US foreign policy)
  Includes bibliographical references.
  United States – Foreign relations. I. Title.
  E183.7.Q56 2009
  327.73 – dc22
                                                                    2009017000

ISBN13: 978-0-415-54965-3 (hbk)
ISBN13: 978-0-415-50052-4 (pbk)
ISBN13: 978-0-203-86767-9 (ebk)

Contents

	Acknowledgements	viii
1	Introduction	1
2	International relations, history and national ideology	10

Introduction 10
Positioning within IR and American history 10
Defining 'ideology' 22
Continuity and change in national ideology 24
The relationship of national ideas and national circumstances, and the relevance of history 25
The usefulness of public statements as evidence 27
Conclusion 29

3 The Founders' Era consensus: 'A Hercules in the cradle'   31
Introduction 31
National and international context 33
The Union as a means of excluding the balance-of-power system 36
Trapped between titans: a divided America's vulnerability to European power politics 41
The Farewell Address and the emergence of the non-alignment consensus 49
Consensus emerges: Jefferson's embrace of Washington's doctrine 52
'Our hemisphere ... of freedom': the Monroe Doctrine as a logical extension of the Founders' Era consensus 55
Conclusion 59

4 Theodore Roosevelt: 'The nation that has dared to be great'   61
Introduction 61
National and international context 63
The 'strenuous life' and the pursuit of national greatness 64
Military strength, restraint and the 'soldierly virtues' 67

Realism in Roosevelt   69
Moralism in Roosevelt   71
The 'Roosevelt Corollary' and American quasi-imperialism   74
The First World War, progress and the moral case for arms   78
Conclusion   83

5   Woodrow Wilson: 'Conquest of the spirits of men'   86

Introduction   86
National and international context   87
Moralism and idealism in Wilsonian foreign policy   88
The expanded Monroe Doctrine as prototype of global Wilsonianism   90
Wilson's justification of war entry and European entanglement   94
Conditional US engagement and the abolition of the balance of power   96
Interests, peoples and international cooperation   100
Universal liberal democracy as a necessary condition of Wilsonian order   102
'Leader and umpire both': American primacy and destiny   105
Wilson's divergence from Roosevelt: 'moral force' and the role of arms   108
Mortality, personal and political   109
Conclusion   111

6   The Truman administration: 'In the struggle for men's minds, the conflict is world-wide'   114

Introduction   114
National and international context   115
From 'one world' to 'two ways of life': Truman's inheritance and the deterioration of US–Soviet relations   116
Truman's conception of the Cold War   119
George Kennan and the sources of Soviet conduct   126
Polarization and militarization: the Clifford–Elsey Report and NSC-68   130
Conclusion   137

7   The George W. Bush administration: 'A balance of power that favours freedom'   139

Introduction   139
National and international context   140
'A balance of power that favours freedom': the National Security Strategy   141
'Universal, human hopes': the universal legitimacy of liberal values   143

*Democratic peace: 'This advance of freedom will bring greater
   security'* 146
'Common interests and ... common values' 150
Peoples and governments 153
The dynamic of historical inevitability 154
*'Military forces that are beyond challenge': hegemonic US hard
   power* 156
Critiques of Bush 157
*The road not taken: ideological choice and the Bush
   administration* 159
Conclusion 164

8 Conclusion: the Bush strategy and national ideology   166

   The historical evolution of American internationalism 167
   *The influence of national ideological history on the Bush
      worldview* 173

Notes   *176*
Bibliography   *202*
Index   *213*

Acknowledgements

It is said that success has many fathers, but failure is an orphan. In that case it is hopefully a good omen that there are so many others for me to thank for making this book possible. On the surface, the categories to be thanked divide into the personal and the professional, though such is the nature of the writing process that this line is far less bright and clear in real life than on paper. The book began as a PhD thesis, and therefore the first and greatest thanks must go to my supervisor and mentor at the London School of Economics, Michael Cox. Apart from the essential assistance he provided in the development and completion of the research project itself, he was also a source of good example and sound advice as I negotiated for the first time the occasionally treacherous waters of academic life more generally. For the role he played in my introduction to a new world, I will always be grateful. Prominent thanks must also go to my examiners, Inderjeet Parmar and Timothy Lynch. Apart from enabling the examination itself to be as enjoyable as such an event can be, their intelligent engagement with the thesis was extremely useful in getting me started with the process of revising it into book form. Thanks again to Inderjeet, and to his co-editor on this book series, John Dumbrell, for their interest in and encouragement of the development of this book from that thesis. Multiplying the numbers considerably, I must thank the great many colleagues who entered the Department of International Relations at LSE with me all those years ago, or followed me through the door not long thereafter, and who were an invaluable source of insight, warmth and wit over the course of my studies. For their willingness to share ideas, offer solidarity through the occasional tough times, and laugh at my jokes more regularly than I imagine they deserved, I thank them, especially (in alphabetical order): Kirsten Ainley, Karen Barnes, Felix Berenskoetter, Chris Berzins, Annika Bolten, Ben Buley, Douglas Bulloch, Stephanie Carvin, Stacy Closson, Patrick Cullen, Alexandra Dias, Bastian Giegerich, Eva Gross, Robert Kissack, Marjo Koivisto, Chris Mackmurdo, Tim Oliver, Sinikukka Saari, Rashmi Singh, Jill Stuart, Marco Vieira, Bill Vlcek and Page Wilson. Finally in this category I must extend a sizeable chunk of gratitude to Nicola Parkin at Routledge, the editorial assistant who was willing to field the numerous queries of an anxious first-time author with efficiency and good grace.

First and foremost on the home front, I must thank my parents, Jim and Margaret Quinn, without whose crucial support – financial and otherwise – it would not have been possible to begin the PhD research that ultimately metamorphosed into this book, or to see it through to completion. Thanks also to the rest of my family, especially my grandmother, Catherine Quinn, and my uncle, David Langan. In their own ways, they all chipped in to the dubious cause of making me what I am today. Finally, there is my adoptive godfather Kingsley Dempsey, without whom there would have been far fewer extended dinners, bottles of Châteauneuf-du-Pape and off-colour imperialist jokes over the years in which this book was written. For his *joie de vivre* and for his boundless generosity I am not alone in owing him the sincerest thanks.

The research comprising this book was funded in part by LSE Research Studentships and by teaching at that institution's departments of International Relations and International History. In that time I was also employed in various capacities by the universities of Westminster, Birmingham and Leicester, before ending up back at Birmingham, where happily I now work as a lecturer. Without all these sources of income, the numbers simply would not have added up. I only hope I gave good value in return.

Lastly, I would like to thank all those scholars, too numerous to name individually, who inspired, assisted and entertained me, either in person or from afar, over the course of my research. Most of those who agreed to talk to me were busy men and women who had no need to see me, and in some cases may well now have forgotten that they ever did. I remember their contributions to my cause, large and small, and will remain ever appreciative. Such errors as are contained in this book – I wish there were few but suspect there may be many – are of course entirely my own.

Permissions

Thank you to the University Press of the Pacific for their kind grant of permission to use the material from the papers of Woodrow Wilson liberally quoted in Chapter 5.

1 Introduction

The notion that their national history might be important is unlikely to shock many Americans, despite the habitual perception of their nation as a 'young' country. In addition to having, in fact, been around for rather a long time by the standards of states – besting the claims of Germany, Italy and a good many others in the Old World to longevity – the United States has also tended to be a rather self-conscious polity when it comes to history. This does not, of course, imply that the majority of Americans know all there is worth knowing about their nation's past; few professional historians could make that daring claim of themselves. But the American people's acquiescence in – indeed implicit demand for – their leaders' daily invocation of tradition and shared values, and their fervent attachment to the symbols and institutions of their system of government, reflect a deep commitment to the idea that the shared story of the national past matters a great deal. More mundanely, American bookshops' brisk and apparently perennial trade in the biographies of long-departed statesmen reflects an interest in dead presidents that stretches far beyond the merely pecuniary.

The central purpose of this volume will therefore make intuitive sense to most readers. That purpose is to combine elements of the disciplines of international relations and history in the hope of saying something worthwhile about why America is the way it is. Its challenge is to say something useful to scholars belonging to the former tribe without doing undue violence to the more particularistic sensibilities of the latter. The broad focus of the book, as the title makes plain, is US foreign policy. More specifically, it is the strategic visions or 'worldviews' constructed by certain US statesmen concerning the nature of the international system and America's role within it. To sum things up in a sentence, the book seeks to argue for some causal connection between these historically evolved ideological constructions and the character of the nation's more recent international strategy. For the sake of simplicity in labelling, it terms this the 'national ideology' approach to explaining foreign policy, though it has features in common with established approaches, as the next chapter sets out.

The research culminating in this book was first motivated by a striking contrast, as this author saw it, between the language used to craft the central concept of the 2002 National Security Strategy (NSS) and the reality of its underlying ideological assumptions.[1] The conceptual centrepiece of George W. Bush's first NSS was the proclaimed aspiration to create 'a balance of power that favours freedom', thus apparently invoking one of the favoured concepts of the realist school of thought, the pursuit of a 'balance of power'. Yet on analysis the document declined to embrace the assumptions upon which an understanding of order based on power balancing should rest, and spurned realism as a guiding mindset.

Unlike realism, it did not base its analysis of America's international situation upon the assumption of inherent conflict between the national interests of rival great powers. On the contrary, it supposed that unprecedented scope existed for a comprehensive alliance of all the world's major powers on a single 'side'. This vision of a thoroughly *im*balanced distribution of power was premised upon the historically inevitable triumph of a set of idealized liberal values with which the United States identifies itself.[2] This prospective universalization of American principles – or, as believers in the theory would have it, the realization in the concrete of universally valid principles – would lay the ground for peaceful concert between all powers. In contrast to realistic approaches, the strategy did not allow for the existence of material counterweights to American power in the international system. Rather, it assumed the existence of an unchallengeable American hegemony in terms of military capacity and supported its entrenchment as the basis of world order for the indefinite future. For these reasons, though it centred on a piece of terminology creatively appropriated from the lexicon of realism, the NSS did not reflect any genuine embrace of realist principles on the part of administration. It embodied their utter rejection.

Based upon this initial analysis, further questions occurred: Was this intellectual tendency a peculiarity of the moment, or was the rejection of balance-of-power thinking about international order an identifiable feature of American history over the longer term? Was President Bush's administration aberrant in adopting this strategic perspective, or was such thinking a recurring characteristic of American leaders' strategic worldview? And if the latter were true, might closer study of America's history shed light on the origins of this national characteristic?

Efforts to address these questions lead one swiftly into an area of long-standing debate within the study of US foreign policy. The classical realist school of thought, including among its notables George Kennan, Hans Morgenthau and Henry Kissinger, has argued since the end of the Second World War that 'unrealistic' thinking has been a relatively consistent feature of American foreign policy.[3] By this they mean that American leaders have been unwilling or unable to see with due clarity that the basis of international relations lies in state power and national interest, displaying instead a preference for what Kennan termed a 'legalistic-moralistic' mindset with inadequate grounding in reality. More recently, neoclassical realists have reprised the spirit of this analysis, arguing that ideological choices to pursue liberal universalist goals have led to repeated mismatches between American aspirations and available resources.[4]

With this impressive tradition of political and social critique as prologue, the aim of this book is to present a historical analysis of American foreign policy's long-term evolution that contributes some supporting evidence to the realist critique while also adding a little causal theorising of its own. As will become evident during the chapters which follow, realists are correct in noting that the mindset displayed in the Bush administration's strategic perspective is far from anomalous, but rather is the recurrence – admittedly in strong form – of impulses already apparent throughout much of US foreign policy's recent past. In arriving at this conclusion, those chapters also find support in American history for classical realism's suggestion – reinforced by more recent constructivist analysis – that 'ideology', broadly defined, can play a significant role in determining how a nation conceives its national interests and international role. They describe in some detail the ideological paradigms constructed by leading American statesmen at key moments in the nation's history, and explore the process by which that ideology has evolved during America's globe-shaping transition from hemispheric separatism to global internationalism.

Finally, the book suggests that these findings might form the basis of a partial causal explanation for reflexive American resistance to balance-of-power thinking. This explanation combines the realist assumption that material and external circumstances have a crucial role to play in shaping national policy with the parallel principle that ideological convictions, once formed, shape and constrain subsequent strategic choices, even when the national circumstances that first spawned them may have moved on. More specifically with regard to the case under study, it argues that while the national strategy created in the early decades of US independence may have been based on the particular circumstances prevailing at that time, it was ideologically constructed in a way that influenced the foundation on which America's twentieth-century internationalism was subsequently established.

In seeking to formulate this argument, the book necessarily provides a significant amount of historical narrative, though this is not its chief objective. More importantly, it aims to isolate for analysis the most crucial of the ideological principles that certain American statesmen constructed and deployed in advocacy of their favoured strategic courses during those key periods selected for study. The chief object upon which the analysis trains its intellectual sights is thus 'ideology', meaning in this instance the intellectual simplifications leaders use to explain and justify the national courses they advocate, both to others and to themselves. In choosing this focus, the book's central argument tacitly embraces the idea that states can have a 'national culture' or 'national character' when it comes to foreign policy making. This implies that the way to fully understand the behaviour of the United States in the international arena is not exclusively through the study of states as a general category and/or the international system, but also through detailed study of the formative influences operative upon the United States in particular.

The specific periods selected for attention were chosen because they present key moments of simultaneous change in US foreign policy thinking and the structure of the international order. During the first period discussed, the Founders' Era, the newly established nation was obliged to construct a foundational foreign policy strategy, while at the same time the international system was shaken by the colonies' success in breaking away from Britain and by the extensive wars arising from the French Revolution. The pair of chapters that follow, which discuss Theodore Roosevelt and Woodrow Wilson respectively, survey the early twentieth-century period from the perspectives of two actors whose different but overlapping worldviews laid the foundations for a new global engagement on the part of the US. This was a key period of change because the United States, vastly grown in power since its foundation, made its first serious moves into the global political arena through imperial acquisitions, a deepening of the Monroe Doctrine, greater involvement in intercontinental diplomacy, and ultimately military engagement on European soil. Meanwhile, the international order was thrown into flux by the outbreak and conduct of the Great War. Similar features were present in the fourth period covered, the administration of Harry Truman (1945–53). During these years the United States made the transition in a more conclusive and lasting sense to a globally entangled grand strategy supported by heavy military investment. At the same time the international order was redefined by the outcome of the Second World War as a bipolar contest between superpowers, one of them the United States.

It in order to avoid disappointing readers – or perhaps merely to disappoint them pre-emptively – it is important to state openly at the outset three things that this book does not attempt to do. First, it does not set out to be anything approaching a comprehensive survey of US foreign policy since independence, and consequently there are several interesting periods in America's journey since 1783 that are left unattended. This is partly for the obvious reason that space is limited. But it is also because, whatever their historical interest, it is contended that other periods do not qualify as key periods of change in the sense defined above. Those periods that have been chosen bore witness both to profound change in the international order and to related change, with significant lasting effect, in US strategic thinking. Other periods cannot claim this to the same degree. To take one example, the Nixon administration, under the influence of Kissinger, made a conscious effort to shift the ideological basis of US policy towards a more realist footing. Yet it is difficult to argue that it succeeded in leaving a lasting legacy to that effect, or that the international system was comparably transformed during that period, even with all appropriate recognition accorded to the significance of the diplomatic opening of China. It would be more accurate to say the period was one of policy variation constrained within the overarching framework set by the Cold War and Truman's Containment strategy.

Second, the thesis on which this book rests is emphatically not that only one single, uniform set of ideas has existed in regard to foreign policy making throughout all US history. The American policy discourse has given air at various times to ideas quite contrary to those set out in any of the worldviews discussed here, i.e. Bush's National Security Strategy, Wilsonian internationalism, Rooseveltian imperialism and the Truman Doctrine. Indeed, those four philosophies are themselves distinct from one another in important ways. To argue that realism has played no part in US policy debates, or that it has had no influence on policy itself, would be quite wrong. The pre-eminent realist thinkers named above were, if not all Americans by birth, at least vocal and influential residents of the United States. This book does not attempt, as would be wholly wrong headed, to deny the existence of the realist contribution to the American discourse. It merely seeks to argue that over the long term other, contrary, ideological principles have carried far more weight in determining US grand strategy. This is, it should be noted, a point that most realists themselves accept; indeed it is a pillar of their own critique of American political culture.

Third, although superficially it may appear to build a case for long-term continuity, the argument presented by this book is in fact about both change *and* continuity. It does not make the simplistic argument that the foreign policy of Bush was 'the same' as that of Truman or Wilson any more than it seeks to argue that Wilson or Roosevelt mimicked the ideas of the Founding Fathers. Each of these leaders, or groups of leaders, was faced with their own quite different circumstance in regard to national capabilities and international circumstances when formulating their policies. Each felt it necessary to seek to significantly alter the foreign policy ideas prevalent in America at the time of their arrival in power in order to better meet the demands of the nation's situation. What this book argues is that these leaders fashioned ways forward that reflected not purely the demands of circumstance but also ideological constraints with their origins in the nation's prior history. Each period saw not the simple continuity of the previously prevailing ideology under new circumstances, but significant shifts in the prevailing ideology. But in each case, the ideological paradigm that emerged was shaped by what had gone before, and the resultant policy reflected the obligation of leaders – unable to begin with a blank slate – to work with an evolving body of ideological principle inherited from the national past.

The book's historical account begins in the period I have labelled the Founders' Era, stretching from American independence to, approximately, the proclamation of the Monroe Doctrine in 1823. In terms of sheer volume of output, this is a neglected period in international relations literature concerning the United States, almost all of which focuses on the twentieth century and later. But starting in this period is essential, because it is here that the first link in the causal chain portrayed by the book as a whole is to be found. In this period, the founding generation of American leaders sought to fashion a worldview designed to fit with both the material power capabilities of the nation and the imperatives and opportunities presented by the international environment. In settling upon the strategic perspective that they ultimately did, they constructed ideological principles that would subsequently serve as a source of constraint upon later leaders, requiring them to tailor justifications for their strategic choices that could sustain a feeling of compatibility with the established and venerated principles of the founders.

In the 1780s, it was in great part the desire to avoid replicating the European 'balance of power' system, and the wish to minimize foreign interference in North America, that led to the establishment of the USA under a new constitution. The establishment of the new nation was then followed by commitment to a policy of detached non-alignment in all political and military matters pertaining to the rival European powers. This policy was then expanded into the Monroe Doctrine, essentially a spheres-of-influence paradigm which held that Europe and the United States should mutually refrain from interference within one another's exclusive domains.

These strategic decisions make ample sense when analysed in realist terms: they reflect the pursuit of a solid strategy of national interest based upon a gradually expanding US level of power, wealth and territory. On the level of ideological construction, however, the strategy went beyond a simple plan for pursuit of the narrow national interest. The strategic consensus forged in the Founders' Era, after a period of acrimonious disagreement, had an ideological dimension asserting that the United States existed in a separate sphere of interests and a superior sphere of values from Europe. In effect, the nation crafted a self-image of itself existing not as a member of or component within the Europe-centred global system based on the balance of power, but entirely apart from that system. Thus detached from the European state system, allegedly without the need to engage in power balancing, the United States could, in its leaders' minds, limit its international role to one of benign hegemonic pre-eminence within the American hemisphere, and freedom from all ties beyond that. By virtue of its 'American' qualities, this cut-out portion of the international system could exist in a more peaceful order than that the Europeans had made for themselves. America's non-alignment was thus based not only on a narrow construction of the national interest defined in terms of material advantage, but upon an ideological conception of America's moral and strategic 'separateness' from the European balance of power, a degenerate Old World basis for order.

The international realities that led to the creation of this strategic paradigm steadily shifted as the size and power of the United States grew and events elsewhere in the international system altered the global strategic balance. Yet the ideological principles created to justify the original American strategic consensus represented a part of the intellectual and political reality facing US leaders when the arrival of the twentieth century brought imperatives for change to a more globally engaged posture. That change thus had to be tailored ideologically to make it compatible with the bedrock principles of the preceding century's strategic consensus, still perceived in the political culture as both prudent and morally correct. This requirement for ideological tailoring had implications in turn for the policies pursued and the manner in which they were presented.

The next chapter, Chapter 4, focuses on the contribution of Theodore Roosevelt. Coming to the presidency immediately after a brief surge in imperialist sentiment during and after the Spanish–American War of 1898, Roosevelt strove determinedly to move the nation towards a more internationally engaged mindset. Proclaiming the interventionist Roosevelt Corollary to the Monroe Doctrine in Latin America, he provided an ideological basis for a much deeper political and economic penetration of that region by the United States, justified by reference not merely to US interests but also to a quasi-imperialistic notion of 'common interests' and the spread of 'civilized' values. With his tireless thumping of the martial drum, Roosevelt also made some progress in convincing Americans of the necessity and virtue of military strength in spite of their historical scepticism of peacetime military investment.

In addition, through engagement with great-power diplomacy and conflict resolution in East Asia and Africa, Roosevelt began the erosion of American taboos prohibiting 'entanglement' in European nations' political–military affairs. He was constrained from going as far as he might have wished by the residual strength of the Founders' Era consensus, but he nevertheless outlined from the bully pulpit of the presidency a perspective on international affairs that embraced interventionism, militarism and a sense of progressive, moralistic and historic mission. He thus sketched for the American people a quasi-imperial worldview that would have an important impact both in his own time and later, after the Second World War. This chapter argues that these aspects of Roosevelt's thought, sometimes seen as an icon of realism in the realm of foreign policy, must to some extent qualify such a reading of his character and significance.

Chapter 5 addresses Woodrow Wilson and 'Wilsonianism', the ideological perspective that bears his name. As president, Wilson broadened and escalated the 'civilizing' interventionism Roosevelt had initiated in Latin America. More significantly for global order, he was also enabled by extraordinary international upheaval to be bolder in his efforts to remould international order and America's thinking about its role within it. With the destruction of Europe's old order during the First World War, Wilson became convinced that America could lead the way in building a 'new world order' founded on universal cooperation and collective security. His confidence that this would be possible stemmed, significantly, from a conviction that history had dictated the universal success of liberty and democracy as the guiding model for the world's nations, thus placing their 'peoples' – assumed to be essentially Wilsonian in their instincts – in command of their governments.

Conscious of the ideological legacy of detachment needing to be overcome in order to establish a new American internationalism, Wilson massaged the ideological debate to make it appear, at least on the level of abstractions, that

8 *Introduction*

the US need not join the world order as it had ever previously existed. Rather, as he made the case, a sort of deal was on the table: a new American global engagement should occur, but on the condition that the old 'balance of power' basis for order should be abolished. It would be replaced by an essentially cooperative 'community of power', predicated on the spread of core American values and practices. In making American internationalism contingent on the pursuit of this ideologically liberal 'deal', Wilsonianism had a profound and lasting effect on the character of American engagement with the world. That being the case, it is important to note that one of the key drivers behind the formulation of Wilsonian ideology was the need to negotiate a way past the established ideology of hemispheric separatism crafted by the Founders over than a century earlier.

Chapter 6 covers the early Cold War, specifically the Truman administration. This is an interesting case because, to some eyes, the entire Cold War would appear to be a counterpoint to Wilsonianism, a period in which a balance of power clearly *was* pursued by US leaders. While acknowledging the emergence in material terms of a kind of balance, the chapter argues that this was not the product of any acceptance by American leaders of legitimate countervailing interests on the part of the Soviet Union, but simply the result of hard practical constraints on America's power. The Truman administration buttressed its strategic posture with an ideological paradigm that, in spite of the de facto balance of power that resulted from containment, was profoundly universalistic, albeit temporarily frustrated in its aspirations. In contrast to some contemporaries who leaned towards a more 'realistic' balance-of-power approach, Truman crafted a worldview that treated the Soviet Union not as a legitimate rival power with its own national interests but as an ideologically illegitimate obstacle to the attainment of the universal peaceful order projected by Wilsonianism. Reprising Wilsonian articles of faith regarding the directionality of history, the Truman administration conceived of and portrayed the Cold War as a global conflict between ideals and systems of government that could only be ended by the capitulation or conversion of the adversary. Even George Kennan, the realist-in-residence of the administration, implicitly endorsed this strategy in his most notable writings of this period.[5]

Diverging from Wilsonsianism's faith in the power of moral force in the international community, however, the Truman administration also reprised Rooseveltian principles regarding the importance of placing military might behind moral conviction, thus enabling the pursuit of the Wilsonian 'deal' partly through the erection of a titanic new national security apparatus. This fusion of Wilsonian ideas concerning the pursuit of what Wilson called the 'dominion of right', i.e. a cooperative world order based on US leadership and universal liberal democracy, with Rooseveltian willingness to embrace the moral righteousness of preparatory militarization, represented a decisive moment in the evolution of US strategy. As the Cold War progressed, Truman himself became a symbol representing this mixture of idealism and hard power, regarded as the ideological model for subsequent administrations.

Introduction 9

By opting to pursue this approach towards post-war order, the US altered its own future and that of the world significantly, and entrenched the national inclination to resist conscious realism and balance-of-power thinking.

Drawing the historical material together in order to illustrate its relevance, the final historical chapter, Chapter 7, concentrates on the administration of George W. Bush (2001–9). There is particular emphasis here on the National Security Strategy, but also extensive reference to other important foreign policy speeches and pronouncements. This chapter aims to illustrate the ways in which the choices made by US leaders at the key historical moments outlined in the chapters gone before, influenced by national and international context, were critical in the evolution of a particular kind of American internationalism, embodied in somewhat extreme form by Bush. In effect, the chapter argues that Bush's core principles, most notably universalism, resistance to 'balance-of-power' thinking, and presupposition of the feasibility and virtue of US hegemony, were a recognizable ideological product of the particular way in which US internationalism had evolved.

The final chapter then draws the overarching argument of the book to a conclusion, demonstrating, it is hoped, the cohesion of the long-term historical account offered by the work as a whole. This book serves to illustrate the way in which, at successive stages, each building on what went before, a series of identifiable ideological 'moves' led America from its foundation to its early twenty-first-century posture. In doing this, it does not wish to convey the impression of believing that the Bush administration's philosophy of international affairs, which many found so traumatic, somehow represented the fulfilment of America's political destiny. It certainly does not intend to suggest that the members of that administration might justify its actions and attitudes in retrospect by reference to some teleological reading of the American national journey. Its aim is simply to place the recently departed administration in its proper context, enabling better understanding of the role of national history in shaping its ideological perspective. Without such a contextual understanding of the depth of its origins, there is a considerable danger of underestimating the magnitude of the task involved in changing the prevailing American approach to foreign policy, which is the outcome that many have hoped for from a change of government. It is not impossible for a nation to fundamentally alter its worldview, any more than it is impossible for an individual man or woman to truly change. But it is rare, it is never easy, and the consequences can never be known in advance.

2 International relations, history and national ideology

Introduction

As explained in the introductory chapter, this book aims to draw together the disciplines of international relations (IR) and history in productive synthesis in what it terms the 'national ideology' approach to the study of US foreign policy. Pursuit of this objective locates it within two vast, occasionally overlapping literatures, exhaustive surveys of which would be unfeasible, unnecessary and – from the reader's perspective – undesirable. That fact notwithstanding, it is appropriate to attempt at the outset a concise explanation of how what follows connects with the broad conceptual frameworks provided by the existing disciplines. The IR and history literatures have often proceeded on parallel tracks, even though they draw on the same core of factual information, albeit at different levels of depth.[1] This chapter seeks, where it can, to draw connections between the two, providing in the process an account of where the national ideology approach most comfortably sits amid the schools of thought used to subdivide the field. In so doing, it seeks not, unless absolutely necessary, to 'pick sides' in the major intra-disciplinary debates, but rather to show that the argument around which the book is constructed is ultimately reconcilable with several of the major analytical schools.

The later sections of the chapter engage with some of the philosophical and methodological issues arising from the approach's focus on the interrelation of ideology and national interests and the role of national history in shaping strategic choice. The purpose of these sections is to render the approach's deeper philosophical assumptions more explicit, complementing some of the conceptual clarification that has gone before. In this part of the chapter, the key concept of 'ideology' is defined, the case is made for studying of ideological change over time, and some methodological implications of this choice of topic are placed in the open.

Positioning within IR and American history

Realism

Because the idea of balance-of-power thinking features prominently in the book's argument, the realist school, which gives significant attention to that concept, is a good place to begin contextualizing it. A common feature of all realist theories is concern with the nation-state and its efforts to obtain relative power – for motives that vary depending on the strain of realism – and the intended and unintended consequences of that quest. Beyond this commonality, there are numerous subdivisions within the realist camp, most significantly that between the neo- or structural realist approach and the older, 'classical' version. The structural approach, because considered more scientific in formulation, has been more prominent in the discipline in recent decades. Advanced with greatest popular attention by Waltz, it takes the international system as its level of analysis and defines it as an anarchical environment in which states seek security first and foremost.[2] It goes on to explain state behaviour by reference to the imperatives of that pursuit. The key variable in this explanatory framework is the distribution of power in the international system, changes in which are used to explain shifts in state alignment.

Within this version of the realist framework, the 'balance of power' is understood as an automatically operative mechanism within the international system. As material power shifts in the system, states react in such a way as to maximize their security, using alliances to balance against any power that becomes too strong. A state that accrues much more power than its rivals will tend to overreach, due to the lack of externally imposed limits on its behaviour, incentivising balancing trends among others that ultimately restore equilibrium. A 'balance of power', therefore, is thought to emerge from the aggregate of state behaviour in much the same way that market equilibrium emerges under classical economics: not as the product of conscious design on the part of the actors, but as the system-level consequence of decisions made at the unit level in response to private motives.

Others have followed Waltz in offering such a structural account, though disagreeing as to whether 'balancing' behaviour is inevitable.[3] Mearsheimer is the best known of the post-Waltz generation of structural realists, though his account emphasizes a more 'offensive' quality to states' pursuit of security than Waltz's 'defensive' reading.[4] These disputes are secondary, however, to the fundamental emphasis on material capabilities, and conception of the 'balance of power' as an impersonal, non-consciously emergent phenomenon.

The classical realist school, though claiming a lineage stretching to Thucydides, is best known to students of US foreign policy through twentieth-century authors such as Morgenthau, Kennan and Kissinger.[5] Such realists engage in what Waltz, in his well-known distinction, terms 'theories of foreign policy', i.e. those seeking to explain the behaviour of particular states, as well as theories of international relations, i.e. those which stick to explaining the operation of all or part of the international system. In pursuit of this objective, classical realists have been more open to explanations of state action that include domestic political factors and to acknowledging the scope for choice and contingency in states' actions. Classical realism does share with the structural variant some effort to identify universal patterns in state behaviour:

it argues, for instance, that as a state's material capabilities grow, its definition of its national interests broadens, along with the scope of its foreign policy actions.[6] But it concerns itself with the role of national politics in shaping particular cases in a way that is largely absent from the system-level analyses of structural realism.[7] Building in some of the more technical vocabulary of modern theory, neoclassical realism has emerged as a revised variant in recent years, using the central principles of classical realism to make a contribution to the contemporary debate.[8]

For classical and neoclassical realist thinkers, the 'balance of power' is not something that emerges spontaneously from states' actions. Rather, states must pursue such a balance as a conscious policy objective in order to attain international stability. States are aided in this quest if they share a core of basic values sufficient to ensure acceptance of one another's legitimacy, and if they are prepared to actively coordinate their policies in pursuit of the objective of stable balance.[9] For these realists, attaining a balance of power requires national leaders to show enlightened restraint in the pursuit of national interests. To be sustainable, an order must offer all its members a sufficient stake to justify their acceptance of the fundamental rules of the status quo. If states do not show the requisite restraint, pursuing instead utopian and universalist objectives, the balance becomes destabilized and war results.

While the classical realist school's *raison d'être* is to argue for the existence of 'reality-based' limits on a state's potential achievements through foreign policy, it does not predict that a stable balance is sure to emerge at the system level from any given scenario, or that balance is the natural condition of international affairs. Indeed, its analysis makes central the idea that national leaders may harm their own interests by their failure to appreciate the limits circumstance places upon them by external reality. Classical realism perceives two major interconnected threats to a successful foreign policy: overreach and idealism. Overreach occurs when national leaders pursue objectives which are unattainable, given the means available, or at least given the means they are in truth prepared to devote to the projects in question.[10] Idealism becomes a problem when leaders do not appreciate that the sole currency of international relations is power, and mistakenly believe that they can advance their objectives by recourse to legal or moral reasoning alone.[11]

The classical realism of IR is intimately linked with the study of history. Indeed, writers such as Kissinger and Kennan aimed to produce works with historical weight as well as contemporary policy relevance. 'Realism' as an interpretive framework has also played a role in the writings of scholars more unequivocally designated as historians, for example in the study of the early Cold War.[12] John Lewis Gaddis, for instance – at least in his post-revisionist period before converting to so-called 'neo-orthodoxy' – wrote the history of US policy with emphasis on realist concerns: the balance of material capabilities, a security dilemma between the superpowers, political expansionism on each side in defining the scope of their interests, and the unintended quality of the Cold War's emergence.[13]

A national ideology approach shares several features with the classical and neoclassical realist approaches. First, it is concerned with foreign policy at the national level rather than merely with international relations at the system level. Second, it concurs that rising material power on the part of the United States was a key driver behind a broadening of its conception of its interests over the span of the period covered. Third, classical and neoclassical realism accept that there is a role for contingency in foreign policy making, and thus are interested in the nationally specific political and cultural forces at work within a given state. Dueck, for instance, argues that the United States could have chosen a number of different courses at various points in the evolution of its foreign policy, but chose the course most compatible with its embedded political culture. This is an argument with which this book agrees, and to which it seeks to lend evidential support. Fourth – a related point – classical and neoclassical realism propose that a balance of power is not a spontaneous systemic phenomenon, but something states need to consciously seek. States, therefore, can adopt 'balance-of-power thinking' as a strategic state of mind – or not. This book argues that American leaders have resisted thinking about international order within the 'balance-of-power' framework prescribed by realists because established ideological considerations draw policy makers away from that mode of thinking. This is an argument that fits with the bulk of classical realist analysis.

The national ideology approach holds back from itself being part of the traditional realist school on a couple of grounds. First, it remains agnostic regarding the normative and prudential prescriptions that realism uses its analysis of history to justify. It does not deconstruct the consequences of the policies it describes or scrutinize counterfactuals to the extent that would be required to build a persuasive argument that an alternative, realist course would be more successful. Classical realism is, at core, an 'error theory' of US foreign policy, arguing that policy has mostly been misconceived and should be reoriented in line with realistic principles. This book, while laying bare the troubling assumptions of the liberal universalist mindset, does not stretch to making that claim. Second, a core conviction of realism has tended to be the argument that the pursuit of 'ideological' objectives leads nations, in this instance the United States, to damage and frustrate their own national interests. Such an argument seems to attribute to 'the national interest' an objective quality that the national ideology approach does not presuppose. It takes interests to be essentially subjective constructs of the nations that pursue them, and thus a nation cannot in the deepest sense be objectively 'wrong' about what its interests are.[14]

Subject to these qualifications, the national ideology approach is in line with classical realist convictions. Indeed, it is the counterfactual realist ideal of what foreign policy should be, and the realist critique of US foreign policy's failure to realize that ideal, that gives the book its central theme. When the later chapters speak of a balance-of-power approach to foreign policy, they are referring to a realist understanding of how order is attained. As

14 *International relations and national ideology*

Morgenthau conceived it, a realistic perspective assumes that ours is 'inherently a world of opposing interests and of conflict among them' meaning that 'moral principles can never be fully realized, but must at best be approximated through the ever temporary balancing of interests and the ever precarious settlement of conflicts'.[15] This is a perspective that US leaders have, with impressive consistency, declined to embrace, opting instead for an ideology of liberal universalism. The historical evolution of that phenomenon is the object of my enquiry here.

Liberalism

The liberal school of international relations differs from realism on at least two significant points. First, it is more directly concerned with the internal structures of state government, believing that democracies differ in important ways from non-democracies in their international behaviour. This often then develops further into a theory of liberal-democratic peace, which posits that the world is made more peaceful by the spread of the liberal form of government, a process that is hoped to end in universalization.[16] Second, while not dismissing the relevance of states' relative material capabilities, it places more emphasis on the importance of norms, institutions and interdependence.[17] Like realism, liberalism contains within itself divergent strands of writers, some of whom prioritize the system level – 'structural liberal' explanations, as it were[18] – and others who pay more attention to choice at the individual state level. On both levels, however, liberals tend to agree that the scope for the pursuit of common or harmonious interests is greater than realists suppose.

The foremost modern analyst combining liberal theorizing about the international system with direct analysis of US foreign policy is Ikenberry. He argues that while America's material capabilities undoubtedly placed it in an advantageous position in the post-Second World War world, its success thereafter was enhanced by the liberal nature of its society and its choice to pursue 'strategic restraint'. Other societies, he proposes, feared the US less than they might have, because its openness as a society meant they could access its decision making and read its intentions more easily. In addition, its restraint in imposing its will on other states, despite superior power capabilities, led them to regard its influence as more benign than the alternatives. Thus, the US was able to create a network of formal institutions and informal understandings in the post-war era that translated its capabilities into effective influence.[19] The idea that 'power' amounts to something distinct from material capabilities, and requires norms and institutions to be useful, is a major theme in liberal analysis.[20]

The concept of the 'balance of power' does not occur so prominently within the liberal paradigm, because of this more multidimensional understanding of the nature of power itself. To the extent that the concept has relevance to liberalism, it is in the sense that a clear power imbalance or hegemony favouring liberal powers – i.e. the absence of a 'balance of power' in the realist sense – is a precondition for the development of liberal order. In the case of the twentieth century, a distribution of material capabilities favouring the United States and its liberal allies enabled its successful pursuit of a liberal agenda. That agenda consisted of more open global economic and political systems pursued through formal international institutions, and embedded over time by the spread to a growing number of states of liberal democratic norms. The policy of the United States, under this reading, has not been the attainment of a stable balance of power, but the maximal spread of its political and economic values and the empowerment of global institutions favouring that agenda.

On this point, liberal and classical realist analyses partly converge: realists can accept that the US, while resting upon a foundation of underlying hard power, uses institutions instrumentally to advance its interests. But there are two clear points of difference. First, liberals argue that America's engagement with such processes goes beyond the pursuit of 'narrow' self-interest, to encompass the provision of global public goods. Second, realists are not convinced, as liberals tend to be, that goals such as universal democracy and effective global institutions are attainable. When realists level their familiar warnings against overreach and idealism, they are usually criticizing liberals, whom they perceive as pursuing these objectives.

The schools of US foreign policy history with clearest links to liberalism are the traditional-orthodox[21] and the progressive,[22] with the former tacitly endorsing the liberal agenda and the latter adopting a critical stance. The traditional-orthodox school tends to accept American good intentions and – albeit with a few caveats – to tell a positive story regarding the US rise to power and influence. It treats the imperialist surge of the late nineteenth century as in essence an aberration from a dominant tradition of anti-colonialism, and follows a narrative of evolution from 'isolationism' to reluctant engagement that judges the decisions of American statesmen mostly sympathetically, based on those statesmen's own perceptions of their context and options. This fits well with the typical liberal portrayal of the United States in IR as an unusually benign great power with the capacity to entice allies into a mutually beneficial world order.

The 'progressive' analytical framework shares liberals' pervasive interest in the role of economic forces and belief in the importance of non-governmental actors. It also accords a coherence and effectiveness to the US government's pursuit of universalistic liberal and capitalist ends that the realist school does not.[23] Progressive history, however, is more negative in its perception of the American 'project'. Some progressives have contained strains of Marxism in their critiques, sharing the liberal analysis of what America's economic goals were as a matter of descriptive fact, but abhorring them on a normative level. In the post-Second World War decades, the progressive school metamorphosed into the revisionist school of foreign policy history, while retaining at its core the conviction that America's capitalist system serves as the root source of a globally ambitious and ethically questionable strategy of US dominance.[24] Some recent work, such as that of Kagan, has the potential to link together this subfield of analysis more tightly by combining a progressive-style embrace of the importance of America's domestic character – including partial acknowledgement of its dark side – with a generally positive sentiment, less coloured by the left-of-centre disillusion and so-called 'isolationist' sentiment of much progressive history.[25]

As with classical realism, the national ideology approach accepts elements of liberalism's descriptive account without entirely sharing its normative conclusions. That it can claim affinity with both perspectives without self-contradiction is an indication that the two approaches are not mutually incompatible to the degree implied by convenient textbook demarcation. One area of commonality between its analysis and that of liberalism is that it accepts that some foreign policy consequence flows from the domestic political character of a state. This book is not a comparative study of democracy and non-democracy, and thus does not set out to enumerate the ways in which America's domestic system makes it different from less liberal nations. Nevertheless, it does suppose that America's foreign policy cannot be understood without reference to the efforts political leaders are obliged to make to justify their foreign policy via the domestic political process.

Classical realism presents us with a factual proposition in want of an explanation: why does the United States reject the prescriptive side of the realist agenda, i.e. balance-of-power thinking? Phrased another way, the question posed is: 'Why do certain liberal tenets – most especially the desire to spread liberal democracy and belief in the essentially complementary and harmonious quality of national interests – play a dominant role in the US foreign policy discourse?' Liberalism offers a partial answer to this question in suggesting that the operations of liberal democracy encourage certain kinds of political reasoning and action on the part of a state and discourage others.[26] In proposing national ideological history as a relevant factor, this book pursues a similar intellectual track to liberalism in looking to America's domestic politics for explanation, but in a sense making liberalism itself, as a belief system, the focus of the enquiry. Part of the explanation for the American resistance to balance-of-power thinking is certainly that American leaders have habitually adhered to liberal ideas, but this merely restates the thing that is to be explained. The manner and causes of liberal universalism's establishment as the prevailing worldview of American leaders are therefore under the microscope.

The national ideology approach diverges from pure liberalism, as with realism, in minimizing normative claims. It does not seek to make judgements regarding the true sources of legitimacy in international affairs, or the means by which the United States might best encourage acceptance of its authority by others under a new world order. Nor is it aimed at testing liberal claims to the effect that the realities of international life reward cooperative behaviour rather than existential competition, one of its key empirical arguments with realism. This book's argument departs from progressive history in that it does not emphasize either secrecy or injustice in its analysis of American leaders' promotion of capitalism. It is concerned with how and why liberal tenets emerged as pillars of US strategic philosophy, not with their truth or falsity, virtue or vice. For a liberal analyst such as Ikenberry, this question of substance is central. For this book, it need not be.

In making an effort, where possible, to take the self-perception of American actors seriously, this book's thesis may be criticized, as the liberal school history and politics often has been, for excessive credulity in its treatment of rhetoric and public pronouncement. Are there not other, darker motives below the surface of what is officially advanced as justification for US policy? On a theoretical level, this concern is addressed in the appropriate section later in this chapter. As to the more political question of whether the argument advanced by this book is simply an exercise in apologetics: it is not. This is intended to be a work of explanation, not of justification.

The 'empire' school

Differing somewhat from mainstream realist and liberal modes of analysis, which generally embrace the conventional IR framework of the state system, another school of thought has argued that the global role of the United States is best understood through intellectual paradigm of 'empire'.[27] Those advancing this case have argued that the relative scale of American power means the US should be seen not merely as one power in a Westphalian state system, but as an imperial entity confronting the challenges historically associated with the creation and maintenance of imperial power and stability.

Some have viewed this as no bad thing, hoping, at least in theory, for a beneficial effect on world order if America willingly embraced something amounting to an imperial role.[28] Others have been critical, arguing that the pursuit of 'American empire' is hubristic and self-destructive.[29] Though divided over the ethics and desirability of the project, these pro and anti analyses nevertheless share common doubts regarding the ability of the United States to sustain the ideological and practical commitment necessary for successful empire, owing to the nation's anti-colonial history and fragile public morale. The empire debate inevitably runs the risk of fixating on a question of terminology: 'should we *call* America an empire?' At its best, however, it has been valuable in focusing debate on assessing the plausible scope, as a matter of practicality and/or legitimacy, of American power and responsibility in the modern world.

Just as the IR debate between those accepting and rejecting the 'empire thesis' has been politically charged, the most closely linked historical literature reveals immense potential for polarization along political lines. The US experienced only the briefest flash of openly avowed imperialism, in Asia at the turn of the twentieth century. As a result, the obvious historical counterpart to the pro-empire 'empire studies' school of IR, i.e. traditional, 'small "c" conservative' imperial history, is not voluminous. To the extent that it exists, it consists of arguments by analogy, drawing parallels between the British and American experience.[30]

On the other side of the political spectrum, however, it is fair to say that the critical work of the New Left embraces the idea that the United States has behaved imperialistically in its foreign policy, using that as starting point for a trenchant critique of US policy. Taking up the essentials of the 'economic explanation' of history favoured by progressives such as Beard, Williams and LaFeber, the New Left added a more comprehensive hostility to the American domestic order, attributing the Cold War primarily and angrily to the imperial ambitions of US elites. At that conflict's end, it used the same principles to criticize humanitarian intervention and democracy promotion as violent neo-imperialism, attributing the problems of terrorism and general global violence to the failures of the capitalist and racially hierarchical American hegemonic project.[31]

The relationship of 'empire' to the 'balance of power' is one of transcendence. Those who argue that the United States should be studied in parallel with imperial history in effect make the case that it needs to be taken out of the context of the state system with which IR has been most comfortable dealing, and studied as some other, qualitatively different sort of entity. If it is an empire, the US should be understood as having relations with others that are essentially hierarchical rather than co-equal, rendering the conventional understanding of power balancing unworkable.

The empire school's core argument that the US is best studied as an imperial power is not entirely convincing, for a number of reasons. First, the geographic demarcation of the 'American empire' has never been clarified sufficiently. Over which territories or nations does the United States exercise imperial authority? If the empire is understood to be global, then the influence of the US does not appear strong enough in most places to justify such an argument. If it exercises imperial power only in some places, then these need to be specified and enumerated. Further, an explanation needs to be provided of how the 'American empire' relates to territories beyond its control differently from those within it. Second, a related point, it does not seem as though the lines of authority between the US and its 'subjects' have been defined with sufficient clarity to make it evident that an empire exists. Aside from Iraq, which from 2003 onwards existed in a quasi-colonial relationship with the United States, the US appears to exercise an external influence over other powers that stops well short of that exercised by past empires over territories considered part of the empire proper. Third, the near-blanket refusal of the American political discourse to embrace an imperial perspective presents insuperable barriers to the implementation of the policies required to make such an enterprise practicable, a point which even proponents-in-principle of empire seem to recognize as a serious problem. Finally, the empire studies school faces a paradox if it makes the claim, as it seems to, that the United States is a 'new kind' of empire. The justification for invoking the politically charged language of empire to describe the US appears to be utilitarian, i.e. that it is useful to draw parallels with empires past, but this is rendered highly problematic by an admission that US power differs qualitatively from any imperial power that has existed previously.

The national ideology approach leads this book to share the view, on which the empire studies school astutely picks up, that a *desire* to 'transcend' the balance-of-power system features prominently in the US strategic outlook, and that this is significant. It also, however, shares the realist concern that maintenance of an *actual* empire is beyond the political capacity of the United States. This is largely for ideological reasons, and this book agrees with liberals that imperialism goes against the grain of American beliefs regarding liberty and legitimacy. The thesis of this book is that within the ideology of American liberalism there are indeed elements of imperialistic sentiment, including tendencies towards universalism, unilateralism and 'exceptionalism'. Crucially, however, this approach is not imperialism as conventionally understood. What American strategy aims for – and sometimes presupposes already to exist – is willing and spontaneous embrace of its own political and economic ideas by others, not submission through compulsion to American authority. Even a power that pursues hegemony can adopt what this book means by a 'balance-of-power mindset', so long as it continues to think of international order as defined by inherently conflicting national interests that must be balanced and manipulated to produce order, as well as reality-imposed limits on even the strongest state's power. The United States resolutely refuses to do this, however.

A note on 'exceptionalism'

A few words on 'exceptionalism' may be appropriate here. This is the body of ideas stemming from the conviction that the United States has emerged as a somehow special political entity because of the unique circumstances in which it evolved. The specific reasons advanced for America's 'special' quality vary, but usually centre on interaction between the values brought by immigrant settlers and the unique environment of the USA's continental territory.[32] This proposition can be used to account for apparently anomalous national traits displayed subsequently, e.g. high levels of religiosity despite advanced economic development, or deep and widespread hostility to socialistic political thought.[33]

Exceptionalism, as sometimes formulated, can imply that a 'chosen' quality on the part of America and its people cannot easily be defended.[34] The national ideology approach offers what is at base an environmental explanation of how the United States came to be as it is, however, and in that respect it has at least something in common with Turneresque exceptionalism. This book makes the argument that, in being averse to balance-of-power thinking, American leaders have in their thinking about international order rejected understandings predominant in other places at other times. It is important to be clear, however, that this has been the result of spontaneous divergence on the part of American leaders, based on some innate moral or intellectual difference between them and the elites of other nations. Nor is it true that no other nation has ever tended towards universalism and away from balance-of-power realism in strategic outlook.

The book's central thesis is that America's circumstances, domestic and international, have interacted to produce particular ideological tendencies over time. The outcome of this process was not predetermined, nor is the present situation fixed. Assessing whether the particularities of the American approach make the US truly unique would require a comparative study beyond this book's scope, though it would be an interesting piece of research. As to whether the United States' particularities make it 'special', that is a thinly disguised nationalist claim to superiority that the contents of this book do nothing to support.

The study of ideas and discourse

In addition to the so-called 'traditional' schools of analysis set out thus far, there are other approaches that concentrate primarily on ideas and the language used to express them. 'Constructivism', as the study of the social emergence of ideas has in recent decades been termed, makes the process by which such ideas are manufactured and disseminated its focus, as well as the use of language in their formulation. Such scholarship varies in the degree of fundamentalism with which it approaches the question. Some is moderate, working within the established IR framework to make the case for the relevance of shared social ideas, especially in establishing norms between nations.[35] Some post-structuralist work, on the other hand – an extension of work in the field of literary criticism – goes deeper in its attempt to deconstruct the separation between the domestic and the international, the social process by which this is done and the political forces underlying the language used.[36] These approaches conceive of the 'balance of power' not, as structural realists do, as a given feature of the international environment, but as a linguistic and ideological construct serving to advance particular political objectives via a prescribed way of thinking about international order and the role of the state. For those critical thinkers who favour radical international reform, balance-of-power thinking is a conservative discourse serving the political ends of those advantaged by the social status quo.

It is crucial to recognize that in its interest in these issues constructivism in fact builds on the ideas of classical realism and liberalism rather than making a decisive break. As set out earlier, both of those approaches are explicitly concerned with the role of shared values and norms. Though realism gives more explanatory weight to material factors than constructivism seems to, classical realists are not unaware that the pursuit of a balance of power is an essentially conservative project, trading on shared notions of state legitimacy and international propriety. As such, it clearly provides a place for ideas, norms and language within its explanatory framework. Hence, there is a good deal more room for integrated overlap than is sometimes supposed between 'traditional' IR philosophies and the theoretically innovative approaches that have emerged in more recent decades. The compatibility of a national ideology approach with both realism and constructivism serves, hopefully, to emphasize this overlap.

Works explicitly on the subject of ideology and US foreign policy

There have been multiple published scholarly analyses claiming to identify dominant strands in the ideology of US foreign policy. The most theoretically grounded is that of Hunt, who identifies three particular features as consistently present throughout the course of the nation's history.[37] There are other examples, however, including the influential contribution of McDougall, and, with more contemporary focus, Lieven's work on American nationalism.[38] The seminal realist work of Osgood, meanwhile, which makes the argument that US policy has oscillated between bouts of exaggerated assertiveness and withdrawal also comes within this subgenre of 'American ideological studies'.[39] One might also point to Klingberg's work on cyclical movements in US social mood regarding foreign policy.[40] More recently, in the political science literature, Monten has linked the so-called 'Bush Doctrine' to long-term historical ideological trends, arguing in theoretical terms for the policy relevance of nationally specific ideological factors.[41] In this he acknowledges a debt to Brands, whose work also fits this category.[42]

This genre of work attempts to identify long-term patterns within the underlying premises of American foreign policy at the grand-strategic level. In so doing, it embraces a conception of ideology similar to that set out by this book, while also reaching into the realm of culture to underpin the analysis. The national ideology approach aims to encapsulate and emulate what these authors have attempted in seeking to discern dominant themes within the particular national culture of policy making in American society, and to explain how these have exercised influence on policy making over the long term. These works do not in the main focus on the same theme identified in this book as linking present policy to the past.[43] That fact notwithstanding, the existence of such scholarship does help to locate this book's approach in an established section of the academic landscape: a genre of long-term historical, political and cultural analysis, aimed at achieving contemporary relevance through cross-cutting analysis of international relations, US foreign policy and history.

In applying a national ideology approach, however, this book does not aim to provide mere replication. For one thing, it focuses on a particular issue – resistance to balance-of-power thinking – that is distinct from the topics of the scholars just named. Further, it differs from Hunt in that his is an argument for continuity, while this book also describes change, even as it attributes causal influence to the past. It argues not that the same core ideological framework has been at work throughout US history, but rather that the American ideology evolved from the interaction between founding principles – themselves a product of contemporary conditions – and changing material circumstances, domestic and international.

This study of change over time puts this book closer, in analytical thrust, to McDougall. Unlike McDougall, however, it does not portray the ideological change it describes as a misguided choice to break with a virtuous founding tradition in favour of a crusader ideology. The chapters to come describe how the modern ideology criticized by McDougall was in fact the product of interaction between the founding principles he praises and changes in national circumstances that made increased US international entanglement inevitable. In this regard, what follows endorses the classical realist view that material circumstances required change, while still allowing that the particular manner in which that change manifested itself was influenced by ideological factors constraining policy choice. Indeed, the book is, on balance, closest to Osgood's realist work in both style and interpretive conclusions, though he looks more deeply at a single contiguous period – roughly 1898 to the Second World War – in contrast to my focus here on a longer-term narrative and five separate key periods.

Defining 'ideology'

In focusing on the concept of 'ideology', and making an argument for evolutionary links between ideas past and present, some definition of terms is appropriate. Hunt defines ideology as 'an interrelated set of convictions or assumptions that reduces the complexities of a particular slice of reality to easily comprehensible terms and suggests appropriate ways of dealing with that reality'.[44] This is a definition which this book is comfortable in proceeding with. Ideology, for its purposes, is understood to be the means by which the human mind takes the infinite data that comprise reality and turns them into a simplified 'worldview', a necessity of mental function which provides a basis for reasoning and, ultimately, action in the political realm. Hence, it should be clear that 'ideology' here does not refer only, as in some pejorative uses of the term, to blinkered political perspectives which wise men should seek to avoid. On the contrary, the argument presented here starts from the assumption that all political perspectives are inherently, and of necessity, 'ideological'.

In this regard, the book embraces the broad definition of ideology offered by Seliger, and appropriated for the study of foreign policy by Macdonald. That is to say, ideologies are:

> sets of factual or moral propositions which serve to posit, explain and justify social ends and means of organized social action, especially political action, irrespective of whether such action aims to preserve, amend, destroy or rebuild any given order. According to this conception, ideology is as inseparable from politics as politics is from ideology.[45]

Thus, ideology is embedded in any and all approaches to the making of foreign policy. In this, the book diverges somewhat from the approach of some others who have tried to take the role of 'ideas' somewhat seriously, e.g. the liberal analysis of Goldstein and Keohane.[46] Those authors seek to argue that 'ideas' – a concept approximating 'ideology' for our purposes here – play a role in determining state action, and see this as challenging theories that assert all state action is the predictable outcome of national interests. But while the resultant enquiry is noteworthy and its findings useful, it often appears to take 'interests' to be an objective and pre-existing factor driving state action in a way that stands outside political subjectivity. In that regard, the authors' approach to the issue actually shares something with the realist theories whose conclusions it challenges.

Rather than seeing ideology as something that competes with national interests for a share of influence in determining state action, the national ideology approach adopted by this book supposes that the very activity of defining the national interest, and judging what it demands in terms of policy, is itself bound up in the mechanism of 'ideology' as defined above. It argues that what matters in deciding a nation's foreign policy is not simply the material reality of the international environment, but the intellectual framework with which policy makers approach that environment. A nation's culture of foreign policy thought develops through the interaction of international circumstances with the reaction of political leaders to those circumstances. This produces and reinforces both dominant factual beliefs concerning how the international system functions and normative ideas as to the role of the particular nation within that system. Being a mental creation that mediates objective reality, simplifying the world in order to enable reasoned action, this framework is by definition ideological. All governing administrations operate within this context, and add to it through their own actions and pronouncements.

This position places the national ideology approach close to the brand of moderate IR constructivism espoused by Wendt, who argues that a state's conception of interest is bound up with a socially created identity that is causally prior to interests. That proposition is not dissimilar to ideology's use here as a determinant of perceived interest. Wendt, however, focuses on shared understandings *between* states in the international arena, while this book opts to pay more attention to the national tradition of foreign policy making of a single state, the United States of America.[47] While that tradition has indeed generated subjective constructions of interest and value governing America's relationship to other states – and done so in interaction with external events – this book does not focus on the agreed inter-subjective quality of such constructions. Instead, it focuses on American political culture's projection of its own ideas onto the world. More radical critical thinkers, such as Campbell, have also shared the view that national identity, culturally produced and reproduced over time, exercises influence over foreign policy, though in focusing on the construction of the concept of 'the international' Campbell enquires a step deeper into the fundamentals of social philosophy than this book does.[48]

Within a given national context, ideology takes operational meaning as the mechanism through which statesmen interpret the world themselves, and by means of which they then proceed to explain and justify policy positions to other political actors and to the public. In order for policy to move forward in practice, leading statesmen must mobilize a critical mass of assent – on the part of political elites and the attentive segment of the mass public – behind their particular construct of the national interest and the programme of action they think necessary to advance it. To put it another way, successful leaders, at least in a society with relatively democratic power structures, need to bring the nation into accord with the fundamentals of their ideological outlook on foreign policy. The essential quality of this process of justification and consent in the political sphere means that ideology and its construction cannot consist purely of private intellectual reasoning on the part of the individual. Rather, it is a social entity, constructed in response to circumstances and used to build coalitions of political support as well as to provide intellectual self-justification in the mind of its formulator.

Continuity and change in national ideology

Sometimes the role of ideology is to serve as the realm of disagreement within a society, allowing for the articulation of divergent conceptions of the 'national interest'. Different groups within a single nation may approach foreign policy with rival premises, reaching differing conclusions about good policy on that basis.[49] But as well as identifying such intra-national division, the social analyst may also seek to identify ideological themes that have predominated with a degree of continuity throughout a given nation's history. There have been disagreements in the United States, as in all nations at all times in history, yet it can still plausibly be argued that one ideological framework has been the dominant one used to support the nation's approach to foreign policy and international affairs.[50] This book argues that this has been an ideology averse to balance-of-power thinking, at first on the basis of regional separatism and then, later, of liberal universalism.

It is important to note clearly that the argument made here is not aimed exclusively at identifying either continuity or change in American ideology. Rather, it is concerned with the manner in which necessary ideological change occurred, and with highlighting the critical influence of interaction between the demands of circumstance and the limits imposed by established ideological principle. Specifically, it argues that America's modern ideological posture is best understood through appreciation of two things: first, the nation's founding tradition of ideological separation from the European 'balance-of-power' system. Second, the manner in which America's leaders – especially presidents (Theodore) Roosevelt, Wilson and Truman – managed the country's ideological transition to global international engagement. The result of these leaders' negotiation of that transition was a nationally specific approach to internationalism which treated American engagement with the international system as conditional upon the reform of international order, shunning balance-of-power *realpolitik* in favour of the pursuit of a cooperative order based on the universalization of American values and practices under US leadership. The central point of the book is to argue that the predominant US ideology today is the product of the particular manner of the nation's ideological transition from Founders' Era detachment to twentieth-century internationalism.

The relationship of national ideas and national circumstances, and the relevance of history

An essential premise of this book's argument is that the ideological past is highly relevant to the present. Intuitively, this seems sensible, and hopefully more rather than less so after reading the chapter thus far. It does carry within it, however, the implication that there can be traditions of foreign policy that are essentially *national*. This idea of 'national character' is a proposition that runs counter to an absolutist structuralist account of the international system.[51] Debate over the appropriate level of analysis for understanding foreign policy is a sufficiently rancorous part of the discipline of IR that to try to offer a definitive answer to the problem here would be too ambitious. In any case, the book as a whole uses history to construct an argument that national factors have been relevant. To seek to prove that point at this stage, before the body of the argument itself has been presented, would therefore be to put the cart before the horse. At this stage all that can sensibly be done is to state assumptions explicitly.

This assertion of a national political culture of foreign policy overlaps with the broader debate within social science generally concerning the relationship between agency and structure, and its parallel counterpart debate over material versus ideational causes. The national ideology approach of this book implicitly embraces the 'structuration' perspective advanced in the field of sociology, and later expanded to other fields, by Giddens.[52] Under this framework, causal primacy is denied either to units or to the whole they comprise. The 'micro' and 'macro' levels of explanation are analysed as inextricably interwoven, yet neither is capable of explaining the other entirely in its own terms.

As applied to international politics, this model tells us that the international system is comprised of units (states) whose actions collectively generate forces that then operate with a 'life of their own' at the macro level. Through the operation of these systemic forces, the system thus becomes causally influential on unit behaviour through the application of power and moral norms. The macro level, however, does not acquire comprehensive explanatory power over the units through this process. The system, having first been produced by state behaviour, is not fixed; it can change over time, influenced by changing practice on the part of units, even as the units continue to be influenced and constrained by existing structures. Efforts to explain change in international affairs are therefore on dubious ground if they rely exclusively either upon the decisions of individual states bereft of context, or on the international system without relating that to the attitudes and behaviour of constituent states. Relying entirely on either level for explanation involves one in a circular 'chicken and egg' argument regarding cause and consequence, because each is meaningful only in interrelation with the other.

With regard to the specific argument of this book, this means that causal supremacy is attributed neither to America's international environment nor to its domestically generated political forces. Likewise, with regard to structure/agency, neither is causal supremacy attributed to the spontaneous decisions of individual statesmen, nor is it accepted that those statesmen are channelled into an inescapably fixed course by the dominant ideological disposition of the nation as a whole. One can only properly understand the reasons for the ideological trajectory of the American nation, and its change over time, by appreciating both its national and international circumstances *and* the decisions made by its leaders in reaction to those circumstances; by appreciating both the ideological principles and innovations constructed by particular American leaders *and* the pressures of pre-existing social ideological conviction within which they had to operate.

The national ideology approach takes a similarly synthesis-oriented view of the interaction between material and ideational factors. It rejects the causally unidirectional, reductionist view that ideology is merely a superstructure determined entirely in content by material factors. Yet, at the same time, the suggestion that ideological postures develop spontaneously in the intellectual realm and take social hold through mechanisms divorced from material circumstances seems implausible. Thus, this book argues that a nation's material circumstances and its ideology interact to produce national policy, and that efforts to grant exclusive causal power to one over the other are inherently misguided.[53]

Turning to the concrete content of the book's historical argument, it is contended that an ideology regarding foreign affairs developed in the Founders' Era that was in great part the product of the circumstances in which the nation found itself, meaning both the international environment and the nation's material resources. The ideology that resulted, however, though produced as a result of circumstances in one period, continued to exercise causal influence over the nation's foreign-policy thinking after those circumstances had changed. In time, the underlying shift in national circumstance – most especially the great increase in American material wealth and power – combined with events in the international system – most importantly the World Wars – to drive change in foreign policy. As a result, the nation's dominant ideological posture had to change too, in order to adapt to new circumstances. The crucial point, however, is that the manner of that change and the ideology that resulted were not simply the product of the new national circumstances dictating course, but the product of interaction between those circumstances and pre-existing ideological principles. The narrative offered here thus serves to illustrate the residual causal influence of ideas even as they are rendered outmoded by changes in the circumstances that originally sparked their construction.

In concluding this subsection, it may be wise to clear up one remaining question: how explicitly must statesmen refer to the thinkers and ideas of the past in order to legitimate this argument? The answer offered here is that the influence of historically prominent national ideologies need not be an entirely conscious affair in the minds of policy makers in order for a sound argument for their relevance to remain viable. This makes sense in light of the principles already outlined concerning national culture, and the definition of ideology as an evolving body of social understanding.

In dealing with the US we have a particularly good case for arguing that ideological influence has transmitted from past to present. As Hunt notes, for all its trials, America has – relatively speaking – known remarkable political stability and continuity since independence. As a result, there has been a relatively stable ideological environment in which political understandings have been transmitted down the generations through multiple rhetorical tropes and touchstones. This means that actors within US politics are, by virtue of their very presence in that context, steeped in inherited ideology. When it comes to assessing the impact of history on contemporary strategic and political ideas, it is therefore legitimate to move beyond merely identifying explicit historical allusions in the speeches of public figures (though in a historically self-conscious society such as the United States there is no shortage of those). A president need not quote Woodrow Wilson, for example, in his speeches for a sound argument to be possible that he is operating on the basis of Wilsonian ideas about international affairs. A figure such as Wilson has been sufficiently integral to the evolution of American foreign policy as to contribute to the intellectual framework inherited by all policy makers, whether or not they are personally familiar in depth with his life and words.[54] Such is the nature of ideology, as outlined above, that its transmission from past eras is as often implicit as explicit.

The usefulness of public statements as evidence

The major sources of evidence used to support the argument of this book include both private documents reflecting the views of the leaders selected for focus and public statements made by those leaders. These are drawn from published collections of speeches and public pronouncements, as well as private and public letters and certain key papers drawn from presidential archives.[55] In addition, the interpretations offered here of individuals' and administrations' views are supported by a balanced portfolio of secondary historical and biographical literature, a first-hand sifting of all relevant primary sources over such a broad sweep of history being impracticable.

There are self-evident criticisms to be made of an approach that accords substantial interpretive weight to public pronouncement, and these have been noted by Hunt, among others.[56] There are sometimes differences between what political actors believe privately and what they find it expedient to say to the mass public. Nevertheless, when focusing specifically on ideology – as opposed, for example, to bureaucratic politics – there is a sound argument to say that public material still represents appropriate source material. As defined above, ideology is a form of socially instrumental thought, not a matter of purely private mental construction. It encompasses the shared assumptions and understandings held by both political elites and the public, of which policy makers make use in order to secure the support necessary to enable the formation and implementation of policy. Hence statements made in public or semi-public forums at the very least give us insight into these shared understandings, even if not always into the private thoughts of the speaker.

There is reason to suppose that individual statesmen are often generally broadly sincere in the ideological framework they offer for their policies at a grand strategic level.[57] This should not be surprising, given that leaders are themselves produced from within the same society in which the public's shared ideological understandings are inculcated. Even if we assume a degree of insincerity, this does not render public statements meaningless. In choosing to outline their perspective in the terms that they do, political leaders themselves reinforce the reality of the socially ingrained ideology to which they tailor their words. Further, by invoking shared ideological principles to justify policy, actors thereby constrain themselves to within the reasonable limits of what those avowed principles permit. While all students of politics are aware that principles are often stretched in practice, or perhaps set aside if secrecy permits, it is equally true that once a principled justification has been presented for a policy, that policy cannot be cast aside publicly without political consequence. At the very least, brazen inconsistency draws politically painful criticism, and a government's very survival can be threatened by total breakdown between policy as implemented and its declared basis in ideological principle.[58]

Policy makers and their successors are thus to some degree bound by views previously propounded both by themselves and by their predecessors, if those predecessors have done so with sufficient frequency to establish a lasting tradition. Disavowal of or disregard for previously ingrained public understandings is a difficult process, necessarily gradual in the implementation and even then not guaranteed success. Thus, leaders are constrained by ideological parameters even as they seek to use them to mobilize support.

The idea that ideology sets parameters is important: ideology does not determine the decisions statesmen make in a narrow sense, but it does construct a framework of limits within which they must operate. Lieven, describing his own work on American nationalism, sums it up well: 'As a study of political culture and its historical origins, this … is not intended to provide a detailed explanation of particular events or decisions, any more than a study of Russian or German nationalism is intended to set out the immediate reasons why the Tsar or the Kaiser took the steps they did in July and August of 1914. Rather, such studies try to provide the ideological and cultural context which made such decisions possible.'[59] The study presented by this book seeks to achieve something similar.

Ideology is not fixed within a nation's collective mind, and it can be altered over time through the application of persuasive leadership and – at least as important – as a result of changes in national circumstances, domestic and external. However, crucially for the argument of this book, this change simply cannot take the form of the abrupt and wholesale discarding of existing ideological understandings. Even radical leaders such as Wilson, on whose ideological innovations a chapter of this book focuses, must explain how the place towards which they want to lead the nation connects with the history from which it has emerged. In the process of this sort of movement, the ideology of the past exercises sizeable influence over the present, and the way in which leaders manage ideological transition has consequences for the parameters within which future policy may be created.

Conclusion

This chapter has aimed to locate the theoretical and methodological approach of this book – which for simplicity's sake it terms a 'national ideology' approach – with regard to the IR and history literatures, and to demonstrate the underlying soundness of the enquiry undertaken. In so doing it has made clear its affinity with some central aspects of classical and neoclassical realist analysis. In particular, it takes realism's account of a balance-of-power approach to international order and sets it as its task to explain America's historical refusal to approach its foreign policy strategy in the way that the normative component of realism prescribes. It accepts realism's argument that growth in a nation's material strength and changes in its international context have consequences for the way it conceives of its interests, and hence for its foreign policy. It also argues that the international environment is not sufficient to explain national behaviour, but that the latter must be understood as the result of interaction between that environment and factors emanating from within the nation itself. In particular, it argues that the national ideological tradition of the United States, evolved over time, has played an influential role in the way the nation has reacted to changes in its national and international context.

In placing this emphasis on the role of ideology, the book's approach shares some ground with moderate constructivist approaches to international relations. In accepting the role that the domestic constitution of the state plays in foreign policy, it shares some ground with liberalism. Its interest in liberalism, however, lies not primarily in assessing the truth of liberalism's theoretical propositions in themselves, but rather in accounting for the emergence of liberal universalism as the dominant ideology guiding US foreign policy. With some similarity, it is sceptical as to the claims of the 'empire school' that the US has as, a matter of fact, constituted itself as an imperial power, but is nevertheless interested in studying the imperialistic features of the liberalism that it believes has guided its strategic thought.

This book proposes that much of the explanation for the way 'America' thinks lies in the study of its national history. Part of the explanation it offers lies in the story of America's material rise as a great power, and then as a superpower. Another part, however, is the emergence on the basis of that rise of a particular American brand of internationalism that rejected balance-of-power thinking, embraced liberal universalism, and made US engagement with international affairs contingent upon pursuit of this reformist international agenda. The book tells the story of how this ideology emerged as a result of interaction over time between America's circumstances and its leaders' ideas, between the embedded principles created by past national context and the demands made by a new context. It is the story of how some of America's greatest leaders constructed for the benefit of the American people, and were themselves convinced by, a narrative that asserted that a rising America need not take its place in the 'balance-of-power' order Europeans had created, but could build a new world order based on its own principles. Like any piece of self-aware analysis, it cannot claim to provide the whole of the truth, or to be the last word on the subject. But the account that it provides does, it is hoped, contribute something of significance to the understanding of the United States and its actions.

3 The Founders' Era consensus
'A Hercules in the cradle'[1]

Introduction

The American states became independent in 1776 or 1783, depending on whether one adopts the American or the British perspective. They did so in substantial part due to international factors. First, the push by the colonies' residents for independence was spurred by tax disputes stemming from the funding of wars to secure and expand the British colonial position in North America, the most proximate being the Seven Years' War (1756–63). Though keen on the idea of expanding their holdings on the continent at the expense of the French and their Indian allies, and willing to contribute directly to the fighting itself, the colonists bridled at 'taxation without representation' and the wider issue of British control over American destiny symbolized by it. There was thus a causal line of sorts between the Franco-British wars in North America and Britain's split with its colonies.[2]

A second international factor, arising after the outbreak of armed conflict, was France's support for the American fight for independence. Spurred by its broader agenda of rivalry with Britain in the European and global arenas, France signed a treaty of alliance with the Americans in February 1778, after the colonists' victory at Saratoga had signalled the military viability of their independence struggle. This broadened the Revolutionary War into an international conflict, providing the Americans with crucial French military support while simultaneously diverting British resources to other theatres where the hostility of France, and its ally Spain, might pose a threat. It is therefore fair to conclude that American independence owed a great deal to the operation of the European balance of power.[3]

This chapter begins its analysis immediately after the attainment of independence, when the newly free American states had to define their relationships with each other, and their collective relationship with the world. The former question was ultimately resolved with the creation of the Union, a project justified in significant part by arguments pointing to international considerations. The US then faced a series of challenges in its relationship with the international system, most especially: (1) how to manage diplomacy with its embittered former colonial master, Britain, (2) how to react to revolutionary turmoil in France, which stirred a colossal wave of war that swept across Europe and beyond, and (3) how, once it had been decided to attempt to do so, to maintain US neutrality in the midst of a global war centred on titanic Franco-British enmity. Having survived this period of international instability, the United States then laid the basis for its policy through the remainder of the nineteenth century with the proclamation of the Monroe Doctrine in December 1823.

The chapter argues that the founding leaders of the United States made decisions that in the end reflected a reasonable interpretation of the national interest, given the national and international context. What emerged was, first, the Union between the American states, and then – after some heated debate – a bipartisan policy of detached non-entanglement with regard to European rivalries and ultimately a spheres-of-influence demarcation of global authority in the form of Monroe's pronouncement. Given that the overarching argument of this book points to a habitual American aversion to the realist mindset, it should be made clear that the argument of this chapter is *not* that the Founders' Era represented a period of policy entirely at odds with a realist reading of foreign policy.[4] What it *does* argue is that the national and international circumstances of the early United States invited its leaders to resolve their founding policy choices not by conscious and explicit engagement with the global balance of power but by mentally withdrawing from it into a local theatre in which the US itself was increasingly unrivalled. Within North America, the United States resolved the problem of potential power rivalries through Union, thus abolishing the independent coexistence of sovereign entities that might have necessitated the armed rivalry of interests in an anarchical setting – in essence, a 'balance of power' as international relations traditionally understands the term. In relation to the rest of the world, the Americans' agreed resolution was exclusion of Europeans from the Americas and a strict taboo against American involvement in European alliances.

The chapter suggests that while these solutions were indeed realistic responses to the circumstances faced by the United States in this period, they were justified ideologically in a way that intellectually 'removed' the United States from the global theatre. In the process they obviated the need for America to conceptualize its international role as one of operation within a competitive system of states pursuing rival interests or, in shorthand, the global/European 'balance of power'. The language used to justify US policy served instead to instil the idea that American interests, and the values underpinning them, were not so much in competition with those of the European states that made up the core of the international system, as essentially separate from them. Thus, the Founders' Era, while on one level generating ostensibly realistic policy, also laid the ideological foundations for an American approach to foreign policy that would last a good deal longer and that would militate against subsequent American engagement with the world on balance-of-power terms.

The chapter assembles this argument in the following sequential steps. First, it establishes the national and international context in which the Founders operated. Second, it shows that the Union itself was the product of aversion to looking to 'the balance of power' as a sound basis for international order. Third, it analyses in some detail the early foreign policy problems faced by the United States, largely a result of spillover from the bellicose rivalries of Europe. Fourth, it then shows how what it calls the 'Founders' Era consensus' on foreign policy emerged, settling earlier disputes between rival political leaders through agreement around the principles of separation and non-entanglement. Finally, it highlights the Monroe Doctrine's role in establishing the principles of this consensus on a hemispheric scale, setting a course for US foreign policy for decades to come. All told, these sections combine to show that avoiding participation in the balance-of-power system of global order, an objective aided by geography, was central to the foundational foreign policy of the United States.

National and international context

The United States was born large but not strong. Americans had won independence not by equalling the British in wealth or military capability – though they did achieve notable battlefield successes at Saratoga and Yorktown – but through a mixture of attrition, foreign support and superior staying power. Once independent, the states were not, strategically speaking, in a position of any great strength; though there was little likelihood they could ever be re-subjugated, they remained vulnerable to military and economic pressure from more powerful European states. Britain retained a presence in North America through its ownership of Canada, and through a series of military outposts within what was, on paper, US territory, de facto possession of which it retained for some years after American independence. To the west, Spain's ownership of the Louisiana territory, though less daunting than the British presence, nevertheless presented a further potential source of vulnerability.

The international system of the 1780s was dominated by European powers. Indeed, through their development of the modern 'state' itself, these European nations were the creators of much that constitutes the 'international system' as subsequent thinkers have understood it. The most significant powers were Britain and France, with a weakening Spain also a significant force. In the east, Russia had steadily risen in power and prominence, attaining the status of great power within the European system. Between France and Russia lay Austria, as well as several lesser powers including the Netherlands and the precursors of the unified German state.

All the greatest powers of Europe were monarchies of one form or another, though with some variation in what that meant in practice, ranging from the British king's relative accountability to elected institutions to the autocratic tsarism of Russia. These states competed with one another for power – meaning a mixture of territory, treasure and control – through frequent wars. Their wars took place in Europe itself and also on other continents, the fighting sometimes done by colonists and other proxies, as in the conflicts between Britain and France in North America. To the inhabitants of the newly independent America, therefore, European politics was associated chiefly with two things, monarchy and war – a perception that was not altogether unfair. The European balance of power was viewed as an amoral – perhaps even immoral – mechanism through which kings and tyrants fought bloody conflicts of self-interest.

American independence was based upon a strident assault on monarchical legitimacy, asserting an extensive programme of rights possessed by individuals even in their dealings with a king. This was, of course, a challenge to one of the pillars of the European order, one of the reasons why the British were keen to resist it. The monarchical basis of that order was disturbed again, more grievously, in 1789 with the commencement of the French Revolution, which brought with it a long and vicious cycle of wars throughout the European continent itself. The story of US foreign policy in the Founders' Era is an account of how it dealt with the old, established European order, the putative new order announced by the French Revolution, and war between the proponents of each to gain the upper hand. It is thus, in short, the story of how Americans sought to manage their relationship to the European balance of power.

Prior to the question of how the United States might relate to Europe, however, was that of how the states should relate to one another. From independence until 1788–89 they operated under the Articles of Confederacy. The central authority established under the Articles, the Congress, struggled to offer coherent government, due to a shortage of powers. Specifically, it could not legislate directly for individuals, levy direct taxes or regulate trade. For funds it relied on requisitions from state governments. The thirteen states each possessed a single vote, with nine required for approval of important matters such as treaties, and amendments to the Articles themselves requiring unanimity. Such constraints reflected the intention at the time of the Articles' formulation that the states should retain their 'sovereignty, freedom and independence'. The arrangement was, in effect, as one of the Articles' drafters described it, more 'a firm league of friendship' than a true union.[5]

Such an arrangement produced predictable weakness of central authority. Demands for money from state governments often went unheeded. Preoccupied with local affairs, the states neglected to appoint representatives to Congress promptly, and as a result it met irregularly and unproductively. The nation's weightier political figures gravitated to state governments, where real power lay. In the absence of revenue, the debts of the recent war went unpaid, and America's overseas credit rating sank. Worse, it became clear that the national authority was not competent to quell civil disorder, relying instead on the loosely coordinated efforts of state militias. Shays' Rebellion, a revolt against debt collection by farmers in Massachusetts in 1786–87, led many to fear a breakdown of basic order. These fears were intertwined with a sense of vulnerability to threats from abroad. In retaining its fortified posts within the north-western border of the US, Britain cited as justification America's failure to enforce payment of debts owed by Americans to British subjects. London also imposed severe restrictions on American trade with the British Empire, aiming to impart a retrospective lesson on the benefits of imperial inclusion. The central government's inability to enforce the payment of the debts even if it chose to, or to retaliate economically against Britain's slights, reinforced the perception of impotence.

It was in this context that the movement for a new constitution arose. Two of the most significant actors were Alexander Hamilton and James Madison, whose backgrounds could scarcely have been more different. Hamilton was an outsider and upstart: an illegitimate boy from the West Indies who had propelled himself upward into the American elite through service as George Washington's wartime aide-de-camp and a good marriage into New York society. Notable for administrative flair, bountiful mental energy and an argumentative streak, by the mid-1780s he was making a reputation for himself in Congress and the New York Assembly.[6] Madison, by contrast, was the scion of a line of Virginia planters needing nothing on the scale of Hamilton's luck and self-promotion to get ahead. Still, he too had 'found himself' during the Revolution, having been drifting unenthusiastically towards the law before it. He spent it not on the battlefield but as an elected representative, becoming acquainted in the process with Thomas Jefferson, who was a few years older and became a mentor of sorts. Madison shared with Hamilton a gift for the written word, a mastery of detail and a formidable work ethic. But while the adoptive New Yorker was a natural executive, the Virginian's talents were those of a parliamentarian. No great orator, Madison nevertheless built a reputation as a quiet but relentlessly logical debater who could extract results from assemblies.[7]

Both men played indispensable roles in bringing about the new constitution. First, their efforts were instrumental in engineering a full-scale constitutional convention at Philadelphia in 1787 on the basis of a loose mandate to revise the Articles. Madison's 'Virginia plan' then served as the starting point for designing a federal government with the powers to levy direct taxes, regulate trade and raise armed forces. Finally, each then put in a heroic performance at the special assemblies elected in their respective home states to consider the Constitution, ultimately turning around hostile majorities led by powerful local figures to deliver ratification. In the course of this battle for a 'yes' vote, the pair collaborated on *The Federalist Papers*, a series of pseudonymous pamphlets published first in New York and then more widely, setting out the catechism of arguments in favour of the Constitution. The judiciary and others have since used arguments contained therein as one of the clearest windows available into the Founders' intentions. In no small part, the rationale presented in the arguments of *The Federalist Papers* was founded in ideological propositions concerning foreign policy and the international system. More specifically, the Union's architects argued for it as a means of avoiding the replication of Europe's balance-of-power system in America.

The Union as a means of excluding the balance-of-power system

Whether rightly or wrongly, the Founders considered the wars that had afflicted North America prior to independence to be something inflicted upon them by British rule: the tie to Britain, they argued, had dragged them into the grinding machine of European power rivalry, contrary to Americans' own interests.[8] Independence was a chance to be free of this kind of warfare, but attaining that objective would require keeping the states together. If the dysfunctional order provided by the Articles faltered, the states might fragment into regional confederacies. Hamilton, Madison and their fellow 'federalist' campaigners held up the spectre of this outcome as the likely consequence of rejecting their proposed new Union. Coexistence of separate confederacies, they argued, would inevitably generate conflict. Just as in Europe, rivalries over commerce and power would sow discord, which opportunistic politicians might then inflame into war. Further, a divided America could be manipulated by outside powers, worsening instability. Thus, the failure of the Union would result in the replication, in even more unstable form, of the European balance of power.

Jefferson missed the Philadelphia convention due to a diplomatic posting in Paris, but in later reflection he provided a neat summary of the case for Union. The Articles, he said, had been 'found insufficient, as treaties of alliance generally are, to enforce compliance'. But if the wartime bond were to expire and 'each state to become sovereign and independent in all things', he argued, 'it could not but occur to everyone that these separate independencies, like the petty States of Greece, would be eternally at war with each other, & would become at length the mere partisans and satellites of the leading powers of Europe'.[9]

This retrospective analysis of Jefferson's matched what Hamilton had been arguing even before independence was won. In 1781, still only in his mid-20s, Hamilton was warning in newspapers of the prospect of internecine strife in the absence of strong union. 'Political societies, in close neighbourhood, must either be strongly united under one government, or there will infallibly exist emulations and quarrels,' he argued, a fact which flowed from 'human nature'. As some American states grew 'populous, rich and powerful', he noted, this would 'inspire ambition and nourish ideas of separation and independence'. Though it would be 'their true interest to preserve the union', they would likely be led by 'vanity and self-importance' to 'place themselves at the head of particular confederacies independent of the general one':

> A schism once introduced, competitions of boundary and rivalships of commerce will easily afford pretexts for war. European powers may have inducements for fomenting these divisions and playing us off against each other ... The particular confederacies, leaguing themselves with rival nations, will naturally be involved in their disputes; into which they will

be the more readily tempted by the hope of making acquisitions upon each other, and upon the colonies of the powers with whom they are respectively at enmity.[10]

Madison expressed such anxieties similarly early. Without a sufficiently empowered central government, he told the Continental Congress in 1783, relations between the states would be poisonous. Minutes record his ominous prediction of how events would then unfold:

> The consequence would be a rupture of the Confederacy. The Eastern States would at sea be powerful & rapacious, the South opulent and weak ... Reprisals would be instituted. Foreign aid would be called in first by the weaker, then by the stronger side; & finally both made subservient to the wars & politics of Europe.[11]

Both Hamilton and Madison hoped for a time that the existing Congress might successfully be exhorted to show the requisite energy, but soon concluded that the structural barriers to strong central action were insurmountable so long as the Articles remained in force. '[T]he present system neither has nor deserves advocates,' Madison concluded, 'and if some very strong props are not applied will quickly tumble to the ground.' Unless something was done soon, he warned: 'The bulk of the people will probably prefer ... a partition of the Union into three more practicable and energetic Governments.' Though 'a lesser evil' than monarchy, he wrote, such fragmentation would be:

> so great a one that I hope the danger of it will rouse all the real friends of the Revolution to exert themselves in favour of such an organisation of the Confederacy, as will perpetuate the Union, and redeem the honor of the Republican name.[12]

At Philadelphia, he touched again on the theme of inevitable destructive rivalry between the states if disunited. Seeking to convince the representatives of smaller states that their interests would be safer under a strong union, he warned that under an anarchical order they would likely be caught in the crossfire of big-state rivalries:

> Among individuals of superior eminence & weight in Society, rivalships [are] much more frequent than coalitions. Among independent nations, pre-eminent over their neighbours, the same remark [is] verified. Carthage and Rome tore one another to pieces instead of uniting their forces to devour the weaker nations of the earth. The Houses of Austria & France were hostile as long as they remained the greatest powers of Europe. England & France have succeeded to the pre-eminence & to the enmity. To this principle we perhaps owe our liberty ... [13]

These arguments reveal essentially realist assumptions on the part of both Madison and Hamilton regarding international behaviour.[14] Both were sceptical as to the possibility of peaceful cooperation between nations in the absence of some higher authority. Only through Union could America's states coexist peacefully. The alternative was a balance of power analogous to Europe's, and that, history taught, meant regular war.

In the campaign for ratification, Hamilton used several of the earlier *Federalist Papers* to make this realist case for the Union. Striking a pessimistic moral tone, he attributed the inevitability of a clash between separate states to the fundamental drives of men and nations, which rendered them incapable of living peacefully side by side without a higher power to maintain order. A man would have to be 'far gone in Utopian speculations', he noted, to doubt that a disunited America in 'partial confederacies' would see 'frequent and violent contests':

> To presume a want of motives for such contests as an argument against their existence would be to forget that men are ambitious, vindictive, and rapacious. To look for a continuation of harmony between a number of independent unconnected sovereignties, situated in the same neighbourhood, would be to disregard the uniform course of human events, and to set at defiance the accumulated experience of ages.[15]

'The causes of hostility among nations are innumerable,' he argued, including 'the love of power or the desire of pre-eminence and dominion – the jealousy of power, or the desire of equality and safety' as well as 'the rivalships and competitions of commerce between commercial nations' and 'others ... which take their origin entirely in private passions; in the attachments, enmities, interests, hopes and fears of leading individuals of the communities of which they are members'.[16] Thus, the 'inducements' for American states to make war would be 'precisely the same inducements which have, at different times, deluged in blood all the nations of the world'.[17]

Thus, Hamilton's case to the voting public was that relying on reason and goodwill to guarantee peace was dangerous. His darker vision did not suggest that nations, or indeed people, were necessarily inherently malevolent, but that they were jealous guards of their power and would seek opportunities to expand it. While there was 'nothing absurd or impracticable in the idea of a league or alliance between independent nations', such ties were 'subject to the usual vicissitudes of war, of observance and non-observance, as the interests or passions of the contracting powers dictate'. Though such arrangements had periodically sprung up in Europe, the 'fondly hoped for benefits ... were never realized'. Despite the complex multiple alliances Europeans formed with 'a view to establishing the equilibrium of power and the peace of that part of the world', he observed, 'they were scarcely formed before they were broken, giving an instructive lesson to mankind about how little dependence is to be placed on treaties which have no other sanction than the obligations of good faith; and which oppose general considerations of peace and justice to the impulse of any immediate interest and passion'.[18]

One could also point, he noted, to America's own experience with the Articles of Confederacy. Optimists had predicted that there would be compliance with federal authority because 'a sense of common interest would preside over the conduct of the respective members'. Yet the Articles' ineffectuality in practice had shown that such optimism 'betrayed an ignorance of the true springs by which human conduct is actuated'. The reason domestic government was necessary was that 'the passions of men will not conform to the dictates of reason and justice, without constraint'. 'Has it been found that bodies of men act with more rectitude or greater disinterestedness than individuals? ... The contrary of this has been inferred by all accurate observers of the conduct of mankind.'

> There is in the nature of sovereign power an impatience of control, that disposes those who are invested with the exercise of it, to look with an evil eye upon all external attempts to restrain or direct its operations. ... [I]n every political association which is formed upon the principle of uniting in a common interest a number of lesser sovereignties, there will be found a kind of excentric [sic] tendency ... Power controlled or abridged is almost always the rival and enemy of that power by which it is controlled and abridged.[19]

Such ruminations on the nature of men and states offered ample basis for pessimism by themselves. But the clinching factor was the strategic influence of Europe. Its potent and hostile states stood ready to foster discord between the Americans as a means of advancing their own interests. 'America, if not connected at all, or only by the feeble tie of a simple league offensive and defensive,' Hamilton argued, 'would by the operation of ... opposite and jarring alliances be gradually entangled in all the pernicious labyrinths of European politics and wars ... *Divide et impera* must be the motto of every nation that either hates, or fears us.'[20]

Thus, disunion would bring ruin to America's interests. Secure union, on the other hand, offered America unique opportunities, given its geographical advantages. 'If we are wise enough to preserve the Union,' he predicted,

> ... we may for ages enjoy an advantage similar to that of an insulated situation. Europe is at a great distance from us. Her colonies in our vicinity are too much disproportioned in strength, to be able to give us any dangerous annoyance. Extensive military establishments cannot, in this position, be necessary to our security.[21]

Madison echoed this thought when he argued in Federalist 41 that the United States, distant from 'the powerful nations of the world', could enjoy the same 'happy security' Britain had from Europe by virtue of its being an island.

Without union, however, it would suffer 'the miseries springing from her internal jealousies', while simultaneously 'plentiful addition of evils would have their source in that relation in which Europe stands to this quarter of the earth, and which no other quarter of the earth bears to Europe'.[22]

Madison and Hamilton were both nationalists, and as such there was a strong strain of concern for national dignity in their writings. They feared that, without union, the disorganized confederacy of states risked contempt in the eyes of foreigners. In 1778, Hamilton wrote a letter of remarkable self-confidence – he was in his early 20s and a mere lieutenant colonel in the Continental Army – to Governor George Clinton of New York, lambasting him and his fellow governors for damaging America's reputation abroad through disregard for the orders of Congress. 'Realize to yourself,' he implored acridly, 'the consequences of having a Congress despised at home and abroad,'

> ... How can we hope for success in our European negotiations, if the nations of Europe have no confidence in the wisdom and vigor, of the great Continental Government? This is the object on which their eyes are fixed, hence it is America will derive importance or insignificance, in their estimation.[23]

In his pamphleteering later, after leaving active service, he revisited the theme more publicly. 'There is something noble and magnificent in the perspective of a great Federal Republic, closely linked in the pursuit of a common interest, tranquil and prosperous at home, respectable abroad,' he observed, 'but there is something proportionally diminutive and contemptible in the prospect of a number of petty states, with only the appearance of union, jarring, jealous and perverse, without any determined direction, fluctuating and unhappy at home, weak and insignificant by their dissentions, in the eyes of other nations.'[24]

Like many Americans of the time, Hamilton resented the perceived attitude of Europeans towards his adopted homeland, and he aspired in the long run to force reconsideration on their part:

> The superiority [Europe] has long maintained, has tempted her to plume herself as the Mistress of the World ... It belongs to us to vindicate the honor of the human race, and to teach that assuming brother moderation ... Let Americans disdain to be the instruments of European greatness! Let the thirteen States, bound together in a strict and indissoluble union, concur in erecting one great American system, superior to the control of all trans-Atlantic force or influence, and be able to dictate the terms of the connection between the old and the new world.[25]

There are two central points of significance to register from this section, with an eye on the overarching thesis of the book. First, the foundation of the

Union was based to a significant extent upon a realistic approach to international politics. Presupposing states to be motivated by power and interest, it was concluded that war between Americans would be inevitable if a European-style balance of power between separate confederacies were allowed to take shape. It would also prove impossible under such circumstances to force Europeans to respect America, a source of concern to nationalist sentiment. Second, the solution derived from this analysis was that a firm Union was necessary. No other means was believed capable of overcoming the problems of international anarchy and producing peace. Thus, the foundation of the United States was brought about in part as a result of Americans' conscious rejection of the balance of power as a desirable system of international order.

Trapped between titans: a divided America's vulnerability to European power politics

Once the Union had been established, the leaders of the nation had to decide how the newly cohesive entity they had created would relate to the international system. There were three key, interconnected issues to be addressed, each of which generated intense disagreement at the highest political level. The first was the relationship with Britain, proprietor of the empire from which Americans had just broken away. The second was how to respond to the French Revolution. The third was navigating a course through the global war between Britain and France that would dominate the quarter century beginning from 1789.

As had been universally assumed during the Constitution's drafting and ratification, the unifying figure George Washington was unanimously elected as the first president, taking office in 1789.[26] Hamilton, who had carefully cultivated his relationship with his former commander since leaving the army, was appointed Secretary of the Treasury, with a brief to repair the national finances and erect a new economic architecture. Madison, also close to the new president, went to the House of Representatives, where he began to push for the Bill of Rights, having conceded the necessity of one during the ratification debate. Jefferson returned from France in 1789 to discover that he had been nominated to serve as Secretary of State, a position he accepted only with a certain unease. Tensions between Jefferson and Hamilton would come to define the first Washington term. The term would end with Madison and Hamilton thoroughly alienated from one another and the former in partnership with Jefferson in constructing, with increasing openness, a party of opposition to Washington's administration.

Jefferson was a figure of some political weight before he took the Secretary of State's office, famous as the man who had drafted the Declaration of Independence.[27] He had previously been governor of Virginia, generally admired for a legacy of liberal legislation, in spite of question marks over his leadership during wartime crises. Like Washington and Madison, he was born to a Virginian inheritance of land and slaves. Possessed of a range of cultural and scientific interests, he cultivated the aura of Renaissance man, gifted and learned across the board. Critical of the aristocratic extravagances of European elites, his dismissive attitude to formality revealed in its own way a sense of easy entitlement to his place in the upper tier of American society.[28]

Even before they differed on policy, it was easy to predict that Jefferson's persona might rub Hamilton's the wrong way. His chosen profile was that of the effortlessly cultured yet humble face of inherited privilege. Having beaten grim odds to become a self-made success, the insecure dandy Hamilton was psychologically primed to find the image of a wine-loving, slave-owning landed gent turned populist hero less sincere and more irritating than the straightforward aristocratic bearing of someone like Washington. As they fell out over policy, he duly came to view 'the Sage of Monticello' as a dangerously ambitious visionary and hypocrite.

British antagonism

First among the pressing issues facing the new government was that of commercial relations with the former motherland. After a brief flirtation with conciliation, the British government under Pitt the Younger had taken to squeezing US shipping, refusing to permit it freedoms it had previously enjoyed in trading with British territories. American production was oriented towards agriculture and natural resources, and dependent on British manufactured goods paid for with export revenues. This meant that salvaging this commercial relationship was an obvious priority.

Adding further to the importance of British trade, immediately upon taking office Hamilton persuaded Congress to use the national government's new powers to levy a tariff on imports. This revenue stream was used to fund the national debt, which had been assumed from the individual states by the federal government and refinanced with fresh loans from abroad. This measure, combined with the controversial establishment of a national bank, served to increase the liquidity of the US economy and restore the credibility of American credit, but also made the continuity of revenue from imports essential to the nation's economic health.[29] At this stage Madison shared Hamilton's conviction that trade was economically essential, and also his anticipation that, in the longer term, a move might be made to assist industrialization by means of government tariffs and subsidies.[30]

Jefferson, however, was not so convinced of the merits of mercantilism. If it were possible, he wished in principle that the US might 'practise neither commerce nor navigation, but to stand with respect to Europe precisely on the footing of China. We should thus avoid wars ...'. But he accepted that this was 'theory only', because public opinion's 'decided taste for navigation and commerce' made government action to curtail trade politically impossible.[31] Hence, though ideologically out of sympathy with the commercial imperative, Jefferson accepted indirectly the need to fight for America's commercial rights and interests. Though in an ideal world, 'we might indulge ourselves in speculating whether commerce contributes to the happiness of mankind', he wrote in a 1784 letter to Washington, in the real world America was obliged to 'endeavour to share as large a portion as we can of this modern source of wealth & power'.[32]

The task before the first national government was thus somehow to pressure the British to grant more rights to American commerce without provoking a ruinous trade war. Part of the original purpose of empowering the new federal government had been to open up the possibility of forcing such concessions from Britain.[33] Yet the US depended sufficiently on British trade that if the confrontation escalated, then the damage to the emergent American economy could be catastrophic.[34] Hamilton, as architect of the import-dependent financial system, was especially sensitive to this risk, and tried to steer the administration away from commercial retaliation. Jefferson, less concerned about the threat to Hamilton's fiscal and monetary house of cards, and with Madison as an ally in Congress, pushed for tough retaliatory tariffs, which he rather optimistically argued would make Britain climb down. One of the final acts of his troubled tenure as Secretary of State was to submit a report to Congress openly advocating commercial tit-for-tat. In it he argued that:

> Free commerce and navigation are not to be given in exchange for restrictions and vexations ... It is not to the moderation and justice of others we are to trust for fair and equal access to the market with our productions ... but to our own means of independence, and the firm will to use them.[35]

This was one of a number of major splits in the administration in a period in which the Secretaries of State and the Treasury took to denouncing one another through newspaper proxies. The row over British commerce was symbolic of broader disagreement over America's social direction and, therefore, the merits of Hamilton's financial system. This period also saw a final break between Hamilton and Madison, their earlier quarrels over the Bank and the federal assumption of war debts hardening into fundamental opposition on Madison's part to the central thrust of Hamiltonian policy.[36]

Though successful in assembling the nucleus of an opposition movement, Jefferson and Madison were thwarted on anti-British tariffs by Hamilton's powerful influence over Congress and the weight of Washington's reputation. Further, Hamilton undermined Jefferson's authority as Secretary of State by establishing his own back-channel relations with George Beckwith, an unofficial representative of Britain in America, in order to ensure the avoidance of a breach.[37] Reassuring the British through this channel that talk of sanctions would come to nothing, Hamilton minimized the risk of a diplomatic crisis, though of course he also undercut any prospect of the British caving in to the threat. By Beckwith's account, Hamilton explained to him that Madison, the public driver of a confrontational policy, was 'very little acquainted with the world ... [H]e has the same end in view that I have, and so have those gentlemen who act with him, but their mode of attaining it is very different.'[38]

The first major point of disagreement between America's early leaders was thus on whether to approach the relationship with Britain chiefly through confrontation or appeasement. Hamilton favoured the latter course, and in the 1790s was largely victorious.

The French Revolution

Friction with Britain was a foreseeable consequence of American independence. Less predictable was the cataclysmic international context created by the fallout from the French Revolution. This had begun to unfold in 1789, while Jefferson was still in Paris to see it. By the time the Washington administration was up and running it had gathered pace, and it entered its radical republican phase in 1792. The following year King Louis was executed by the revolutionary government and war broke out between France and most of the other states of Europe, including Britain. France's turmoil presented difficult choices to America's new leaders. Of most immediate significance was the fact that the United States still had a treaty obligation left over from the War of Independence, calling for wartime support of France. Was this still binding even though 'France' was no longer the same political entity with which the Americans had agreed the alliance? Even more profound, there was the strategic, ideological and moral question of whether France's republican cause, now pitched in existential combat against hostile monarchies, represented an international extension of the Americans' own fight for liberty.

These questions divided the cabinet. Hamilton, rather sceptical of the Revolution itself, sought to convince the president that the treaty alliance had been rendered void by the change of regime. Jefferson, more sympathetic to the revolutionaries' cause, argued that both the 'tribunal of our consciences' and 'the opinion of the world' obliged America to consider the alliance still binding.[39] He sought to play down the material consequences of such a position, suggesting that America's only obligation might be assisting in the defence of France's West Indian colonies, and that it was not clear that the French were asking even for that.

Present in France at the first outbreak of Revolution, Jefferson had a declared sympathy with its aims. Before his departure for home, he was optimistic regarding the events unfolding before him:

> I have so much confidence [in] the good sense of man, and his qualifications for self-government, that I am never afraid of the issue where reason is left free to exert her force; and I will agree to be stoned as a false prophet if all does not end well in this country. Nor will it end with this country. Hers is but the first chapter of the history of European liberty.[40]

Equating the revolutionary cause with that of liberty, and seeing historical forces at work that would lead to a wave of liberation in Europe, Jefferson saw America's interests as entwined with this cause, and therefore with France's. Taking up his position as Secretary of State, he wrote to a French friend that among 'the circumstances which reconcile me to my new position ... the most powerful is the opportunities it will give me of cementing the friendship between our two nations'.[41]

As a result of his deep sympathy for the underlying principles of the Revolution, at least as he perceived them, he was prone to intemperate statements of support even as the political atmosphere in France shifted from reformism to radicalism and finally to bloody ferment. As war was breaking out across Europe, he wrote to an associate to defend the Revolution in spite of the trend towards demagoguery and political execution that ultimately culminated in the Reign of Terror. 'The liberty of the whole earth', he wrote, was 'depending on the issue of the contest':

> ... and was ever such a prize won with so little innocent blood? My own affections have been deeply wounded by some martyrs to this cause, but rather than it should have failed, I would have seen half the earth desolated. Were there but an Adam & an Eve left in every country, & left free, it would be better than as it is now.[42]

This was not a momentary aberration on Jefferson's part. Late in his life, though by that stage well aware of what had followed for France in the form of terror, coup and empire, he stood by his early support for the Revolution. In his *Autobiography*, he excused the misjudgements of the revolutionaries, or at least those who had launched the first wave of revolution: 'They were unconscious of (for who could foresee?) the melancholy sequel of their well-meant perseverance.' Still he identified the early Revolution's cause with America's, stating that it represented an 'appeal to the rights of man, which had been made in the U.S. [and] was taken up by France, first of the European nations'. He stood by his prediction that the cause of liberty was 'irresistible' and that 'the condition of man thro' the civilized world will be finally and greatly ameliorated' by its spread.[43] In 1823, as in 1793, he appeared at ease with the human cost of liberty's progress. Writing to the sceptically conservative John Adams, he told him that in his view, 'rivers of blood must yet flow, and years of desolation pass over. Yet the object is worth rivers of blood, and years of desolation for what inheritance so valuable can man leave to his posterity?'[44]

Hamilton, as well as others within the administration at the time of the Revolution, differed from this view, to put it mildly. Contrary to what Jefferson implied, they early on sensed potential for tragedy in France's political upheaval, and expressed that fear aloud. In 1789, Hamilton wrote to the Marquis de Lafayette,[45] alongside whom he had served in the War of Independence, that he viewed events in France 'with a mixture of pleasure and apprehension'.

As a friend to mankind and liberty I rejoice in the efforts which you are making to establish it, while I fear much for the final success of the attempts ... I dread the vehement character of your people, whom I fear you may find it more easy to bring on than to keep within Proper bounds, once you have put them in motion; I dread the interested refractoriness of your nobles, who cannot all be gratified and who may be unwilling to submit to the requisite sacrifices. And I dread the reveries of your Philosophic politicians ... who being mere speculatists may aim at more refinement than suits either with human nature or the composition of your Nation.[46]

This divergence in levels of enthusiasm for the Revolution made Hamilton and his supporters suspicious of Jefferson's enthusiasm for the French cause. By inference from his views on that topic, they feared that the Secretary of State might steer America into the war in Europe out of ideological sympathy with France – go to war, as he would see it, to advance the cause of global 'liberty'. As the unpleasant reality of the Terror unfolded, the Hamiltonians, increasingly known by the factional label 'Federalists', were unnerved by the solidarity shown by a sizeable body of Americans for the French cause. Numerous 'Democratic' clubs and societies sprang up throughout the country in the 1790s and looked to Jefferson to represent pro-French sentiment in public life. These societies overlapped with the informal machinery of the 'Republican' party of opposition being assembled steadily by Madison, acting as Jefferson's right hand.

Already resentful after clashes over the domestic agenda, Hamilton became convinced that Jefferson's faction represented a dangerously pro-French fifth column in the foreign policy debate. Their views on foreign policy, he wrote excitably, were 'unsound & dangerous. *They have a womanish attachment to France and a womanish resentment against Great Britain.*' If 'left to pursue their own course', he proclaimed, the pair would produce 'in less than six months *an open War between the U States and Great Britain.*' Insisting that he himself had 'a due sense' of America's debt to the French nation for its previous aid, he argued that there was nevertheless 'a wide difference between this and implicating ourselves in all her politics; between bearing good will to her, & hating and wrangling with all those whom she hates'. Jefferson, he alleged, had come into the Cabinet 'electrified ... with attachment to France and with the project of knitting the two countries in the closest political bands'.[47]

In a 1794 memo, Hamilton complained that 'the effect of Experience' had been 'much less than could reasonably have been expected' with regard to popular views of France. The 'predilection' for the Revolution, he lamented, was still 'extensive and ardent', and continued to attract those in a position to know better. 'The error entertained is not on a mere speculative question,' he warned. 'The French Revolution is a political convulsion that in a great or less degree shakes the whole civilized world and it is of real consequence to the principles and of course to the happiness of a Nation to estimate it rightly.'[48] He had earlier argued, in favour of a policy of neutrality, that 'gratitude' for assistance in the War of Independence offered no better a basis for signing up to France's wars than ideological sympathy. France, he noted with realist cold blood, 'in assisting us was and ought to have been influenced by considerations relative to its own interest'.[49]

Though Washington accepted Jefferson's argument that the treaty of alliance was still binding in spite of the change of regime in Paris, Hamilton did convince him, after heated debate with Jefferson in cabinet, to issue a 'Proclamation of Neutrality'.[50] As well as declaring neutrality on the part of the government itself, the proclamation threatened prosecution for any Americans who independently sought to involve themselves in the conflict on either side. Jefferson and Madison opposed the measure, arguing that the pronouncement overstepped the president's constitutional limits, usurping Congressional authority to declare any state of war or, by implication, peace.[51] The administration's policy enraged pro-French forces in the country at large, who regarded the official line as the product of elitist, pro-British sentiment.

In analysing this period, it is important not to overreach as one sets up the dichotomy of positions within the cabinet. Jefferson served as Secretary of State in the very administrations his incipient party criticized, and never committed himself to US entry into the war in support of France.[52] Warier than some of his supporters of the consequences of an actual war, the farthest he went was advocacy of the much vaguer notion of somehow tilting neutrality so as to make it favourable to the French, perhaps through sympathetic access to US ports.[53] Meanwhile, neither administration policy nor even Hamilton personally was quite as pro-British as portrayed in Republican propaganda. While Hamilton certainly doubted the French Revolution's virtues, his aversion to clashing with Britain was chiefly pragmatic in motive rather than the product of deep Anglophilia.[54] Thus, while each leader had evident biases towards cultivating good relations with his favoured power, both were sufficiently pragmatic to see the limits imposed on either strategy by the brute fact that war would entail gross military, economic and political costs. As such, a course deliberately targeted at war was in truth the policy of neither Hamilton nor Jefferson, even if some of their supporters were less restrained.

Nevertheless, the second challenge facing the nation was clear: to decide whether the French Revolution, and the wars that flowed from it, presented a sound reason for the United States to take sides in European conflict. In short, did the American national interest encompass the cause of France, its friend during the War of Independence and now its brother in 'liberty'?

Neutral rights in wartime

The fact that the international system was on a war footing made it especially difficult to tread a middle course between Britain and France. The US parties' rival desires to tilt towards either the commercially important monarchy or the ideologically sympathetic republic led to controversy over how firmly to assert America's commercial rights as a neutral in the midst of a global war. US policy was thus poised precariously at the centre point of a see-saw of rival antagonisms, a posture that pleased neither of the belligerent great powers. The British navy being pre-eminent upon the oceans, the French were unable to transport goods freely under their own flag. As a result, they sought to use US shipping to keep supply lines open, by granting Americans the right to ship goods between France and its colonies. The British, unimpressed by such efforts to circumvent their squeeze of the enemy through embargo, began to waylay American ships plying this new trade and seize their cargoes. Predictably, such seizures prompted vocal outrage among pro-French Republicans in the United States. Invoking the principle of 'free ships, free goods', they insisted that America had an inviolable right as a neutral to trade with whomever it saw fit.

Jefferson and Madison, the leaders of the incipient Republican faction, had foreseen the likelihood of just such a scenario some years before the actual European war broke out.[55] When American ships began to be interfered with, public anger at British behaviour put wind in the sails of their movement for commercial sanctions against Britain. Temperamentally averse to war, Jefferson had fostered the theory that economic sanctions could serve as an alternative. This war, in the 1790s, he told Madison, could be a test case, furnishing 'a happy opportunity of setting another example to the world, by showing that nations may be brought to do justice by appeals to their interests as well as by appeals to arms'. The use of economic sanctions, he anticipated, 'would work well in many ways, safely in all, & introduce between nations another umpire than arms. It would relieve us too from the risks & the horrors of cutting throats'.[56]

Hamilton, by contrast, thought this prediction delusional. Britain, he was convinced, would never back down as Jefferson assumed. Worse, the imposition of economic sanctions in wartime – in effect a declaration of economic war – would in all likelihood provoke a hot war too, for which America was ill prepared. Faced with rising war fever in the country, Hamilton therefore sought to steer the president away from the Republicans' preferred course. War, he warned Washington, was in danger of breaking out as a result of 'angry and perverse passions' rather than of 'cool calculations of Interest'. He believed that the Republican faction was looking to manipulate the situation in order to engineer 'a more complete and permanent alienation from Great Britain and a more close approximation to France'. Even if their leaders, such as Jefferson, didn't support war outright, Hamilton argued, they considered it 'a less evil than a thorough and sincere accommodation with Great Britain'.[57]

The theory that Britain would simply agree to American demands if faced with sanctions was a 'folly ... too great to be seriously entertained by the discerning part of those who affect to believe the position':

She cannot do it without renouncing her pride and her dignity, without losing her consequence and weight in the scale of Nations – and consequently it is morally certain that she will not do it. A proper estimate of the operation of human passions must satisfy us that she would be less disposed to receive the law from us than from any other nation – a people recently become a nation, not long since one of her dependencies, and as yet, if a Hercules – a Hercules in the cradle.[58]

Americans needed to be honest with themselves – as the Republicans were not being, Hamilton thought – and accept that their position was defined by weakness, not strength. That being the case, sound policy was to avoid conflict, even if that meant enduring shoddy treatment. 'Tis our error to overrate ourselves and underrate Great Britain,' he warned. 'We forget how little we can annoy and how much we may be annoyed ... To precipitate a great conflict of any sort is utterly unsuited to our condition, to our strength and to our resources.'[59] Hamilton was more easily reconciled to such a position because he in any case lacked the underlying sympathy for the French war effort that added fuel to the Republican argument.

While the Federalists still held sway in the 1790s, this Hamiltonian position won the day. He convinced Washington, in the face of popular opposition, to despatch John Jay to London, where he negotiated a soft treaty laying the ground rules for peace with Britain. Though Jay's 1794 treaty obtained some limited but worthwhile concessions, there was no acceptance of the principle of American neutral shipping rights. This, combined with various concessions made to the British, caused fury in the country when the treaty became public. Motivated by the logic that almost anything was better than war, however, Washington and Hamilton rammed ratification through the Senate at speed, achieving victory by a single vote. But the country was left profoundly divided by the deal. Washington's administration was increasingly viewed as a creature of a pro-British Federalist faction, while the Republican opposition mobilized irritation in the country at large into a solid base of support.[60]

The Farewell Address and the emergence of the non-alignment consensus

It was in the context of these acrimonious political divisions that Washington, already making history with his decision to relinquish power voluntarily at the end of his second term, further deepened his presidency's historical impact with the publication of his 'Farewell Address'. Despite the title, the 'address' was published via newspapers rather than delivered as a speech. Its purpose was twofold. Its first aim was to defend the Federalist/Hamiltonian policies of the administration. Its second was to craft a potentially partisan message in such a way as to avoid the appearance of partisanship. When first contemplating the address, the president was disposed to include some defensive passages with a rather bitter and divisive quality. But, in collaboration with Hamilton, he ultimately produced instead a document that adopted a tone of unity-seeking centrism while still defending the essentials of Federalist policy.[61] In adopting this moderated approach, America's ruling class took the first major step towards creating the ideological framework for the consensus on foreign policy that was the ultimate product of the Founders' Era.[62]

The Address's first substantive passage attacked the 'spirit of party', a message that served simultaneously as a veiled stab at Jefferson's faction and also as an entreaty to Americans to consider the prevalence of political division unhealthy. The residual strength of Washington's popular reputation aided the plausibility of striking this pose of non-partisan patriotism. The Address then turned to its primary topic: foreign policy. First, it underlined the foundational Federalist argument, dating from the push for the Constitution, that the great benefit of Union and unity at home was the exclusion of balance-of-power politics from America. That being the case, the US should regard it as imperative to avoid subjecting itself to the evils of that system via embroilment in European conflicts. Regardless of the ideological appeal of France or the commercial imperative for good relations with Britain, aligning with either politically would be disastrous. Unlike other nations, the Address noted, a united America was gifted with geographical advantages that made non-alignment genuinely viable.

The Address sought to portray its position as founded on cool reason and a sound grasp of the national interest. Neither 'permanent, inveterate antipathies' nor 'passionate attachments' for other states, it said, could form the basis of sensible policy. 'The nation which indulges towards another an habitual hatred or an habitual fondness is in some degree a slave,' it warned, with either 'sufficient to lead it astray from its duty and its interest'. It was, it emphasized, important to know that it was not only grudges against others that could harm the national interest. Favouritism also risked it:

> Sympathy for the favorite nation, facilitating the illusion of an imaginary common interest in cases where no real common interest exists, and infusing into one the enmities of the other, betrays the former into a participation in the quarrels and wars of the latter without adequate inducement or justification ...

This was a clear if not explicitly targeted warning of the danger presented by the Republican faction's fondness for France. Such 'attachment of a small or weak, towards a great and powerful nation,' Washington warned, 'dooms the former to be the satellite of the latter'. Thus basing its case on the need for autonomous pursuit of the US interest, the Address set forth a doctrine of strict non-alignment in dealings with the European powers. The United States, it argued, should seek to 'extend' its 'commercial relations', but its 'great rule' should be that in doing so it must 'have with them as little political connection as possible'.

In justifying this maxim, the Address argued that the interests of European nations were neither identical with those of America, nor necessarily opposed to them. Rather, they were essentially separate, concerned with fundamentally different issues, in a geographically distant place:

> Europe has a set of primary interests which to us have none; or a very remote relation. Hence she must be engaged in frequent controversies, the causes of which are essentially foreign to our concerns. Hence, therefore, it must be unwise in us to implicate ourselves by artificial ties in the ordinary vicissitudes of her politics, or the ordinary combinations and collisions of her friendships or enmities. Our detached and distant situation invites and enables us to pursue a different course.

The United States, the address argued, was on a trajectory of growth in its power. So long as the Union held, the time was 'not far off' when it might be strong enough to shrug off 'external annoyance', compel others to respect its neutrality and ultimately 'choose peace or war, as our interest, guided by justice, shall counsel'. To risk war now, as some wished, would be to 'forgo the advantages' of America's 'peculiar ... situation' and 'entangle our peace and prosperity in the toils of European ambition, rivalship, interest, humor or caprice'. This was not a position of ideologically rigid resistance to any cooperation with European states. The Address explicitly referred to the permissibility of 'temporary alliances for extraordinary emergencies'. But its central principle was that the United States' 'true policy' was to 'steer clear of permanent alliances with any portion of the foreign world'.

Assuredly, the address was on one level a party political document: in its advocacy of neutrality it implied that its opponents were straining to enlist as belligerent France's ally. Jefferson and his supporters no doubt thought that analysis disingenuous, feeling the Hamiltonians had tilted towards Britain. That fact notwithstanding, the address was notable for its effort to reach out through moderate language rather than deepen division. It was neither a sharp-edged intellectual tract like *The Federalist Papers*, nor shrill propaganda of the sort the rival parties had exchanged in the press. Rather, it was a document aimed at mass opinion, making an explicit ideological pitch aimed at generating consensus around the central principle of non-alignment, and thus reaching out beyond the Federalist base. Absent was any detailed defence of the more controversial elements of the Federalist programme: this was an effort at mobilization of public opinion through the formulation of a new foundation for strategic consensus.

The argument made by the address was on one level pragmatic and interest-oriented, based on national and international circumstances. Yet it was also ideologically significant. It focused on the idea that European nations had 'primary interests' that were separate from the United States', and with which, advantaged by geography, the US need not concern itself. This analysis implicitly dismissed alternative readings of the American interest that could with equal plausibility have been constructed. For one, it rejected the idea, embraced by some at the time, that France was fighting a war in defence of liberty and that the US must support such a conflict as a moral duty. Transnational ideological causes that might justify war were thus 'defined out' of the US national interest. Likewise, it was restrained and long term in its projections. Even setting aside the question of shared ideology, short-term calculation might have led policy makers to think it worthwhile to side with one of the major European powers against the other in the hope of some territorial or other strategic gain at the loser's expense. Instead, the Address took the view that the potential gains of any such strategy were outweighed by the risks, and that the long-term trend of growth in US power in the absence of war made a policy of neutrality and avoidance of conflict the wisest course. This was not an inevitable choice. It was based on a particular reading of America's circumstances and how best to seek national advantage within them.

The Address was intended to be a strategic guide based on the prevailing national and international context. Though meant to be of lasting value, it was not intended as a proclamation of eternal verities. Nevertheless, the manner in which it expressed itself – in the pursuit of a wide base of political support – lent to its being read as an ideological formula of lasting resonance. Rather than locating the United States within the international balance of power and mapping a path of maximal advantage within that context, it justified American non-alignment by emphasizing America's 'detached' situation, and the essentially separate character of its interests from those pursued within the rest of the European-dominated international system. Such choices in terminology and ideological tone would ultimately matter a lot.

Though spawned thanks to the operation of the balance of power, and in practice obliged by circumstance to work within it, the United States developed in the Farewell Address the basis for a tradition of thought that located the US intellectually 'outside' the balance-of-power system. Europeans might pursue their interests in that system – self-destructively as Americans saw it – but geographical circumstance, in Washington's phrase, 'invited and enabled' the United States to think of itself as separate, in terms of both its strategic interests and its moral code.

Consensus emerges: Jefferson's embrace of Washington's doctrine

Hopes for the consensual spirit of the Farewell Address's text seemed precarious during the grimly confrontational one-term Adams presidency that followed Washington. As the Federalists had foreseen quite clearly, Jay's Treaty had moved the pro-French section of the country to outrage.[63] And it was not only American Republicans who were enraged by the treaty: in the zero-sum mindset of the French Revolutionary Wars, France regarded the treaty as an American realignment behind Britain, jettisoning the Franco-American alliance. This perception was worsened by the presence of James Monroe, a Republican ultra, as the US representative in Paris, where he fanned the flames of France's perceived grievance instead of fighting them.[64] Thus, the price of Hamilton's peace with Britain was perilous breakdown in relations with France. This reached its nadir under Adams, when an undeclared naval 'quasi-war' erupted between the two nations. These hostilities, worsened by a botched attempt at negotiation that spawned charges of dishonour and corruption, held the US on the precipice of full war for an extended period.[65]

The president even went so far as to authorize raising an army – under Washington's command on paper and Hamilton's in practice – to stand ready for the threat of invasion.[66] These final four years of Federalist administration also witnessed the passage of draconian sedition laws – at least by American standards – targeted at the Republican opposition. Jefferson and Madison, meanwhile, reacted to being squeezed by federal authoritarianism by inciting state legislatures to threaten nullification of federal laws. The end of the crisis with France, however – thanks to Adams's decision to break with Hamiltonian hardliners and seek a deal with Paris – brought on the implosion of the Federalist party in an orgy of internal rancour. This, as well as the superior grassroots machine assembled by Madison over the preceding decade, allowed the Republicans to triumph in the election of 1800, and Jefferson to accede to the presidency in 1801.

This 'revolution', as Jefferson termed it, gave the Republicans control of foreign policy for the first time, generating suspense in the country, given their history of pro-French advocacy. By the turn of the century, however, external circumstances had moved on from the debates of the Washington era. The wars of the French Revolution had elevated an autocratic general to dictatorial power in Paris: Napoleon Bonaparte was now 'First Consul' of France under a constitution of his own design. Within a few years he would declare himself emperor for life. The imagined fraternal bond of political values between the American and French Revolutions, central to the Democratic Societies' activism in the 1790s, had thus been severed. Jefferson himself had moved on somewhat, too, perhaps chastened by the looming responsibilities of government as well as by events in Paris. The steady degeneration of France's republicanism, which culminated in Bonaparte's coup of 1799, was already apparent by the time of the Farewell Address. During Jefferson's term as an antagonistic absentee Vice President in the Adams administration, he had already begun to edge away from his prior identification with the French cause and to advocate an even-handed neutrality rather than one tilted towards France.[67] 'Better to keep together as we are,' he wrote to one associate, 'hawl off from Europe as soon as we can, & from any attachments to any portions of it. And if we feel their power just sufficiently to hoop us together, it will be the happiest situation in which we can exist.'[68] During the crisis over the XYZ affair, not long before Bonaparte's coup, Jefferson wrote to a friend insisting that he now favoured complete detachment from European wars. Foreshadowing the words of his first inaugural address, he wrote that '[c]ommerce with all nations, alliance with none, should be our motto'.[69]

In that first address as president, in March 1801, he sought to cloak himself in the spirit of the Farewell Address, minimizing partisanship. Now in power, he wanted to heal the political divisions he had helped foster in the 1790s, and calm fears that he would implement a recklessly anti-British policy.[70] To that end, he used phraseology so closely emulating Washington's strategic proposition that one of the key phrases – 'entangling alliances' – is often misattributed to the Farewell Address itself. America, Jefferson declared, was a 'rising nation'. Retreading Washington's steps, he noted that it was 'kindly separated by nature and a wide ocean from the exterminating havoc of one quarter of the globe', 'too high minded to endure the degradations of others'. It was in many ways 'a chosen country'. The correct policy was thus clear: to seize on these advantages by pursuing 'peace, commerce and honest friendship with all nations, entangling alliances with none'.[71]

Omitting reference to his own pro-French disposition in the decade gone by, President Jefferson was soon celebrating the wisdom of America's having refused to entangle itself in the war across the ocean. '[L]et us bow with gratitude,' he said in his third annual message, 'to that kind Providence which ... guarded us from hastily entering into the sanguinary contest, and left us only to look on and pity its ravages.'[72] Happily, America was 'separated by a wide ocean from the nations of Europe, and from the political interests which entangle them together'. '[I]t is our duty,' he told Americans, 'to look on the bloody arena spread before us with commiseration indeed, but with no other wish than to see it closed ... .'[73] It did not matter to America who beat whom in European wars, only that the United States should stay out of them.

This beginning of the Jefferson presidency was, more so than the Farewell Address itself, the key to embedding the principle of 'detachment' from Europe in US foreign policy thought. Washington had crafted a potentially unifying ideological text preaching the separateness of American and European interests and the basis in rational interest of a policy of strict non-alignment. But it was Jefferson's decision to echo these tenets that signalled the moment at which the Founders reached a fundamental intellectual consensus on America's world role.

The emergence of consensus was aided by circumstances, not least the changed nature of the European scene, where conflict was now transparently between rival empires rather than rival ideals. It was also aided – though of course no one would have said so out loud – by the sudden death of Washington in 1799, which allowed his posthumous re-establishment as a non-partisan figurehead and facilitated the invocation of his ideas as transcendent principles rather than party political positions. After a decade of heated disagreement over the fundamentals of America's strategy in foreign affairs, the entwined, mutually supportive pronouncements of the departing Washington and the 'arriving' Jefferson crafted consensus around a version of the American national interest and how to pursue it that would serve to guide the nation throughout the nineteenth century.

'Our hemisphere ... of freedom': the Monroe Doctrine as a logical extension of the Founders' Era consensus

However well issues of principle might have been settled, in the messy world of practice there was still turbulence in foreign affairs under the governments of Jefferson and Madison that opened the nineteenth century. This included a tense stand-off with France, ended only by the 1803 Louisiana Purchase, which finally terminated French territorial influence in North America. There was also Jefferson's economically and politically ruinous imposition of an embargo on the entirety of US–European trade in reaction to an exchange of blockade and counter-blockade between Britain and France as their long war dragged on into the new century. 'Jefferson's Embargo' (1807–9) was a strategic failure, and also the beginning of a chain of events that led to an ill-planned and ultimately stalemated military clash with Britain in 1812. Nevertheless, through all this instability, the core essence of American strategy remained that which had been encapsulated in the Washington–Jefferson consensus: remain rigorously neutral between the European powers, shore up the Union at home, and seek to minimize foreign influence in America.

By 1815, the autonomy and viability of the United States had been firmly established, as had its unwillingness to play a role in the European balance-of-power system. Much as US leaders might wish otherwise, however, the Old World remained intimately involved in the affairs of the New by virtue of its territorial holdings there, particularly the vast colonies of South America. This presence undermined the reality of the United States' desired exclusion of the balance of power from America and its ability to refrain from dealings with Europe beyond the commercial.

The cardiac arrest of Spanish imperial power in the early decades of the nineteenth century was a tipping point in resolving this tension between America's hemispheric ambitions and reality. By the 1820s, long-smouldering independence struggles throughout the region appeared destined for success. The vanquishing of Napoleon's empire at Waterloo in 1815, however, had extinguished one threat to American security, only to potentially spawn another. By the 1820s, the 'Holy Alliance' of European monarchies – Russia, Austria and Prussia – in league with a rehabilitated France, was threatening to reimpose European power on Latin America. This was the grave international worry with which James Monroe, the last president of the founding generation, contended.[74] In collaboration with his Secretary of State, John Quincy Adams, he ultimately crafted in response the doctrine that later came to bear his name.[75]

The Monroe Doctrine came in the form of a proclamation by the president before Congress on 2 December 1823. Its more important audience, however, consisted of foreign governments rather than American legislators. Having planned the statement in collaboration with Adams, Monroe set out a series of interlocking principles designed to obstruct any re-subjugation of the Americas to European power, and to form the spine of American policy into the foreseeable future. They were: (1) no new European colonization in the Americas would be permissible; (2) no existing colonies in the Americas should transfer between the hands of European nations; (3) finally, and more generally, Europeans should refrain from interference in the affairs of American nations outside the confines of their own vestigial colonial holdings. Any violation of these principles would be considered a trespass against vital US interests.

The message took as its starting point the consensus within the United States on non-intervention in Europe: the US, it made clear, had explicitly set aside any thought of a global push to spread any particular form of government. American policy towards Europe, Monroe asserted, was 'not to interfere in the internal concerns of any of its powers; to consider the government *de facto* as the legitimate government for us'. In reciprocity for this blanket disengagement from casting political judgement, he explained, the US expected Europeans to refrain from interfering with the politics of American nations. In the Americas, circumstances were 'eminently and conspicuously different' from elsewhere in the world, he said. It was 'impossible' that the European monarchies 'should extend their political system to any portion of either continent without endangering our peace and happiness; nor can anyone believe that our southern brethren, if left to themselves, would adopt it of their own accord'.[76]

Adams, as Bemis characterizes his view, thought that there were 'two separate systems, two spheres' in operation.[77] The purpose of Monroe's message, he felt, should be to assert American principles, and

> while disclaiming all intention of attempting to propagate them by force, and all interference with the political affairs of Europe, to declare an expectation and hope that the European powers will equally abstain from the attempt to spread their principles in the American hemisphere ... [78]

Compared with the hegemonic charter that the Monroe Doctrine would become later in the nineteenth century, the pronouncement itself was mild. It was accompanied by no military mobilization of the sort necessary to enforce the sweeping prohibitions it purported to declare.[79] In another of the ironies hovering around America's intellectual aversion to the European balance of power, Monroe's aspiration in fact depended for implementation on a coincidence of interests with Britain: it was Britain's control of the seas, and its ability to apply pressure in Europe, that gave practical effect to America's 'hands off' proclamation. Even so, the Monroe Doctrine was still a significant ideological pronouncement. Later, it would provide the political basis for a raft of regional police actions. More immediately, it rounded out intellectually the logic of the Washington–Jefferson consensus on foreign policy.

The Monroe Doctrine announced a spheres-of-influence arrangement of sorts with Europe – a realistic attempt to maximize benefits to the United States, given its capabilities and the international context. However, like

Washington's and Jefferson's pronouncements, it formulated that strategy in such a way as to intellectually 'remove' the United States from the broader international system and the European balance of power. The US portrayed itself as different from the European nations, who fought for their interests in an inescapable and competitive system of rival states. Instead, it extended Washington's formulation of 'separateness' to imply that in the Americas a new system of states was coming into existence, and that the members of that system had interests that were not so much in conflict with those of European nations as, in some abstract sense, separate or detached from them.

As one of Washington's ministers abroad, John Quincy Adams had concluded that 'it is our duty to remain the peaceful and silent, though sorrowful, spectators of the European scene'.[80] This agreement with the emerging dominant philosophy of detachment stayed with him as he rose higher on the political ladder, and was captured for the ages in his epigrammatic contribution to US strategic thought that 'America is the well wisher to the freedom and independence of all. She is the champion and vindicator only of her own.'[81] In line with the prevailing consensus, he took the view that the 'political system of the United States is ... extra-European ... [F]or the repose of Europe, as well as of America, the European and American political systems should be kept as separate and distinct from each other as possible.'[82]

The Adams–Monroe expansion of the US sphere was a development of national strategy based on changing national circumstances. The economic strength, geographical size and geopolitical weight of the US were all increasing, while the ability of the Europeans to project power in Latin America was constrained by internal division. The Monroe Doctrine was thus part of the process of the United States raising its ideological horizons to the hemispheric level, as classical realism would predict in such circumstances, while retaining and reinforcing the parallel ideological dimension of separation. In 1825, Adams, now president, explained how he conceived of the strategy as a steady evolution from Washington's Farewell:

> [T]he period which he predicted as then not far off has arrived ... *America has a set of primary interests which have none or a remote relation to Europe*, ... [and] the interference of Europe, therefore, in those concerns should be spontaneously withheld by her upon the same principles that we have never interfered with hers ... [I]f she should interfere ... we might be called ... to take an attitude which would cause our own neutrality to be respected, and choose peace or war, as our interest, guided by justice, should counsel.[83]

Interestingly, as they looked ahead to a future in which the Americas would be populated by a multiplicity of newly independent states, US leaders did not reprise the arguments of their own constitutional debate in the 1780s to infer that an American balance-of-power system, and therefore insecurity, might loom as a result. Instead, the overwhelming preponderance of power enjoyed by the US within the Western Hemisphere served to convince them that a benign and cooperative 'American system' would emerge, distinct in character from that of Europe. Exclusion of Europeans was required in order to prevent the emergence of countervailing power centres that could threaten this assumption of benign US hegemony and corrupt the system with the values of European power politics. The assertion of unchallengeable US primacy in its own environs, implicit even in the first arguments in favour of Union, had now emerged as an entirely explicit feature of the ideological consensus. Both Adams and his Secretary of State Henry Clay used the phrase 'American System' to describe the interrelation of states in the Western Hemisphere. This was intended to communicate the idea of a separate sphere of international relations operating on somehow distinctively 'American' principles, i.e. without the compulsive war of the European balance of power.

The aged Jefferson approved thoroughly of this new hemispheric scope for US policy. In retirement in 1813, he wrote of his doubts concerning how well democracy might flower in Latin American nations, but nevertheless felt that their proximity to US influence and the exclusion of European interference would maintain the separation between American and European affairs:

> In whatever governments they end, they will be *American* governments, no longer to be involved in the never-ceasing broils of Europe. The European nations constitute a separate division of the globe; their localities make them part of a distinct system; they have a set of interests of their own in which it is our business never to engage ourselves. America has a hemisphere to itself. It must have its separate system of interests, which must not be subordinated to those of Europe. The insulated state in which nature has placed the American continent, should so far avail it that no spark of war kindled in the other quarters of the globe should be wafted across the wide oceans which separate us from them. And it will be so.[84]

In a letter to his former acolyte Monroe, towards the end of his life, Jefferson endorsed the principles of the doctrine the president would shortly be proclaiming to the world:

> Our first and fundamental maxim should be, never to entangle ourselves in the broils of Europe. Our second, never to suffer Europe to intermeddle with cis-Atlantic affairs. America, North and South, has a set of interests distinct from those of Europe, and peculiarly her own, separate and apart from that of Europe. While the last is labouring to become the domicile of despotism, our endeavour should be, to make our hemisphere that of freedom.[85]

The intellectual and political journey made by Jefferson and his party is illustrated by his easy acceptance by this period of the British role in enforcing the Monroe Doctrine. By 1823 the former devotee of the French Revolution could observe with pleasure that Britain was a highly useful ally in preserving America's separateness, and was a nation with which America 'should most sedulously cherish a cordial friendship'.[86] If Hamilton had lived, he might just have appreciated the irony.[87]

Conclusion

This account of what American leaders thought and said during the emergence of the Founders' Era consensus tells us that American strategy in this period had, on the whole, a realistic character. The creation of the Union itself was the conscious product of realist philosophical assumptions about international order, and was an effort to avoid the replication of the European balance of power in America. Showing sound awareness of America's capabilities after Union, and seizing on the unique advantages conferred upon the US by geography, the Founders ultimately judged that the new nation's interests would best be served by the pursuit of a strict policy of non-interference in European affairs in order to avoid war. As the nation grew stronger, they built on this foundational consensus by seeking to exclude powerful outsiders from the Western Hemisphere and to establish a hegemonic role for the US in the region. These were not inevitable choices: the rejection of the 1787 Constitution, or US entry into Europe's wars in the hope of either ideological gratification or material gain, were serious alternatives to the choices actually made by America's early leaders. Their decision to act as they did can be explained as the pursuit of a particular vision of the national interest.

The strategy pursued in this period, however, also had ideological consequences for the longer term. Entering the Founders' Era, Americans faced two issues: relations between the American states themselves and also relations between the states collectively and Europe. The former issue was resolved not by a scheme for the coexistence of sovereign equals in a competitive balance of power, but by a Union that averted the prospect of such a system emerging in America. The latter issue was resolved not by the acceptance of a role for the United States competing in the global balance of power with Europeans, but again by rejection of the 'balance-of-power' system: Washington, Jefferson and their successors argued that geography and political circumstance afforded the US the opportunity to separate and insulate itself from global balance-of-power politics. The language with which America's leaders crafted their consensus did not facilitate thinking of America's national interest in terms of a competitive global balance of power. Instead, it encouraged the belief that the balance of power was a European system from which the United States could and should remain detached. The United States did not have interests in competition with Europeans; rather, its interests existed in a conceptually separate geopolitical space. The US refused to engage with political and military issues in Europe, and sought to exclude Europeans – the dominant powers in the global system – from the affairs of the Western Hemisphere. The 'American system' was to be a separate domain, one of cooperation, dominated by the United States.

It cannot be denied that in reality the destiny of the US was much affected by the international balance of power. Americans achieved independence through the operation of the European balance of power, and pursued Union because they were aware of the nature of that system. In their pursuit of neutrality and their management of relations with Europe during its extended wars, America's leaders displayed a good deal of realism and intelligence in their efforts to seek national advantage in a challenging international environment shaped by brutal competition for power. Ultimately, the strategy that they pursued successfully achieved a spheres-of-influence division of the world. Crucially, however, amid all of this realist practice, they did not lay the intellectual ground for America to conceive of itself as operating within a balance-of-power system, pursuing its national interests in competition with others. Instead, their discourse of separateness encouraged a perception of American detachment, of existence in a sphere of interests unconnected with the European/global system. This ideological legacy of the Founders' Era provided the basis of the foreign policy perspective often simplified analytically by the label 'isolationism'.

When national and international circumstances changed – when growing American power and events in the international system called for increased American involvement beyond the Western Hemisphere – US leaders thus had to contend with an established ideological consensus that conceived of the United States not as an interested participant in the global balance-of-power system, but as a morally superior outsider. This would have significant consequences for the nature of American internationalism.

4 Theodore Roosevelt
'The nation that has dared to be great'[1]

Introduction

The United States had come a long way by the dawn of the twentieth century. Territorial expansion had given it possession of land stretching from the Eastern Seaboard to the Pacific Ocean, encompassing a vast expanse of North America. Immigration and fertility had taken its population from four million in 1790 to more than 76 million in 1900.[2] The expansion of industry and commerce had transformed the primarily agricultural nation of early independence into one of the economic powerhouses of the developed world. All the ingredients were in place for the United States to play a major role in the global balance of power.

This chapter and the next cover the presidencies and ideas of Theodore Roosevelt (1901–9) and Woodrow Wilson (1913–21), which in terms of the book's portrait of ideological evolution form an interlinked pair. In so doing, they describe the process by which America reasoned its way towards embracing the desire to translate this potential for power into concrete global influence. Realist logic can tell us that the huge growth in America's power capabilities by 1900 naturally led it to expand the scope of its definition of the national interest.[3] Structural analysis of events in the external environment during this period, especially during Wilson's presidency, can highlight in addition the pressures for increased US activism brought to bear by the international system. The destructive operation of the European balance of power, which once again brought about global war, created circumstances in which US leaders felt pushed to pursue a more globally engaged foreign policy.

While accepting the merits of both these analyses, these chapters seek to argue the importance of a parallel ideological dimension to events. Roosevelt and Wilson did not exist in a political vacuum, free to change the established course of US foreign policy by fiat. They needed to offer coherent strategic explanation of the need for a change in national course. In doing so, they were significantly constrained by the established ideological tradition of US foreign policy. In other words, they needed to contend, even as they broke new ground, with the deeply rooted consensus dating from the Founders' Era. To paraphrase a later president, they needed to build a bridge to the twentieth century. These chapters seek to argue that the nature of the American internationalism constructed in this period was significantly shaped by this need to fashion a traversable ideological path between the prevailing tradition of 'non-entangled' aversion to the balance-of-power system and the new necessity of engaging with the global international system.

The result – as set out in detail in the body of this chapter and the next – was an American internationalism that emphasized liberal universalism, concerned itself inextricably with the internal politics of other states, and considered the price of US engagement to be the pursuit of a cooperative new order among nations. The 'road not taken' was a self-conscious realist strategic perspective, conceiving of the United States as an ordinary participant in the global balance of power and seeking to advance its interests, narrowly defined, in competitive coexistence with that system's other states. Even Theodore Roosevelt – the focus of this chapter – who was among the most 'realistic' of America's historical leaders, characterized the expansion of America's international role in highly moralistic terms, justifying a new militarism and internationalism by reference to the progress of 'civilization' and liberal imperialist assumptions regarding relations with other nations.

The chapter first describes the national and international context in which America was operating in this turn-of-the-century period. It then sets out, over several sections, the ways in which Roosevelt's bold internationalist ideology sought to push back the limits imposed by the inherited tradition of detachment, hoping to gain favour for a more globally active US policy. In the course of doing so, it acknowledges the realist aspect of his thought, but also emphasizes the equal if not greater importance of the elements of moralism and liberal imperialism in his contribution to American political ideology. Further, it shows how his deepening of the Monroe Doctrine, combined with his civilizational imperialism, prefigured Wilsonianism in laying a template for the universalist and interventionist American internationalism of later decades. The importance attributed by Roosevelt to military strength even in peacetime is also highlighted. This was out of step with the traditions of American thought prior to, and indeed during, Roosevelt's time, but his views would become established as mainstream after the Second World War.

In providing this detailed portrayal of Rooseveltian thinking on foreign policy, the aim of the chapter is to show that even as the shifting circumstances of the nation, internal and external, pushed it towards a new global engagement, the ideology that began to take shape was not balance-of-power realism, but something more universalist, perhaps even imperialist, in character. In the past, the realism of American leaders had led them, based on their reading of America's capabilities and circumstances, to shun the global balance of power. Now that the imperative was instead to engage with the global system, America's embedded ideology of detachment faced a challenge. The ideological visions that contended to displace the Founders' Era consensus, however, were themselves inheritors of that era's aversion to balance-of-power thinking, and the result was a new American internationalism significantly at odds with realism's recommended attitudinal approach to foreign policy.

National and international context

The watershed event symbolizing the United States' arrival as a global power came with the Spanish–American war of 1898. The conflict was prompted by Spain's weakening grip on Cuba, its last remaining possession of significance in the Americas. The US saw opportunity in the crisis on the island not merely to do a good turn for the Cubans – who had risen up in rebellion and faced harsh Spanish countermeasures – but also to further its own project of US dominion in the Western Hemisphere. Roosevelt, serving during the run-up to the war as Assistant Secretary of the Navy, and a vocal advocate of military action, summed up its justification as follows: '[F]irst, the advisability on the grounds of both humanity and self-interest of interfering on behalf of the Cubans, and of taking one more step toward the complete freeing of America from European dominion; second, the benefit done our people by giving them something to think about which isn't material gain, and especially the benefit done our military forces by trying both the Navy and Army in actual practice.'[4]

The incumbent administration of William McKinley was not especially devoted to foreign policy. It had won power in 1896 chiefly for domestic reasons, because the populist railing of the Democrats' William Jennings Bryan against plutocracy and the gold standard had startled the conservative Gilded Age establishment. But the growing underlying strength of the United States in terms of men and money had already done enough to turn some minds to the nation's untapped potential as an international actor, and Spain's problems on its doorstep presented a very public opportunity. Pressure for action was thus already intense when the actual spark for war arrived: an explosion on the American battleship *Maine* in Havana harbour, sinking the vessel along with more than 250 of its crew. Though no Spanish involvement could be demonstrated, in the tense context it gave American hawks enough basis to launch their first war with a European power since 1812.[5]

Though possessed only of relatively small armed forces with limited equipment and training, the Americans triumphed against sclerotic Spain, a well-chosen enemy. In the space of a few months, American forces occupied Cuba, as well as Puerto Rico. In the Pacific, in accordance with secret Navy Department plans, pre-positioned ships pulverized the Spanish fleet at Manila, adding the Philippines to the haul. Adding further to the expansionists' satisfaction, Congress took advantage of the exuberance of wartime to annex the islands of Hawaii via a joint resolution, a project that had been stalled in the machinery of government for years. It was, as Ambassador to England and soon-to-be Secretary of State John Hay jauntily observed, 'a splendid little war'.[6]

The national and international context of the United States in this period was, then, defined by strength and confidence, in stark contrast to the Founders' Era. America's underlying basis – in wealth, territory and population – for projecting power had reached unprecedented levels. Abroad, it had announced this new reality by dealing the death blow to a sickly European empire, and reinforced the supremacy of the Monroe Doctrine in the West.

The broader world was, however, as a hundred years before, still dominated by European states. Britain had recovered from the loss of America to build a vast global empire. France, after many experiments, had adopted constitutional democracy, and rivalled Britain in its pursuit of imperial possessions around the globe. At the heart of Europe, the state of Germany had been united by Prussian conquest and diplomacy, placing a rising new power at the continent's centre. Russia still struggled with the economic and political primitivism of its huge territory, but its sophisticated ruling class could still leverage its sheer scale to sustain great-power status.

Through colonialism and the evolution of an increasingly complex international economic system, the world had become more thoroughly 'Europeanized' than ever before. The modern bureaucratic states evolved in Europe, and the balance of power in which they vied with one another for influence, had become de facto the global system. Asia had become an increasingly important arena, for two reasons. First, Japan's successful emulation of Western methods had set it on track to become the first non-Western member of the modern great-power state system. Second, the fragile Chinese state, simultaneously preserved and dominated by the great powers, had become a theatre for the pursuit of economic and political rivalry between them.[7] In this period, the United States needed to envision a strategic role for itself. Its power capabilities enabled it to join this 'Europeanized' world as a great power; indeed, the scale of its power rendered non-involvement extremely difficult. Yet its foreign policy tradition encouraged non-entanglement in the balance of power between Europeans. It would be difficult, but ultimately necessary, to reconcile these facts.

The 'strenuous life' and the pursuit of national greatness[8]

The celebrated seizure of the Philippines was partly thanks to Roosevelt's tenure as Assistant Secretary of the Navy. The Secretary being out of Washington, Roosevelt was 'misguiding the Department in his absence' and ordered the pre-positioning of the necessary ships.[9] That plan in motion, he promptly resigned his post and took to the Cuban battlefield, where he saw heavily publicized action with a volunteer cavalry regiment, the so-called 'Rough Riders'. Prominent association with a short, triumphant war made him an overnight national hero. This he used as a springboard to political office, capturing the governorship of New York as a front man for the machine of local party boss Thomas C. Platt.

Within two years he had been kicked upstairs to the vice presidency of the nation after proving rather too independent minded for the comfort of his backroom sponsor. The elevation at first appeared of dubious benefit to a man of ambition; Roosevelt only accepted because he felt he had little choice, and was soon uttering the complaints of alienation from power familiar to many holders of the office. 'The man who occupies it may at any moment be everything,' he lamented, 'but meanwhile he is practically nothing.'[10] Fortunately for Roosevelt, though not for his immediate superior, the meanwhile did not in this case last long. Shot and mortally wounded by an anarchist after a speech in September 1901, McKinley yielded to 'Tecumseh's Curse' and the presidency fell to his turbulent understudy. Or, as Senator Mark Hanna, the Republican fixer behind McKinley's successes, despairingly put it: 'Now look – that damned cowboy is President of the United States.'[11] He was 42.

Such was Roosevelt's personal exuberance that he appeared to many a larger-than-life, even cartoonish character. Playing tennis in rain or shine, indulging in boxing and martial arts to unwind – with a predictably long list of injuries – and notorious for forcing lunch guests, foreign dignitaries included, to accompany him on arduous outward-bound treks, he was by some distance America's most physically adventurous president. His company could also be overpowering verbally: guests were 'overwhelmed in a torrent of oratory' which even his friend Henry Adams sometimes found 'mortifying beyond even drunkenness. The worst of it is that it is mere cerebral excitement, of normal, or at least habitual, nature. It has not the excuse of champagne, the wild talk about everything ... [it] belonged not to the bar-room but the asylum ... When I was let out and got to bed, I was a broken man.' 'Theodore is never sober,' he observed on another occasion, 'only he is drunk with himself and not with rum.'[12] It is not difficult to see why one recipient of the Roosevelt treatment advised visitors, tongue in cheek, 'you must always remember that the president is about six'.[13]

The compulsive dynamism was the product of a philosophy of self-improvement through incessant activity. TR was committed to, even obsessed by, the idea that, to be good, a man had to embrace the path of action; to 'be the man who is actually in the arena, whose face is marred by dust and sweat and blood'. Win or lose, such a man was superior to the 'cold and timid souls who know neither victory nor defeat'.[14] Leon Bazalgette, author of the first TR biography, noted that: 'To live, for him, has no meaning other than to drive oneself, to act with all one's strength. An existence without stress, without struggle, without growth has always struck him as mindless. Those who remain on the sidelines he sees as cowards, and consequently his personal enemies.'[15]

Crucial to understanding Roosevelt's foreign policy thinking is to appreciate that he considered the same philosophy to apply to nations as to men. Acutely conscious that the United States had risen to potential great-power status, he made it his work to exhort, cajole and scold the American people and their representatives until they embraced the role and responsibilities this entailed. Accepting the vice presidency, he expressed his expectations by means of aggressive rhetorical enquiry: 'Is America a weakling to shrink from the world work of the great world powers?' The answer, he declared, must be 'No'.[16]

Indeed, the purpose of the 'Strenuous Life' speech, which famously set out his personal ethos, was to draw precisely this link between how each American should live and how America as a whole should carry itself. 'As it is with the individual, so it is with the nation,' he proclaimed. 'Far better it is to dare mighty things, to win glorious triumphs, even though checkered by failure, than to take rank with those poor spirits who neither enjoy much nor suffer much, because they live in the gray twilight that knows not victory nor defeat.'[17] The country most to be admired was that prepared to 'boldly face the life of strife ... provided we are certain that the strife is justified, for it is only through strife, through hard and dangerous endeavour, that we shall ultimately win the goal of true national greatness'.[18]

In advancing such views, TR signalled himself as the first top-tier political leader to openly confront the mindset of the Founders' Era consensus and argue the case for a bold new global role. America's tradition of shunning involvement in non-American affairs was, to his mind, becoming dangerously outmoded. 'There is scant room in the world at large for the nation with mighty thews that dares not to be great,' he had told an audience in 1901, and he would not rest until the American people had been persuaded that modern conditions demanded a more active foreign policy.[19] Having resoundingly defeated the colourless Democrat Alton Parker in 1904 to win a term in his own right, Roosevelt used his inaugural address to remind the nation that:

> Much has been given us, and much will rightfully be expected from us ... We have become a great nation, forced by the fact of its greatness into relations with the other nations of the earth, and we must behave as beseems a people with such responsibilities.[20]

Likely thinking of Jefferson's expressed ideal of emulating China's relation to the world, TR more than once cited China as an example of repugnantly passive foreign policy, lambasting those politicians who he believed sought to 'Chinafy' the nation. 'We cannot, if we would, play the part of China,' he expounded, 'and be content to rot by inches in ignoble ease within our borders, taking no interest in what goes on beyond them, sunk in a scrambling commercialism; heedless of the higher life, the life of aspiration, of toil and risk.'[21] If the United States opted to pursue this policy, it would eventually 'go down before other nations that have not lost the manly and adventurous qualities'.[22] A published historian himself, TR identified himself with the pro-army, strong-state ethos of the Federalists and had a marked dislike of Jefferson, whom he described as 'perhaps the most incapable executive that ever filled the national chair; being almost purely a visionary, he was utterly unable to grapple with the slightest actual danger'.[23]

It was simply impermissible, TR was insistent, to seek to 'opt out' of America's responsibility to act as a global power, as a matter both of prudence and of ethics. Drawing a parallel with the individual's simultaneous responsibilities to family and society, he argued that 'a nation's first duty is within its own borders, [but] it is not thereby absolved from facing its duties in the world as a whole; and if it refuses to do so, it merely forfeits its right to struggle for a place among the peoples that shape the destiny of mankind'.[24] The attainment of this historical 'place' was essential to Roosevelt, and underlay his determination that the US should make its mark on the development of what he termed 'civilization'. This was his ultimate test of national success, and by passing it, America might achieve a kind of notional immortality. Nations, like men, were transient, but 'the nation that has dared to be great, that has had the will and the power to change the destiny of the ages ... really continues, though in a changed form, to live forevermore'.[25]

In making such claims Roosevelt drew parallels with the historical legacies built by Rome and Britain.[26] The embrace of imperialism inherent in such comparisons was not out of character. Especially in pre-presidential days – the practicalities of running the likes of the Philippines later dimmed his ardour – Roosevelt was explicitly and proudly imperialist in outlook, albeit with the qualification that his was an imperialism that nodded to the liberal principle that subject peoples should be beneficiaries of the process. As Britain had done in Egypt and India, he mused in his 'Strenuous Life' address, 'we will play our part in the great work of uplifting mankind'.[27]

Military strength, restraint and the 'soldierly virtues'

A key step towards the embrace of global 'responsibilities', in Roosevelt's mind, was expansion of the military, one of the most significant areas in which he used his leadership to challenge the existing consensus. Indeed, enlarging, strengthening and modernizing the armed forces, particularly the navy, was the single most prominent concrete end sought by all his political pronouncements. One of the first addresses of importance that he made in national office, to the Naval War College in 1897, was on the theme of 'Washington's Forgotten Maxim', by which he meant the old epigram that 'to be prepared for war is the most effectual way to promote peace'.[28] The prevailing attitude at the time, in the tradition of Jeffersonian republicanism, was that permitting a large military establishment in peacetime would be the prelude to foreign wars and a threat to liberty at home. Roosevelt sought to turn the tables, arguing that weakness invited slights from other powers that could force the nation into conflicts for which it was ill prepared.

There was 'not the slightest danger of an over-development of warlike spirit' in America, he declared.[29] On the contrary, the true danger lay in its underdevelopment. Paper guarantees of peace offered by the sort of arbitration treaties popular in this period had their place, he felt; as president he engaged with efforts at an international regime for arbitration of disputes. But they were insufficient. 'Arbitration is an excellent thing,' he insisted, 'but ultimately those who wish to see this country at peace with foreign nations will be wise if they place reliance upon a first-class fleet of battleships rather than on any arbitration treaty which the wit of man can devise.'[30] Far from undermining domestic liberty, Roosevelt believed that armed strength was the key to preserving it:

> It may be that at some time in the dim future ... the need for war will vanish. But that time is yet ages distant. As yet no nation can hold its place in the world, or can do any work really worth doing, unless it stands ready to guard its rights with an armed hand. That orderly liberty which is both the foundation and the capstone of our civilization can be gained and kept only by men who are willing to fight for an ideal.[31]

He put forward an unsentimental but probably accurate view of the European great powers, warning that 'we shall keep the respect of each of them just so long as we are thoroughly able to hold our own, and no longer'. 'If we got into trouble, there is not one of them whose friendship we could count on to get us out; what we shall need to count upon is the efficiency of our own fighting men and particularly of our navy.'[32] 'I have fought,' he later wrote to the English diplomat Cecil Spring-Rice, '... to make our people understand that unless freedom shows itself compatible with military strength, with national efficiency, it will ultimately have to go to the wall.'[33]

As well as shipbuilding, national preparedness meant something less tangible: the inculcation of a fighting spirit in the people. '[T]he nation', he insisted, 'should have physical no less than moral courage.'[34] Without this, it would be the prey of tougher powers. Americans had to 'secure peace by being ready to fight for it', and this necessitated holding on to 'those most valuable of all qualities, the soldierly virtues', 'fighting qualities for the lack of which in a nation, as in an individual, no refinement, no culture, no wealth, no material prosperity can atone'.[35] To Spring-Rice he wrote: 'I abhor and despise that pseudo-humanitarianism which treats advance in civilization as necessarily and rightfully implying a weakening of the fighting spirit and which therefore invites destruction of the advanced civilization by some less-advanced type.'[36]

He posited a virtuous chain of intertwined goods. A proper navy and army would prepare the nation to face external threats. This would enrich the national character with martial virtues and manly self-respect. With both physical and spiritual strength thus in place, America would be well placed to stake its claim to national greatness. The alternative was to remain in denial regarding the necessity of translating America's size and status into global engagement. This meant immersion instead in base materialism or, worse, ideological pacifism, bringing both vulnerability to external threats and moral degeneration. This was a worldview that gave rise to a plethora of 'Rooseveltian' maxims: 'A nation that cannot fight is not worth its salt'; 'Mere bigness, if it is also mere flabbiness, means nothing but disgrace'; 'An unmanly desire to avoid a quarrel is often the surest way to precipitate one.'[37]

Yet, despite his militarism and a fixation on 'manliness' that it would not overly tax a gender theorist to deconstruct, Roosevelt did not see himself as an advocate of international aggression. Clearly – irrefutably, indeed – he had a deep emotional and intellectual attachment to an idealized notion of war. In spirit he always remained the man who told the Naval War College that 'no triumph of peace is quite so great as the supreme triumphs of war'.[38] But his ideals of manly virtue, importantly, also encompassed a kind of moral restraint. Military strength might enable aggression abroad, but it could not justify it any more than individual power justified being a bully, a species Roosevelt insisted he despised. 'I am as intolerant of brutality and cruelty to the weak', he insisted, 'as I am intolerant of weakness and effeminacy.'[39]

Indeed his most famous single sentence on foreign policy illustrates his desire that the wielding of hard power be understated, though it is not always interpreted in this way. Borrowing what he alleged was a West African proverb, he summed up his prescribed ethos for policy in the Western Hemisphere thus: '*Speak softly and carry a big stick: you will go far.* If the American nation will speak softly, and yet build, and keep at a pitch of the highest training, a thoroughly efficient navy, the Monroe Doctrine will go far.'[40] It is tempting, in deconstructing this remark, to emphasize the eye-catching stick. But it sits better with what Roosevelt was trying to achieve at the time – to persuade a war-averse political class of the benefits of military spending – and with a wider reading of his thought, to conclude that he intended his invented proverb's two elements – strength and restraint – to share equal importance. He had spelled out the need for balance between underlying power and diplomatic caution in a prior observation on the theme: 'If a man continually blusters, if he lacks civility, a big stick will not save him from trouble; but neither will speaking softly avail, if back of the softness there does not lie strength, power.'[41]

This aversion to 'bluster' was not purely theoretical. When Admiral Dewey, a darling of the nation's hawks after the triumph at Manila, later made public statements playing up America's role in forcing Germany to pull back from an intervention in Venezuela, Roosevelt warned him sharply against such talk in public: 'Say nothing that can be taken hold of by those anxious to foment trouble between ourselves and any foreign power ... We are too big a people to be able to be careless in what we say.'[42] Hand in hand with power, as he saw it, came the need for circumspection.

Realism in Roosevelt

Roosevelt has won more approval from realist analysts than many American presidents can claim. Kissinger argues that he 'commands a unique position in America's approach to international relations. No other president defined America's role so completely in terms of the national interest, or identified the national interest so comprehensively with the balance of power.' Highlighting his appreciation of the limits of international law and his emphasis on the value of military strength, Kissinger suggests that TR 'taught an especially stern doctrine for a people brought up in the belief that peace is the normal condition among nations, that there is no difference between personal and public morality, and that America was safely insulated from the upheavals affecting the rest of the world'. His willingness to accept the idea of regional hegemony of the strong over the weak in a spheres-of-influence system shows him to be possessed of 'European-style views', according to Kissinger: 'He approached the global balance of power with a sophistication matched by no other American president.'[43]

There is some truth to this. It is correct that Roosevelt was vastly closer to the realist perspective than his near-contemporary Wilson, whom realists have always loathed for his perceived embodiment of high-flown liberal idealism unconstrained by appreciation for reality's limits. If realism is defined by its focus on the national interest, then certain key events in Roosevelt's presidency do lend weight to his credentials. His grandest project was realizing concrete progress in the long-standing but ever-delayed scheme to link the Caribbean to the Pacific by canal. This was made possible by Roosevelt's apparent involvement, in 1903, in the Panamanian conspiracy to secede from Colombia after the Colombian Senate had rejected a canal deal previously agreed with the US.[44] An immense strategic gain – an isthmian canal under American control – was thus achieved by means of a covert plan that vitiated the sovereignty and territorial integrity of another nation. 'I have no use for a government that would do what that government has done,' Roosevelt observed dismissively of the authorities in Bogota, upon learning of their rejection of the original deal.[45]

In dealing with weightier powers he was similarly hard nosed. The reinvigoration of the Monroe Doctrine, which purported to exclude European powers from Latin America, was a central feature of Roosevelt's presidency.[46] In one notable instance, he apparently used back-channel threats to fend off Germany's desire to exploit Venezuelan debts as a means of establishing a colonial foothold in the Americas.[47] In so doing, he successfully defended the US sphere of influence through willingness to raise the threat of force – diplomatically and in secret, but evidently with sufficient firmness.[48]

One of Roosevelt's most celebrated diplomatic achievements, ultimately rewarded with a Nobel Prize for Peace, was convening successful talks to close the Russo-Japanese War. TR was personally pleased at the bloody nose delivered to Russia in that conflict, but knew that even though they had won the fighting, the Japanese needed a formal peace before their limited resources ran out.[49] In negotiating a peace, he hoped to leave the two powers 'locked in a clinch, counterweighing one another, and both kept weak by the effort'.[50] The deal struck at Portsmouth, New Hampshire, achieved something resembling just that. In pursuit of the settlement, Roosevelt was prepared to endorse Japanese control over Korea, and thus to engage in *realpolitik* at the expense of previously professed American commitments to the territorial integrity of China and to the principle of self-determination.[51] This new degree of initiative and involvement in global great-power affairs – manipulating a regional balance of power to American advantage – is perhaps the clearest example in support of the realist portrayal of Roosevelt, and Kissinger predictably underlines it.[52] Of the Portsmouth deal, Roosevelt observed: 'It's a mighty good thing for Russia, and a mighty good thing for Japan ... [and] a mighty good thing for me too.'[53]

Finally, we might note Roosevelt's cautious involvement in the 1906 Algeciras Conference on the control of Morocco. American participation was a sign of the rising global esteem in which the nation was held, but also a potential infraction against the non-entanglement consensus. As such, the president was obliged to be careful, and kept American involvement to a reserved minimum. The United States agreed to attend the talks, but resisted weighing in on matters of substance, disappointing Germany's hope that the US should boldly assert the principle of the 'Open Door' in such a way as to favour the German case in Morocco.[54]

In each of these instances, Roosevelt appeared comfortable treating the international system as a competitive arena in which states battled for their interests. This was not out of tune with his pre-presidential philosophy. During his time in the Navy Department he expressed the view that resisting German interference in Latin America was not a matter of abstract law and justice, merely of conflicting interests:

> [T]wo nations with violently conflicting interests may each be entirely right from its own standpoint ... [A]s a German, I should be delighted ... to defy the Americans and their Monroe Doctrine in South America ... As an American I should advocate ... keeping our Navy at a pitch that will enable us to interfere promptly if Germany ventures to touch a foot of American soil. I would not go into the abstract rights and wrongs of it; I would simply say that we did not intend to have Germans on this continent ... and if Germany intended to extend her empire here she would have to whip us first ... I should adopt [this course] without in the least feeling that the Germans who advocated German colonial expansion were doing anything save what was right and proper from the standpoint of their own people. Nations may, and often must, have conflicting interests, and in the present age patriotism stands a good deal ahead of cosmopolitanism.[55]

Moralism in Roosevelt

Kissinger argues that Roosevelt offered a 'stern doctrine' that sought to correct the American people's wrong-headed assumption 'that there is no difference between personal and public morality'.[56] While the elements of realism in Roosevelt are there and must be acknowledged, this particular way of posing the argument is misleading, and difficult to reconcile with Roosevelt's stated beliefs. While his geopolitical sensibility was indeed strong, TR also had a potent moralistic dimension to his foreign policy thought. In one of his most important messages on foreign affairs, he declared that 'a nation has no more right to do injustice to another nation, strong or weak, than an individual ... the same moral law applies in one case as in the other'.[57] And in a high-profile address in 1910 he pronounced that: 'I do not for one moment admit that political morality is different from private morality ... I do not for one moment admit that a nation should treat other nations in a different spirit from that in which an honorable man would treat other men.'[58]

The determined sceptic may argue that such rhetoric concealed contrary beliefs. Yet one must wonder why Roosevelt would deliberately raise the issue in such terms at all if he did not sincerely believe his own portrayal of his position. He was not, after all, under enquiry as to whether he harboured realist sympathies. And such claims to being driven by a moral imperative do fit the broader pattern of Roosevelt's thought. In contrast to Kissinger's observation, it is striking the degree to which Roosevelt's view of optimal foreign policy was an outgrowth of his moralistic standpoint regarding social life in general. It has already been noted that his advocacy of 'the strenuous life' served to draw a parallel between the good life for an individual and for a nation. Similarly, in his distaste for bluster and bluffing he was apt to draw parallels with individual good conduct. In a statement to Congress condemning lofty declarations bereft of capacity for follow-through, his chosen phrase was that the practice was 'contemptible, for a nation, as for an individual'.[59]

The sentiment emergent from Roosevelt's analogies between what good men and good nations ought to do was usually that leaders needed to maintain balance between insisting on American rights and respecting those of others. While not crusading in tone, this philosophy of determined self-assertion was certainly framed in moral terms, and often linked to the idea that the only truly acceptable peace was a 'righteous' one:

> [J]ustice and generosity in a nation, as in an individual, count most when shown not by the weak but by the strong. While ever careful to refrain from wronging others, we must be no less insistent that we are not wronged ourselves. We wish peace, but we wish the peace of justice, the peace of righteousness. We wish it because we think it is right and not because we are afraid. No weak nation that acts manfully and justly should ever have cause to fear us, and no strong power should ever be able to single us out as a subject for insolent aggression.[60]

His programme of military strength and self-reliance was not justified simply by reference to the narrow national interest. The argument was broader: that America had a duty to contribute to the furtherance of civilization – through struggle, risk and sacrifice – and that only the strong could fulfil such a duty. This was, in essence, the 'moral case' for a more militarized United States, and Roosevelt used it to justify his programme of naval expansion:

> The little powers of Europe, although in many cases they lead honorable and self-respecting national lives, are powerless to accomplish any good

in foreign affairs ... because they lack the element of force behind their good wishes. We on the contrary have been able to do so much ... because, and only because, together with the purpose to be just and to keep the peace we possess a navy which makes it evident that we will not tamely submit to injustice, or tamely acquiesce in breaking the peace.[61]

There was nothing inherently moral about peace, Roosevelt believed – he was vocal about his loathing for pacifists – and certainly nothing intrinsically immoral about war, which was often necessary to preserve or advance justice. And yet some of his thoughts on the question of war's righteousness in the pursuit of an ultimate just peace look more like precursors of Wilsonianism than a *realpolitik* counterpoint to it. In his foreign policy address to Congress in 1904, for example, TR pointed an accusatory finger at tyrannical governments and seemed to imply that only a grand reshaping of the political order could finally bring a world peace founded on just principles:

There are kinds of peace which are highly undesirable, which are in the long run as destructive as any war. Tyrants and oppressors have many times made a wilderness and called it peace ... The peace of tyrannous terror, the peace of craven weakness, the peace of injustice, all these should be shunned as we shun unrighteous war. The goal to set before us as a nation, the goal which should be set before all mankind, is the attainment of the peace of justice, of the peace which comes when each nation is not merely safe-guarded in its own rights, but scrupulously recognises and performs its duty toward others. Generally peace tells for righteousness; but if there is conflict between the two, then our fealty is due first to the cause of righteousness.[62]

These were views in which he would find himself coinciding with Wilson after American entry into the Great War in 1917. During the neutrality that preceded American involvement, however, he criticized the president in harsh moral terms for his strenuous efforts to stay out of the conflict. Roosevelt convinced himself that Wilson's clinging to neutrality signalled him as either a coward or a cynical political operator manipulating anti-war sentiment for advantage. To his son Kermit he wrote in 1915: 'I agree with all that you say about German brutality and ruthlessness. But after all, a brute is not any worse than a coward. Wilson is at heart an abject coward; or else he has a heart so cold and selfish that he is entirely willing to sacrifice the honor and the interest of his country to his own political advancement.'[63] It was a charge he was happy to repeat to his political friends, and which he continued to make up until the eve of war.[64]

It is thus clear that designation of Roosevelt as a realist must be qualified by the observation that he was fervently moralistic in the way that he thought about foreign policy, and self-aware about that fact. He argued that America should translate its wealth into military strength, not for the simple advancement of self-interest but as a weapon for use in the service of 'righteousness'. That righteousness certainly included the solid defence of the nation's interests, but there was also a broader agenda: the nation's duty to arm itself was not merely prudential, but also a moral imperative. As he prepared to leave the White House in 1908, Roosevelt – not at that time foreseeing the European war – observed that his departure was probably timed right, because politics was turning ever more towards technocratic economic problems. Of such problems, he observed, 'I am not deeply interested in them: my problems are moral problems and my teaching has been plain morality.'[65] Though certainly a militarist, who desired American participation in the arena of global power politics, there was a moral and civilizational dimension to Roosevelt's ideology that should not lightly be dismissed, and which undermines Kissinger's portrayal of a clear dividing line between the personal and the international in the Rooseveltian moral schema.

The 'Roosevelt Corollary' and American quasi-imperialism

During Roosevelt's presidency the United States still held back from full engagement with the strategic balance between the European powers, despite the president's general enthusiasm for an activist foreign policy. This was because, in the absence of a great external upheaval of the sort that would later confront Wilson, Roosevelt was still significantly constrained by the non-entanglement consensus that had held sway for the previous century. His ideas regarding increased national self-assertion and a civilizing mission could still be expressed in other arenas, however, and most thoroughly in the Western Hemisphere. Here an ideological and practical base for US hegemony already existed, thanks to the Monroe Doctrine, and Roosevelt sought to build on it.

In the aftermath of the German–Venezuelan crisis early in his presidency, Roosevelt was acutely aware that a blanket US guarantee to protect Latin American nations from European intervention had created moral hazard. If shielded by their northern neighbour from any threat of retribution, states could run up bad debts with impunity. This dilemma provided the inspiration for Roosevelt's famous 'corollary' to the Monroe Doctrine, which expanded the doctrine into the interventionist's charter that the term conjures in most minds today. The Corollary stated that if the US was expected to defend Latin American states in a crisis, then it was justly entitled to act preventively against any wrongdoing on the part of states that might by their actions provoke such a turn of events. This ideological *quid pro quo* served – from the US perspective, at least – to legitimize 'temporary' seizure of parts of the Venezuelan fiscal apparatus to ensure sound management. This was the first instalment in a wide and deep pattern of regional interventionism that would unfold under Roosevelt and his successors.

Roosevelt's concept of 'civilization' played a foreground part in the construction of the imagined legitimacy of this framework for regional relations. The Corollary was based on the idea that civilized nations had a duty to monitor and re-educate those states where civilization was less developed. Under conditions where 'chronic wrongdoing, or ... impotence ... results in a general loosening of the ties of civilized society', he argued, 'intervention by some civilized nation' might be required. Within the area covered by the Monroe Doctrine this meant the 'exercise of an international police power' by the United States, 'however reluctantly'. He was naturally eager to disavow any 'land hunger' on the part of the United States; the proposed interventionism was argued to be for the good of the nations in question, improving internal order and ensuring that no pretext for European predation might emerge. 'All that this country desires is to see the neighboring countries stable, orderly, and prosperous,' he professed.[66]

Perhaps the single most important conceptual move in the ideological legitimization of the Roosevelt Corollary was the assertion that 'our interests and those of our southern neighbors are in reality identical'. This ideological conflation of US interests with those of others meant that even as the United States asserted the power to decide unilaterally when and where to intervene, it could also argue that the affected nations ought not to perceive US oversight as an intrusion based on an imposed hierarchy, but as a mutually beneficial process. This sort of thinking would later also be central to Wilsonianism. So long as 'the reign of law and justice' held sway within their borders and they obeyed 'the primary laws of civilized society', Latin American states need fear no interference under Roosevelt's model.[67]

Here we find shoots of ideological divergence from realist thinking regarding the state system. On one level, the Monroe Doctrine was and had always been a realist proposition: a spheres-of-influence arrangement dividing up the world's regions and allocating them to the local management of the great powers. At the same time, however, the United States' management of the 'American System' within the Western Hemisphere had provided it with a laboratory within which to develop the alternative ideas of international order that it would later seek – via Wilsonianism – to apply on a global level. These ideas are perhaps best described as liberal quasi-imperialism.[68]

Within the American System, the United States considered itself to be engaged not in power balancing or outright exploitation, but in the management of an order based on (1) its own hard-power hegemony, (2) a conception of 'civilization' defined by the US in its capacity as benign hegemon, and (3) an insistence that this civilized order was based on fundamentally identical or harmonious national interests. Though the point was not explicitly spelled out, it was a fundamental assumption of this model for order that the prerogative of identifying and acting on the 'common interest' lay with the United States alone. This unarticulated but central principle of unaccountable-yet-legitimate leadership is key to understanding the ideology of American interventionism that would follow, including Wilsonianism and its successor creeds.

Without an understanding of the self-justificatory role played by this ideological assumption, subsequent US policy appears cynically disingenuous.

With it, it takes on the aspect of a sincerely well-intentioned but deeply chauvinistic – even solipsistic – enterprise, and that is, on balance, a more accurate portrayal of the bulk of American thinking. Roosevelt's ideological position was relatively liberal in the sense that it viewed freedom, development and self-government as the ideal for other nations, but also imperialistic in seeking to impose American parameters on the values and practices 'free' societies should adopt. '[E]very nation ... which desires to maintain its freedom, its independence,' he argued, 'must ultimately realize that the right of such independence cannot be separated from the responsibility of making good use of it.'[69]

Roosevelt is rightly associated, because of his writings and political lobbying, with the formal imperialism of the United States that followed the territorial acquisitions of 1898. By the time of his presidency, however, the nation had lost its enthusiasm for formal empire. Resistance on the part of subject peoples, combined with prevailing attitudes regarding race, served to convince most Americans that assimilation of the newly acquired populations into the domestic structures of US government would be impossible. Yet simple colonial rule would generate unwelcome contradictions within the ideological culture of American politics, which in principle opposed all unrepresentative government. The remaining option, therefore, was the 'third way': to pursue, on as swift a schedule as practically possible, the ultimate liberation of the subject peoples and their 'education' in how to make 'good use' of their freedom.[70] This set of ideas, applied first and foremost to Cuba and the Philippines, came to have relevance to the whole of US Latin American policy.[71]

'Barbarism', Roosevelt argued, could have 'no place in a civilized world'. 'It is our duty toward the people living in barbarism to see that they are freed from their chains, and we can free them only by destroying barbarism itself ... We must raise others while we are benefiting ourselves.'[72] In the Philippines, it was his view that: 'We are not trying to subjugate a people; we are trying to develop them.'[73] This meant attempting to instil American political mores in the hope they would ultimately become self-sustaining. As Morris observes: 'Expansion to [Roosevelt] meant a hemispheric programme of acquisition, democratisation and liberation.'[74]

Because he thought in these terms, Roosevelt did not – as others well might – perceive using violence to repress the Philippine rebels or erecting an unstable quasi-independent state in Cuba as cynical efforts by the United States to harvest power for itself. He was confident – up to a point – that it was possible to 'rapidly teach the people of the Philippine Islands ... how to make good use of their freedom', and thought it irresponsible to expect them to thrive if propelled directly into sovereignty without stewardship. Those who criticized America's educative imperial role, he said, were 'jack fools who seriously think that any group of pirates and head-hunters needs nothing but independence in order that it may be turned forthwith into a dark-hued New England town meeting'.[75] This attitude was not limited to Latin America. In China, Roosevelt supported the other great powers in repressing the Boxer

Rebellion and resisting Chinese demands for greater autonomy. This was similarly based on the imperialist logic that the Chinese were not equipped to cope with full sovereignty, and needed continued tutelage to protect them from doing themselves harm. There was a harsh circularity in Roosevelt's thought: a people only deserved respect, he insisted, if they could demonstrate strength and independence, something for which he praised the 'civilized' Japanese; yet he accused those who pushed forcefully for more independence, as the Chinese did, of child-like irresponsibility for doing so.[76]

Like many imperialists, Roosevelt tended to think of himself as the reactive party in the relationship, compelled to intervene when really he would have preferred otherwise. Further, he considered his interventionist policies to be so self-evidently for the benefit of all involved as to merit compliance and gratitude. Faced with the absence of either, he was therefore prone to disillusionment and anger. Forced, as he saw it, into renewed intervention to suppress disorder in 'independent' Cuba in 1906, he took on the rhetorical character of an enraged Caesar: 'Just at the moment I am so angry with that infernal little Cuban republic that I would like to wipe its people off the face of the earth,' he fumed. 'All that we wanted for them was that they would behave themselves and be prosperous and happy so we that we should not have to interfere.'[77]

When pressure mounted for the US to take the Dominican Republic's finances into receivership, he lamented: 'I have about the same desire to annex it as a gorged boa constrictor might have to swallow a porcupine wrong end to.'[78] Even in the case of Colombia, in whose dismemberment he conspired during the Panama affair, he maintained the line that 'this country, so far from wronging Colombia, made every possible effort to persuade Colombia to allow herself to be benefited'.[79] Even before he proclaimed the Roosevelt Corollary, he had arrived at the view that 'sooner or later it seems to me inevitable that the United States should assume an attitude of protection and regulation to all these little states in the neighbourhood of the Caribbean. I hope it will be deferred as long as possible, but I fear it is inevitable.'[80]

In effect, his view was that he was obliged to impose his own solutions on others because they could not see the truth: that their own interests lay in line with his prescriptions. To be sure, there was an element of rationalization to this talk, of the sort practised by liberal imperialists in other times and places, but the ideas themselves were sincerely held. Roosevelt did, in his own way, believe in 'self-determination' for nations. But he accompanied this with the heavy qualification that certain developmental preconditions, including stability and political good order, needed to be in place before independence could succeed, especially when it came to non-white peoples.

Beyond that, he also seemed to assume, in line with other American 'progressives', that a free nation was, in a sense, defined as truly free by its choosing to become the right kind of society, and that this meant adopting at least the most basic of the United States' particular principles and practices. It might be acknowledged in theory that free societies could vary in how they structured themselves, but their differences had to be purely superficial: on central political and economic principles, they were expected to share the same values, paving the way for a network of essentially harmonious interests within and between nations. In this way, 'liberty' was not viewed as a condition allowing for a multiplicity of alternative paths of development. Rather, 'true' liberty was taken to contain fixed social outcomes within it, or at least narrow parameters limiting acceptable outcomes, within which 'free nations' should develop. To put it more concisely, it was assumed by a great many American thinkers that *liberty for* a state ought to produce something resembling *liberalism within* that state, for such was the meaning of 'progress', as they understood it. If this proved not to be the case, it was axiomatic that the nation in question had not truly become free, thus rendering further intervention to rectify that flaw entirely legitimate.

This was the ideological basis of Roosevelt's liberal quasi-imperialism in Latin America. In the Philippines, this meant restructuring the social order while maintaining occupation. In Cuba, it meant underwriting a brittle liberal order with the promise of US intervention, should backsliding occur. In other states less completely within the United States' administrative grasp, it meant preventing European intervention by policing behaviour, and intervening more deeply if a crisis should arise. Under Roosevelt's direction, therefore, the Monroe Doctrine realized its conceptual potential in supporting an 'American System' of states under US hegemony. Based on an assumed right to assert common or identical interests, the US created an international order in the Western Hemisphere based not on a balance of power but on a universalistic and progressive model of national development towards approved liberal values. This expanded version of the Monroe Doctrine would later serve as the basis for American ideas regarding the reform of the entire global system.

The First World War, progress and the moral case for arms

Roosevelt's views on global affairs also had some features reflective of his status as a participant in the Progressive movement in early twentieth-century American politics. He was aware of the potential for complex changes in technology and economic patterns – phenomena that would later be bundled under the term 'globalization' – to affect the nature of international relations. Even well before the political rupture brought about by the First World War, he predicted major reform of the international order in the foreseeable future. 'As civilization grows, warfare becomes less and less the normal condition of foreign relations,' he observed. 'More and more the increasing interdependence and complexity of international political and economic relations renders it incumbent on all the civilized and orderly powers to insist on the proper policing of the world.'[81]

Where he fell out of step with much of the mainstream liberal internationalism of his era was in his belief that the process of 'civilizing' international relations was still in early development rather than on the brink of full flower. Unlike those who seemed to think world peace just around the corner, he was sceptical of predictions that the role of force was on the verge of becoming an irrelevance. Perhaps some day war might be obsolete and the world's nations cohabiting in a harmonious system, he thought, but for now the world was inhabited by a mixture of good, upstanding nations and others of more dubious character. In such a world, it was imperative that the good, including the United States, develop their military strength.

The outbreak of the Great War in Europe in 1914 served to underline this necessity, he thought. During the three years of American neutrality that followed, he cited the war as evidence that force was far from obsolete in international affairs. 'We hope ultimately that the day will come on this earth when wars will cease. But at present the realization of that hope seems as far in the future as the realization of that other hope, that some day in the future all crime will cease,' he argued.[82] It was clear to him that some kinds of great power were more dangerous than others: their strength used to bully and their respect for the rights of others negligible. He saw Germany as one such threat. As the first wave of war consumed Europe, he criticized Germany in harsh terms for having precipitated the conflict with 'no regard for anything except its own interest ... For the last forty-three years Germany has spread out everywhere, and has menaced every nation where she thought it was to her advantage to do so.'[83]

His call for a stand against Germany was not quite immediate. At the moment of the war's outbreak, he hesitated, agreeing that Belgium had been wronged but suggesting that it was 'eminently desirable that we should remain entirely neutral'. Indeed, he echoed President Wilson's position – one he would subsequently pillory – in arguing that 'neutrality may be of prime necessity in order ... to conserve our influence for helping toward the reestablishment of general peace when the time comes'.[84] This phase, however, was fleeting. In the early stages of the war he wrote to Spring-Rice that had he still been president, he would have led a multilateral effort to restore Belgian neutrality, which had been guaranteed under recent Hague treaties.[85] It was not long before he became a vociferous convert to the cause of full American intervention, far earlier than most American politicians of either party.

The US had every reason to be concerned about the outcome of the war in Europe. Any outcome that put control of the Continent in the hands of a hegemonic power would represent a grave threat to American security. And, as a century before, America's commercial ties to the belligerents made its indirect entanglement in their respective war efforts hard to avoid. Part of Roosevelt's desire for US war entry was founded in the clear and present danger of Germany to US strategic interests. If Germany came to dominate Europe and 'smashed the English Fleet', he predicted, 'within a year or two she would insist upon taking the dominant position in South and Central America'.[86] This was not a newly dawning realization: years earlier he had noted that America had an interest in preserving a balance of power in Europe:

> [A]s long as England succeeds in keeping up the balance of power in Europe, not in principle but in reality, well and good. Should she, however, for some reason or other fail in doing so, the United States would be obliged to step in, at least temporarily, in order to re-establish the balance of power in Europe, never mind against which country or group of countries our efforts may have to be directed.[87]

His preference for Britain over Germany as a dominant naval power was partly pragmatic as opposed to ethical or civilizational: he believed that the US–UK relationship could be managed more advantageously because 'Canada is a hostage for her good behaviour'.[88]

Even taking all of this into account, however, it is evident that Roosevelt projected a moral dimension onto the European conflict that went beyond simple conflict between national interests. It was also, for him, a war with implications for civilization as he understood it, and part of his concern in judging what the war demanded of America was assessing what would best advance the interests of 'civilization' as a transnational concept. In making that judgement, he had some ambivalence: might crushing Germany open the door to 'a great military danger in the future' from Russia? But on balance he decided that 'there is no question where the interests of civilization lie at this moment'. That was in opposition to Germany. He even held out hope for a win-win scenario under which 'this war may see the dawn of the reaction against militarism and that Russia may tend to grow more civilized and more liberal'.[89] In his later discussion of the war, the attribution of blame was important, and it was clear to him that it lay with Germany. The 'most tremendous tragedy in the history of civilization', he said, had been brought about by 'the cynical treachery, brutality and barbarism and the conscienceless worshipping of revolting cunning and brute force which made the German people what it was in 1914 (and what, except that it is defeated, it is now)'.[90]

Though an earlier a convert to war than Wilson, Roosevelt was less millennial than Wilson would ultimately become in conceptualizing the proper objectives of the war. America should fight, he argued, for a 'peace of justice'

> based on ability to guard ourselves from injustice, and determination not to do injustice to others, a peace in which some step shall have been taken toward putting international force behind an international desire to secure at least a reasonable approximation toward justice and fair play.[91]

Such talk of a 'reasonable approximation' of justice was more measured than Wilson's contemporary vision of new world order, but it is nevertheless evident that he considered notions of righteousness, as opposed to mere power balancing, important to his thinking about the post-war world. This was consistent with his long-standing arguments that civilization could be advanced only by the strong, and that sometimes justice was a higher goal than peace.

Before American war entry, Roosevelt was quick to hold the 'ultrapacifist' Wilson responsible for America's failure to join the defence of civilization. He blamed him for America's lack of readiness, military and political, for war, due to his 'trusting to fantastic peace treaties, to impossible promises, to all kinds of scraps of paper without any backing in efficient force' in place of armed preparedness.[92] In planning for post-war order, they again diverged on the role of arms and force. Looking to the future, Roosevelt did not call for the re-establishment of the balance of power in Europe with a new role for America: he was broadly supportive of plans for a more cooperative order in its place, and of a role for some new global institution.[93] But whereas Wilson's plans included substantial disarmament even of the victorious Allies, Roosevelt thought this foolhardy. Such disarmament, he thought, would weaken the most civilized nations in the face of future threats.

The lesson to be drawn from the events of 1914, to Roosevelt's mind, was that civilization needed muscle to defend it, not just solemn words. 'We must recognize that to enter into foolish treaties which cannot be kept is as wicked as to break treaties which can and ought to be kept,' he argued. Instead what was needed was 'an international agreement among the great civilized nations which shall put the full force of all of them back of any one of them, and of any well-behaved weak nation, which is wronged by any other power'. Until that was in place, however, America had to be 'ready ... to back our fights with our strength'.[94] 'There is just one way in which to meet the upholders of the doctrine that might makes right,' he insisted. 'To do so we must prove that right will make might, by backing right with might.'[95] For Roosevelt, security began at home, with America's own military strength: 'Until we make the world safe for America,' he observed in 1917, '... it is empty rhetoric to talk of making the world safe for democracy.'[96]

He had spelled out his views on disarmament when resisting campaigns for it during his own presidency, and his opposition was only confirmed by the events of the First World War. 'To have the best nations, the free and civilized nations, disarm and leave the despotisms and barbarisms with great military force, would be a calamity compared to which the calamities caused by all the wars of the Nineteenth Century would be trivial,' he had warned in 1906.[97] Disarmament would only be safe, hypothetically, 'if there was some system of international police; but there is now no such system'.[98] Lessons might wisely be drawn from history, he suggested in a letter in 1905, to the effect that peace usually only comes when 'some strong and on the whole just power has by armed force, or the threat of armed force, put a stop to disorder'.[99] The issue in 1918 remained the same: in an essentially ungoverned international environment, the civilized powers needed to be strong enough to protect themselves first if they were to be in any position to do good for others.

Perhaps the best summary statement of Roosevelt's views on the importance of armed strength as a tool of civilization's defence came in his 1904 Congressional message on foreign policy:

> When one nation wrongs another or wrongs many others, there is no tribunal before which the wrongdoer can be brought ... Until some method is devised by which there shall be a degree of international control over offending nations, it would be a wicked thing for the most civilized powers, for those with most sense of international obligations and with keenest and most generous appreciation of the difference between right and wrong, to disarm. If the great civilized nations of the present day should completely disarm, the result would mean an immediate recrudescence of barbarism in one form or another ...
>
> [A] self-respecting, just, and far-seeing nation should on the one hand endeavor by every means to aid in the development of the various movements which tend to provide substitutes for war, which tend to render nations in their actions toward one another, and indeed toward their own peoples, more responsive to the general sentiment of humane and civilized mankind; and on the other hand ... it should keep prepared, while scrupulously avoiding wrongdoing itself, to repel any wrong, and in exceptional cases to take action which in a more advanced stage of international relations would come under the head of the exercise of the international police. A great free people owes it to itself and to all mankind not to sink into helplessness before the powers of evil.[100]

In other words, progressive reform of the international system might well be possible, and collective security arrangements desirable, but American armed strength was crucial to any such project.

Interestingly, Roosevelt's belief in the moral case for physical force even extended to what we might today term 'humanitarian intervention'. A case in point was his attitude towards Turkey's efforts to kill or displace its Armenian population during the war, which he described as 'the greatest crime' of the conflict. For this he believed America should accept some responsibility, since its 'failure to act against Turkey' served in effect 'to condone' its actions. Once America had entered the war, Roosevelt argued it should also declare war on the Ottoman empire in order to live up to its principles: '[T]he failure to deal radically with the Turkish horror means that all talk of guaranteeing the future peace of the world is mischievous nonsense ... [W]hen we now refuse to war with Turkey we show that our announcement that we meant to "make the world safe for democracy" was insincere claptrap.'[101]

He was also, to some degree, an advocate of the view later advanced as a pillar of Wilsonianism, that tyrannous governments were inherently threatening to international order. Beyond the Armenian slaughter's intrinsic horror, TR also argued that the presence of despotism of the Turkish sort in Europe was also a barrier to post-war peace and stability. 'While the Turk is left in Europe and permitted to tyrannize over the subject peoples,' he wrote, 'the world is thoroughly unsafe for democracy.'[102] In previous years he had also suggested that the liberalization of Russian politics would be necessary if that society and its environs were to prosper.[103] '[D]own at bottom,' he told to the Harvard academic Hugo Munsterberg in 1916, '... the Russian is just like you or me.'[104] Thus, even as he displayed a cold realism in insisting on the continuing necessity, and moral righteousness, of armed power to secure the defence of nation and civilization, Roosevelt displayed flashes of the liberal universalism that would establish itself as America's dominant ideology in the years that followed.

Conclusion

Theodore Roosevelt did not have the opportunity to participate personally in the great debate over post-war order that followed Wilson's return from the Paris Peace Conference in 1919. Weakened by a tropical fever caught during adventures in the Amazon jungle after his defeat (as a third-party candidate) in the 1912 presidential election, his health had become shaky, but no one suspected he was mortally ill. It therefore shocked the nation when, in January 1919, the ebullient exponent of the strenuous life passed away in his sleep at only 60 years of age, victim of a coronary embolism.

His 20-year career at the highest level of politics had coincided with the United States' emergence as a great power at the global level. Hugely significant increases in territorial size, economic scale and population since the foundation had elevated it to a higher level in the international hierarchy of strength. Before 1898, however, America had not begun in earnest the process of translating its underlying potential into great-power status in the global international system. One of the greatest constraints on its doing so was the continuing ideological dominance of the Founders' Era consensus, which stated that the United States should not entangle itself in the European balance of power. Europe's great powers being the pre-eminent powers in the global system, and the European balance of power therefore overlapping mightily with the global balance, this prohibition severely limited America's ability to participate in global affairs.

Thus, at the beginning of the twentieth century the United States was simultaneously being pushed towards greater international activism by its own growing strength and yet held back by its ideological aversion to embroilment within the Europe-dominated order. The chapter that follows describes how the implosion of the European order after 1914 provided the opportunity – seized upon by Woodrow Wilson – to craft a new American internationalism. Roosevelt, in contrast, was in the main obliged to govern within the ideological limitations he inherited – though he was inclined to test his boundaries – because the international context was comparatively stable during his time in office. Nevertheless, he did initiate the process of ideological transition on the part of the United States from a consensus on detachment from the global balance of power towards a new internationalism.

The first key element of this transition was his consistent advocacy of increased military strength, which prepared the ground for the nation to later take on the role of a significant military power. Further, by tying hard power into a narrative of national greatness and a historic mission to serve and extend civilization, Roosevelt gave the acquisition of military strength a dimension that was moral and nationalistic, broadening its appeal to a reluctant body politic. His careful balancing of the need for strength against the distastefulness of excessive national self-assertion, and his argument that military power was essential in order to do useful service for the greater good would serve as the basis of a later generation's case for unprecedented peacetime mobilization. His conviction that peace depended upon the arming of 'civilized' powers in readiness to check aggression would in time become a dominant pillar of American thought, far more influential than Wilsonian theories of disarmament.

Roosevelt was, up to a point, a realist. He readily acknowledged the crucial role played by power and national self-interest in international politics. He successfully executed a number of diplomatic operations that displayed his comfort with pursuing the country's interests in a competitive international system, and cautiously raised the horizon of America's diplomatic activities. At the same time, however, he was also strikingly – even stridently – moralistic, highlighting the importance of pursuing 'righteousness' even at the expense of peace, stability or wealth. This side of his thought, obsessively focused on virtue and manliness, must serve to qualify the realist tag, if that term is taken to imply a school of thought defined by dispassionate focus on self-interest. In this regard, Roosevelt's moralistic version of realism can be seen as the forerunner of later US policy, more so than the European-style strain of realism advocated by, for example, Henry Kissinger.

Though still operating under the Monroe Doctrine's division of spheres, and thus not fully engaged in European affairs, Roosevelt's foreign policy expanded the scope of that doctrine, making it a charter for deeper and wider US intervention in the Western Hemisphere. As well as exercising a 'police power' to avoid malfeasance in international relations, the United States also adopted a quasi-imperial attitude of tutelage over the political and economic development of the region's states. Operating in a strategic environment of US hegemony, Roosevelt argued that US interests were identical with those of Latin American states, that the US had the right to identify those interests unilaterally, and that it was a responsibility of the US to teach those within its sphere how to use their 'freedom' appropriately. This liberal-imperialist position evolved out of the political indigestion caused by the territorial acquisitions of 1898, and was based on 'progressive' assumptions regarding fixed appropriate outcomes of national liberty and self-determination. Such progressivism asserted the justness of US intervention in the event that states should diverge from a baseline of prescribed political mores. This expanded version of the Monroe Doctrine would serve as America's ideological model for global order when the international system became – or so it appeared – amenable to radical reform during Wilson's presidency.

Roosevelt did not succeed during his own career in implementing the scale of change that he might have wished in the relation of the United States to the world, though he certainly made incremental changes of lasting significance. He did, however, make a substantial contribution to the ideological transition of the United States from the ideas of the Founders' Era consensus of hemispheric detachment towards a policy of greater militarization and global engagement. This Rooseveltian ideological contribution would be critically important in later years, especially when combined with its overlapping ideological contemporary, Wilsonianism, to which the next chapter devotes its attention.

5 Woodrow Wilson

'Conquest of the spirits of men'[1]

Introduction

This chapter argues that international circumstances provided Woodrow Wilson with both need and opportunity, even more so than in Roosevelt's case, to radically increase America's level of international engagement. It further argues that enthusiasm for that engagement was intellectually predicated upon a set of interlocking liberal universalist principles – subsequently tagged in political shorthand as 'Wilsonian' – and that this was a consequence of Wilson's need to manage the transition to internationalism within a political culture that rejected balance-of-power thinking about international order.

The chapter begins, as the others do, with an outline of national and international circumstances. The sections that follow then outline in detail the components of Wilsonian thought and their significance. First, the moralistic and idealistic approach Wilson brought to his leadership is discussed, and some parallel with Roosevelt noted. The next section, covering the period before America's embroilment in the First World War, describes how Wilson continued and extended Roosevelt's pursuit of a hegemonic, imperialistic policy towards Latin America. This deepened Monroe Doctrine would serve as the model for his later proposals for international order more globally. The section after this discusses Wilson's making of the case for US entry into the European war, in which he made the justification for American entanglement dependent upon the prospect of a new world order following that war's end. The remaining sections go on to set out the intellectual framework of that imagined new order, including Wilson's crucial distinction between governments and peoples, the posited commonality of interests between peoples, the need for the universalization of liberal government, and the assumption that America would exercise global leadership in the future. Finally, the chapter notes the divergence between Wilson and Roosevelt with regard to the role of military strength in the new world order.

The chapter seeks to illustrate the way in which Wilson seized upon American participation in the war to advance an agenda that broke with the Founders' Era consensus on hemispheric detachment which had constrained his predecessors. As part of the same process, however, the prior existence of that consensus's prohibitions on entanglement in the European balance of power crucially shaped his formulation of the ideological arguments for a new

American internationalism. Rather than arguing that the US should join the existing global system, Wilson argued that America's new global engagement was inextricably linked to the emergence of a new, cooperative international order, a perception rooted in his own liberal universalist ideas. As realist assumptions can tell us, the emergence of a new American internationalism during this period was partly the result of America's increased strength, combined with major shifts in the international distribution of power. Also extremely important, however, was the ideological dimension of Wilson's leadership in reaction to those circumstances. This interaction between circumstance and ideology led to the emergence of a particular American internationalism that believed the nation's new engagement with the world could be contingent on the pursuit of liberal reform of the global order and the states within it.

National and international context

At the beginning of Wilson's term of office – he was elected in 1912 – the global order retained much of the character it had possessed at the turn of the century. The international system was still centred on the European great powers – especially Britain, France, Germany and Russia – and their competition for advantage both in Europe itself and other theatres such as China. Japan's increasing military strength and effectiveness had forced others to recognize it as a significant power, and that fact, in combination with the rise of the United States, signified a challenge to Europe as the sole locus of significant national power. Nevertheless, Europe remained the key power centre, and the balance of power between the Europeans almost synonymous with the global balance.

The United States had its own sphere of hegemonic influence in the Western Hemisphere, from which it had been largely successful in excluding the Europeans. It had not yet developed its military capability in proportion to its size and wealth, though it had expanded and modernized its navy somewhat thanks to Roosevelt's determined efforts. If the US took an interest in affairs beyond this Western sphere, its politicians feared, it would risk entanglement in European rivalries. It therefore by and large avoided taking such an interest, with a few limited exceptions such as its involvement in a multi-power consortium dealing with China.

The First World War, which defined Wilson's second term and led to the emergence of Wilsonianism as a global ideology, signalled the beginning of the end for this world. The war's outbreak was the product of several convergent trends in European strategic affairs, including increasing rigidity in alliances, a destabilizing arms race and the development of military mobilization plans that incentivized early strikes and made reverses of course risky. The unprecedented cost and inconclusive nature of the violence that sprang from the war also reflected the development of technologies that favoured defence and increased terribly the price in lives of traditional tactics.[2]

The breakdown of the existing international order brought about by the First World War demanded that the United States take a new, deeper interest in intra-European politics, and presented Americans with an opportunity to pursue radical reform of the ideological basis of the European and world orders. The Wilsonian policy and ideology that emerged was in this sense a reaction to international circumstances. The nature of that reaction, however, was shaped by the pre-existing American ideological consensus, and the need to bridge the gap between the demands of the present and the embedded convictions of the past.

Moralism and idealism in Wilsonian foreign policy

Like that of Roosevelt, Wilson's rise to political power was a relatively sudden affair. An academic at the head of Princeton University, he mirrored TR in being spring-boarded to elected office as a state governor (of New Jersey) by party bosses and propelled from there to the national level at speed. His 1912 election made him the first Democratic president for a generation, thanks in great part to a split of the Republican vote between the incumbent president William Taft and Roosevelt, who had fallen out with his own chosen successor and run again as a third-party candidate.[3] It was the height of the Progressive Era, and most thought that the pressing issues of coming years would be domestic and economic rather than foreign and military. Wilson himself reportedly remarked that it 'would be the irony of fate if my administration had to deal chiefly with foreign affairs, for all my preparation has been in domestic matters.'[4]

Wilson and Roosevelt have often been set in stark contrast to one another, with Wilson cast as ivory-tower idealist and Roosevelt as robust action man. Such a dichotomy obscures the reality that, outside of politics, Roosevelt was an author and intellectual, and Wilson was a skilful politician who, at least before his health deteriorated, displayed a good deal of passion and dynamism. More importantly, they also had similarities in their thinking.[5] For all his fondness for abstract principles, Wilson too emphasized the merits of action over pure thought and of sentiment over cold reason. 'We are not put into this world to sit still and know,' he wrote as a young man. 'We are put into it to act.'[6] In his historical writings, he mostly joined Roosevelt in siding with the Hamiltonian Federalist tendency towards 'energetic' government and criticizing Jefferson as excessively theoretical.[7]

Unlike in Roosevelt's case, however, analysts have not downplayed the moralistic dimension to Wilson's political thought; on the contrary, emphasis of that aspect of his character pervades the literature. His most extensive and sympathetic biographer judges him to have been 'primarily a Christian idealist' in foreign policy, who 'almost always tended to judge policies on a basis of whether they were right ... not whether they brought immediate material or strategic advantage'. He based policy on 'the assumption that a nation as much as an individual should live according to the law of Christian love, and by a positive repudiation of the assumptions of the classical "realists" about international behaviour'.[8] Like Roosevelt, he saw moral uprightness on the part of citizen and nation as the necessary foundation of national greatness. 'As the individual is the type of the nation,' he believed, 'so the nation should embody the highest individual ideals of civil perfection, in order to assert and maintain its honorable position in the world-family of commonwealth.'[9]

This mindset would in time become the basis of his thinking concerning post-First World War order. In April 1917 he told Congress that in the future order 'it will be insisted that the same standards of conduct and of responsibility for wrong done shall be observed among nations and their governments that are observed among the individual citizens of civilized states'.[10] This commonality between Roosevelt and Wilson in equating the moral status of the nation and the individual should not surprise us: they were, after all, both American 'progressives', ideologically speaking. As Dawley, a historian of Progressivism, puts it:

> [T]he itch to improve the world, whether the world wants it or not, did not stop at the border ... [I]n combining moralism and realism in foreign policy – the itch to uplift and the itch to control – they were a perfect pair ... As Christian moralists, both thought of the US role overseas as morally redemptive. Both would have agreed with Albert Beveridge, a close associate of Roosevelt, that the United States had a messianic mission as God's chosen nation to lead in the regeneration of the world.[11]

Complementing this moralism, Wilson was inclined towards an idealistic conception of what drove – or at least could drive – national policy, that downplayed the importance of material interests. In this he shared Roosevelt's sense that the nation could better attain greatness through the pursuit of grand historic projects for the moral uplift of civilization rather than through the pursuit of mere treasure. America was established, he asserted, 'not to create wealth ... but to realize an ideal'.[12] 'America is not going to be immortal because she has immense wealth,' he admonished in 1919, but rather 'because of the ideas she has conceived ... the purposes she has set herself to achieve ... because she has seen visions that other nations have not seen' and because it sought 'the liberty of mankind'.[13] Economic strength was important, but only as a means to an end. As Clements notes, Wilson's 'goals were more moral and political than economic, but he understood that the power that made the achievement of his goals conceivable rested upon economic strength and upon the military might that depended upon economic power'.[14] Wilson would later cite America's entry into the Great War as vindication of his belief that material prosperity could be subordinated to the service of ideals, arguing that America's sacrifice would 'show that we were not accumulating that wealth selfishly, but were accumulating it for the service of mankind'.[15]

Keen to elevate the tone of US policy after four years of so-called 'dollar diplomacy' under Taft, especially in Latin America, Wilson asserted that 'our greatness is built upon our freedom – is moral, not material'.[16] The nation should therefore be 'more concerned about human rights than about property rights' in dealings with weaker nations. America should 'think of the progress of mankind rather than the progress of this or that investment, of the protection of American honor and the advancement of American ideals rather than always of American contracts'.[17] He expressed similar concerns regarding the use of US power to further vested interests rather than moral ends in China.[18]

Though idealistic, such statements did not betray a complete lack of self-awareness on Wilson's part regarding the results of America's policies. He acknowledged that in continuing to pursue the 'Open Door' into other economies, America was seeking 'commercial conquest of the world', a 'righteous conquest of the world's markets'.[19] In a moment of borderline Marxist analysis of his own policy, Wilson would later tell Europeans that:

> A country is owned and dominated by the capital that is invested in it ... In proportion as foreign capital comes in amongst you and takes its hold, in that proportion does foreign influence come in and take its hold. And therefore the processes of capital are in a certain sense the processes of conquest.[20]

To some, this analysis might give ethical pause, but any tension between Wilson's enunciation of high principles and his acknowledgement of commercial imperialism remained largely invisible to him, because he assumed harmony between America's interests and the fulfilment of its moral ideals. He could do this because he equated the civilized liberty that America's ideals mandated it to spread with the advance in tandem of a brand of economic liberalism advantageous to American interests. American principles were thus 'not incompatible with great material prosperity' – on the contrary, they were 'indispensable to it'.[21]

When leading America through its involvement in the war and subsequent peace, Wilson was generally open in arguing that there was a case based on economic self-interest to be made for US participation.[22] But he always insisted on expressing at the same time his view that such a justification lowered the tone of the American debate, and exhorted the people to share that sense. When mentioning the commercial arguments for supporting the League of Nations, he swiftly followed with the observation that 'I do not like to put it on that ground because that is not the American ground.'[23] The economic argument was only 'the lowest basis' on which to justify what was a more profound effort to 'guarantee and underwrite civilization'.[24]

The expanded Monroe Doctrine as prototype of global Wilsonianism

Latin America served as testing ground for the idea of a cooperative order of states progressing towards 'civilization' under US hegemony. Wilson took up the liberal imperialist framework of the Roosevelt Corollary and expanded it still further, establishing a regime of wide-ranging interventionism in the United States' sphere of influence. Though he disapproved of what he saw as the money-driven character of his predecessors' policy, he had no qualms regarding interventionism per se. The United States' task, as he saw it, was to set aside selfish considerations and help America's neighbours to develop more democratic, liberal and constitutional political orders. In practice this meant more intrusion into others' affairs, not less.

Wilson imagined the US could drive forward liberalization of states in Latin America while also increasing stability, because the two were interrelated. He thought the US should push nations towards elections, and then seek to ensure the results were upheld if challenged by disgruntled political forces. Once proper order had been established in Latin nations, 'interruptions of civil order' would thenceforth not be tolerated. In time, order and stability would become self-sustaining. 'Each conspicuous instance in which usurpations ... are prevented will render their recurrence less,' he predicted, eventually assuring 'the peace of America and the untrammelled development of its economic and social relations with the rest of the world'.[25]

His most substantial intervention came in neighbouring Mexico, where he sought to depose General Victoriano Huerta, who had taken power in a bloody coup not long before Wilson's inauguration. Wilson had previously professed wariness of the idea that liberty could be 'handed down from above', but he was insistent that Mexico did provide suitable soil for self-government. 'When properly directed there is no people not fitted for self-government,' he said. The Mexicans might not be 'at present as capable of self-government as other people – our own, for example – but I do hold that the wide-spread sentiment that they never will be and never can be ... is as wickedly false as it is palpably absurd'.[26] By the time he began to engage with Mexico, the nation was already in the throes of civil conflict. US policy under Wilson then went through sequential phases of interference and retreat. At first the policy was one of 'watchful waiting', before 1914 saw direct intervention in the form of a sizeable US military incursion at Vera Cruz. This proved counterproductive, however, uniting all Mexican factions in opposition to foreign encroachment. This failure led Wilson to abandon plans for further military intervention against Huerta's government, which in any case was soon toppled by its domestic enemies. Still, however, Wilson persisted in seeking to shape Mexico's internal politics, supporting the Constitutionalist faction in the civil war. Then, in 1916, he repeated his earlier misjudgement by sending troops back into Mexico, this time in response to deliberately provocative cross-border incursions mounted by rebel leader Pancho Villa.

Throughout this extended episode of neighbourly interference, Wilson was driven by a paradoxical combination of objectives: insistence on Mexican freedom to pursue 'self-government' sat uncomfortably side by side with his own liberal ideas prescribing the form that government should take. Repeatedly he took an interest in the policies and intentions of the rival Mexican factions, with a view to securing the 'right' kind of order there, a posture the

Mexicans naturally found intrusive. Though professing to believe that the Mexicans should resolve their own affairs, underlying Wilson's demands for 'good government' was always the threat of intervention, whereby the US 'would be constrained to decide what means should be employed ... to help Mexico save herself and save her people'.[27] As one critic has noted:

> No distinction seemed to exist in Wilson's thinking between United States intervention and Mexican self-determination. He considered the legitimate objectives of both nations to be identical. Intervention thus became no more than a means to expedite self-determination.[28]

To his mind, intervention in Mexico was necessary to create the pre-conditions for the Mexicans to rule themselves. The success of US efforts at control would thus mean not US domination, but 'an enlargement of the field of self-government'.[29] As Bell puts it, 'intervention was not really intervention, because the intentions of the United States were for the best and the consequences would be beneficial to Mexico'.[30] It was the role of the US in the Western Hemisphere to provide the necessary guiding hand to other states: 'helping them compose their differences, starting them on the road to peace and prosperity, and leaving them to work out their own destiny, but watching them narrowly and insisting that they shall take help when help is needed'. As Notter notes, it was clear that 'we [Americans] were to judge that need'.[31]

Because he believed that his interventions favoured the spread of self-government and liberty, Bell notes, it made sense to Wilson to think that:

> an expanding American system was not only to be beneficial to the United States but beneficial to the rest of the world. If one believed this then one might assume that one had no special interest but that which is right. Those who opposed Wilson's program could be regarded as being unrepresentative of the real aspirations of their own people.[32]

Wilson, he argues 'gradually reached a definition of America's needs and interests, and this he defined as right ... The coercion of Mexico by the United States was not in conflict with the principle of self-determination, because "real" self-determination came from doing what Wilson thought should be done.'[33]

During his first term, Wilson also set in train highly interventionist policies in Cuba, Haiti, the Dominican Republic and Nicaragua. These involved the deployment of US troops and American administrative 'assistance', and the creation of new constitutional systems. Sometimes, when those systems failed to sustain themselves, the process reached its logical conclusion with the institution of US military government to rescue basic order.[34] As well as helping to draft constitutions, these interventions established US control of substantial parts of the government revenue apparatus, effectively annexing chunks of national sovereignty. In each case the objective was to take weak, illiberal and insolvent states in hand and create something resembling constitutional market-oriented democracy. The usual result was a fragile state with shallow popular commitment to its institutions and a dependence on the US to underwrite the political order. In pursuing this strategy, Wilson applied the same ideological jujitsu as in the Mexican case: he rationalized an expansion of the scope of US intervention within other sovereign states, based upon the principle of advancing self-determination. Even as the US's controlling role in Haiti, the Dominican Republic, Panama and Nicaragua was reaching its peak, the president was telling Congress of a new footing of 'genuine equality and unquestioned independency' in Latin America, which sprang from a 'more vital community of interest'.[35]

From a purely military-strategic perspective, this interventionism made eminent sense: it ensured US control of all the key potential launch-points for any hostile naval thrust at the Panama Canal. Under the logic of the Roosevelt Corollary, it also forestalled European interference against vulnerable states. No doubt the preservation of US investments in the countries in question also entered into consideration, though these were hardly enormous in the grander scheme of the US economy. But most important in Wilson's reasoning were political and ideological priorities. Clements sums up Wilson's Latin American policy thus: 'Security concerns and economic interests played only small parts ... its main motive was genuine, albeit patronizing, benevolence. Its result was a dangerous, destructive, and ultimately unsuccessful moral imperialism.'[36] As Wilson supposedly – and perhaps apocryphally – summed up the project himself, his goal was to 'teach the South American Republics to elect good men'.[37]

Wilson did not deliberately seek to imitate European colonialism. On the level of abstract principle, he idealized the independence of Latin American nations. Although he embraced the Monroe Doctrine, based on 'the premise that American influence was liberating compared to the exploitative nature of European influence', he was somewhat concerned about its one-sided nature.[38] But the Monroe Doctrine could and should be reconceived, he thought, as 'a common guarantee ... of political independence and territorial integrity'.[39] His grand project for the region, never realized, was a 'Pan-American Pact' to turn the unilateral doctrine into a mutual security agreement.[40]

Like Roosevelt, Wilson spoke and acted as though there was an overlap – even an identity relationship – between the interests of the US and the Latin American nations. In seeking 'the lasting interests of the people of the two continents', he was sure that his policies would 'redound to the profit of both and interfere with the rights and liberties of neither'.[41] His policy, he said, was 'Pan-Americanism', which had 'none of the spirit of empire in it. It is the embodiment ... of the spirit of law and independence and mutual service.'[42] He was largely oblivious to the depth of suspicion with which the United States was regarded in Latin America, believing that people there welcomed US oversight because the United States – as he saw it – had a proven track record of disinterestedly aiding its neighbours. In 1919, 21 years after the 'liberation' of Cuba in the war with Spain, Wilson felt confident in proclaiming that 'we redeemed our honor to the utmost of our dealings with Cuba. She is weak but absolutely free; and it is her trust in us that makes her free. Weak peoples everywhere stand ready to give us any authority among them that will assure them a like friendly oversight and direction.'[43]

Wilson was even more deeply immersed than Roosevelt in the view that liberty and progress must necessarily result in an approximation of liberalism in order to deserve those labels. All right-thinking people aimed towards the same universal progressive ends, he believed, noting that 'throughout this hemisphere the same aspirations are everywhere being worked out, under diverse conditions but with the same impulse and ultimate object'.[44] True freedom and independence meant the maintenance a liberal, democratic capitalist order. This belief served to justify substantial US intervention to ensure that a country did not drift away from the 'correct' developmental path and towards dictatorship, economic radicalism or anarchy. His problems in achieving lasting success in Latin America were thus founded on what Bell terms an 'inability to understand the nationalistic sentiments of other peoples'. This made him misguidedly confident that others would understand 'that what was to the interest of the United States must work for the good of all others', and doomed him to a struggle to 'create an empire of good will' which in practice could only 'generate disbelief and hostility'.[45] The Wilsonian strategy was thus, at root, an extension of Roosevelt's desire to 'civilize' Latin America.

These features of Wilson's Latin American policy are especially important because they served as the ideological model for his later efforts to reform global order. After the First World War had brought about entanglement in Europe, he consciously regarded his reimagining of the Monroe Doctrine and his efforts at a Pan-American Pact as the template for America's new global diplomacy.[46] In 1919, he argued that under the proposed League of Nations the Monroe Doctrine would become 'the doctrine of the world'.[47] His assumption that other nations would gladly embrace such an idea revealed his complacently US-centric perspective on the nature of the Monroe Doctrine. For Wilson it did not have the connotations of US imposition and interference with which others in the Americas associated it. It simply affirmed, Wilson thought, that 'no nation should seek to extend its polity over any other nation or people, but that every people should be left free to determine its own polity, its own way of development'.[48]

Wilson's justification of war entry and European entanglement

The collapse of the European balance of power into extreme violence in 1914 seemed to confirm most Americans' worst preconceptions regarding the degeneracy of the European system of order. At the outset Wilson responded by reaffirming the prevailing consensus that Europe was, geographically and politically, a world apart. The unfolding conflict was, he said, 'a war with which we have nothing to do, whose causes cannot touch us'.[49] The United States would stay out. In practice, however, as the Founders had discovered generations earlier, neutrality amid a major European war was easier declared than sustained. US commerce was interrupted by a British naval blockade of the Central Powers, and then also by retaliatory German submarine attacks. With American ships and lives at risk thanks to the U-boat attacks, Wilson fretted presciently that 'I am afraid something will happen on the high seas which will make it impossible for us to keep out of the war.'[50]

The American journey to war was not a swift one, although with hindsight it had an inexorable quality. Even after 128 Americans died in the sinking of the unarmed British liner *Lusitania* in May 1915, Wilson sought to maintain a pacific course, telling the American people that there was 'such a thing as a man being too proud to fight ... a nation being so right that it does not need to convince others by force ...'.[51] He was, however, prepared at the same time to send a diplomatic note to Germany threatening a breach unless its submarine policy was moderated. This was successful at first, but the same crisis was recreated two years later, when the Germans declared their intention to wage unrestricted submarine warfare on vessels entering an exclusion zone around Britain. As the final diplomatic break loomed, Wilson shifted his ideological position on the conflict as a whole, implicitly dismissing his own earlier assertion that the war and its causes need not concern the United States. 'The war inevitably set its mark from the first ... upon our minds, our industries, our commerce and our social action,' he argued in 1917. 'To be indifferent to it or independent of it was out of the question.'[52] Once Americans citizens began to be killed under the new German policy of unlimited strikes at sea, the matter came to a head and Congress declared war, at Wilson's request, on 6 April 1917.[53]

Wilson, re-elected in 1916 as the candidate more likely to keep America out of the war, was now a war president. This departure, not only from his previous policy but also from the standing doctrine of non-involvement in European wars, demanded political justification. Despite its status as the official *casus belli*, the issue of submarine strikes did not remain in the foreground for long. More important in Wilson's political case for war was the argument that that aspect of German behaviour was merely a symptom of the deeper threat posed by that nation and its desire for domination of Europe. Speaking of the Kaiser's plans for supremacy, Wilson warned the American people that if Germany were victorious 'America will fall within the menace'. With Germany dominating Europe, America would be forced into heavy militarization in order to be 'ready for the next step in their aggression'.[54]

He still talked, as he had during neutrality, of ending the war with a peace uniting all sides, but now argued that the ground first had to be cleared by the defeat of Germany and the destruction of its system of government. 'The rulers of Germany', he would later allege, had sought to accomplish 'purposes which would have permanently impaired and impeded every process of our national life and have put the fortunes of America at the mercy of the

Imperial Government of Germany'. The US needed to join the war because German victory would mean rule 'by sheer weight of arms, and the arbitrary choices of self-constituted masters, by the nation which can maintain the biggest armies and the most irresistible armaments ... in the face of which political freedom must wither or perish'.[55]

Wilson faced a sizeable ideological challenge in seeking to justify America's entry into the war and subsequent global engagement. He needed to overcome over a century of ingrained tradition whereby America's leaders had argued that the US interest lay in separation from the set of interests and values instantiated in the European balance of power. He accomplished the task in two stages. First, he cast the conflict as one concerning not merely narrow national interests, but a fundamental clash of political morality: a war between the virtuous ideals of liberal democracy and the warped values of militarist autocracy. Second, he argued that American intervention did not amount to what had heretofore been prohibited – the embroilment of the US in the European system – but rather an opportunity to strike a blow demolishing that order. Despite their long-standing tradition of detachment, he argued, Americans, including himself, had become convinced that the war 'was not a European struggle ... [but] a struggle for the freedom of the world and the liberation of humanity'.[56] 'It is not an accident or a matter of sudden choice that we are no longer isolated,' he later told the Senate, '... It was our duty to go in, if we were indeed the champions of liberty and of right.'[57]

To create an ideological bridge away from the Founders' Era consensus, Wilson advanced the ideological proposition that the United States would not be joining the system of international relations as it had operated before, but rather stepping in to finally dismantle the European order and replace it with one based on American – i.e. liberal and universally valid – principles:

> We are provincials no longer. The tragical events of the thirty months of vital turmoil through which we have just passed have made us citizens of the world. There can be no turning back. Our own fortunes as a nation are involved, whether we would have it or not ... And yet we are not the less American on that account. We shall be the more American if we but remain true to the principles in which we have been bred. They are not the principles of a province or of a single continent. We have known and boasted all along that they were the principles of a liberated mankind.[58]

Key among those principles was the tenet that 'peace cannot securely or justly rest on an armed balance of power'.[59]

Conditional US engagement and the abolition of the balance of power

The old, Europe-centred order had been based on the theory of a competitive balance of power maintained between rival nations, heavily armed, pursuing mutually exclusive interests in perpetual contest. Despite acknowledging that the scale of the Great War in Europe had threatened US interests beyond the point of tenable neutrality, Wilson did not draw the conclusion that America had at last been forced into playing its part in this old order. Instead, he concluded that the war had presented an opportunity for comprehensive reform of the international system in line with American ideals. The principles that had previously mandated America's arms-length relationship with the global system could now, therefore, through their conquest of European minds, enable and justify a new international engagement.

This idea entered public life in the months before US war entry, when, in January 1917, Wilson told Congress that there must be 'not a balance of power, but a community of power; not organized rivalries, but an organized common peace'.[60] Thereafter, the rejection of the balance of power as an organizing concept was a leitmotif of his discussion of post-war order. During that American phase of the war, he rebuffed exploratory German enquiries pointing towards a negotiated peace, on the grounds that they invited what he termed 'the method of the Congress of Vienna'. By this he meant a conservative peace based on the balancing of armed great powers' rival interests. What was needed, he said, was 'a new international order based upon broad and universal principles of right and justice', not a return to 'the great game, now forever discredited, of the balance of power'.[61] This war was 'much more than a war to alter the balance of power in Europe', he insisted:[62]

> Henceforth, alliance must not be set up against alliance, understanding against understanding, but there must be a common agreement for a common object and at the heart of the common object must be the inviolable rights of peoples and of mankind.[63]

In 1919, he would say of the Paris Peace Conference that the participants 'were trying to make peace on an entirely new basis, and to establish a new order of international relations'.[64]

This rejection of balance-of-power thinking has been highlighted by many of Wilson's biographers. Pierce notes that 'he saw the whole notion of basing peace on a balance of power as flawed'[65]:

> Wilson could not condone the balance of power as a guide for foreign policy. He saw the obsession with a geopolitical solution to the world's problems as not only contrary to the American way, but also as a major reason for the advent of war ... The United States would shift the balance to the Allies' favour only to render balance-of-power tactics obsolete.[66]

He told a London audience before the Paris conference that Allied and American soldiers had fought 'to do away with an old order' the 'center and character' of which was:

that unstable thing which we used to call the 'balance of power' – a thing in which the balance was determined by the sword which was thrown in the one side or the other; a balance which was determined by the unstable equilibrium of competitive interests; a balance which was maintained by jealous watchfulness and antagonism of interests which, though it was generally latent, was always deep-seated.

The new order demanded 'not a balance of power, not one powerful group of nations set off against another, but a single overwhelming, powerful group of nations who shall be the trustee of the peace of the world'.[67] This was a reference to his plan to reform global order by the provision of 'collective security' through a League of Nations.[68] Such a scheme could overcome American taboos against entanglement in Europe because US engagement with a thoroughly reformed global order would no longer be 'entangling'. There would not be an alliance *with* some states and *against* others, but rather American leadership of a universal cooperative effort to preserve good order. Hence the commitment was asserted to be qualitatively different from those that the Founders' Era consensus admonished US leaders to shun.

By this reasoning, Wilson felt he could claim to 'read Washington's immortal warning against "entangling alliances" with full comprehension and an answering purpose', and at the same time endorse extensive commitments on America's part to defend global order. This was because 'only special and limited alliances entangle; and we recognize and accept the duty of a new day in which we are permitted to hope for a general alliance which will avoid entanglements and clear the air of the world for common understanding and the maintenance of common rights'.[69] In fact, he claimed, not only was his foreign policy tolerable in the light of Washington's injunction against alliances – it was positively mandated by it:

> [T]he thing [Washington] longed for was just what we are now about to supply; an arrangement which will disentangle all the alliances in the world ... Nothing entangles a nation, hampers it, binds it, except to enter into a combination with some other nation against the other nations of the world.[70]

What Washington had opposed, on the other hand, was 'exactly what [opponents of the League] want to lead us back to. The day we have left behind us was a day of alliances. It was a day of balances of power ... The project of the League of Nations is a great process of disentanglement.'[71]

This was a bold argument by any standard. Wilson was suggesting that the US must become a guarantor of the global order, yet he cast this as a fulfilment rather than an abandonment of the Founders' Era tradition, because the new world order would be a cooperative one based on American principles.[72] To further his case, he characterized America's choice as one between two stark alternatives, in the process casting opponents of his strategy, by implication, as supporters of US entanglement in the old order:

> We must go forward with the concert of nations or we must go back to the old arrangement, because the guarantees of peace will not be sufficient without the US, and those who oppose this Covenant are driven to the necessity of advocating the old order of balances of power. If you do not have this universal concert, you have what we have always avoided, necessary alignment with one or other nation or with some other group of nations.[73]

'Our task,' he said, 'is no less colossal than this, to set up a new international psychology.'[74] His hope was that this would be rendered achievable by the spectacular failure of the old order, which would prompt Europeans to embrace change:

> We know that there cannot be another balance of power. That has been tried and found wanting ... [T]here must be something substituted for the balance of power ... a thoroughly united league of nations. What men once considered theoretical and idealistic now turns out to be practical and necessary.[75]

Advancing his case in this way, Wilson considered himself to be the true 'realist' among world statesmen, while any wanting a return to the old order were surely the impractical ones.[76] 'The old order is gone,' he intoned, 'and nobody can build it up again.'[77] 'A war in which [the people have] been bled white to beat the terror that lay concealed in every Balance of Power must not end in a mere victory of arms and a new balance,' he told the Senate. The causes of the First World War sprang from the structure of international order: the war was 'the logical outcome of the process that had preceded it'. The purpose of gathering at Paris was to 'destroy that system and substitute another ... based upon an absolute reversal of the principles of the old ... '.[78]

In constructing an ideological bridge from past to present on this basis, Wilson's argument in effect made American global internationalism conditional. Without the radical reform of global order that he projected, a return to the old strategy of detachment would be the appropriate response:

> If the future had nothing for us but a new attempt to keep the world at a right poise by a balance of power, the United States would take no interest, because she will join no combination of power which is not the combination of all of us. She is not interested merely in the peace of Europe, but in the peace of the world. Therefore it seems to me that in the settlement that is just ahead of us something more delicate and difficult than was ever attempted before is to be accomplished, a genuine concert of mind and purpose.[79]

America had agreed to enter the world not to join the pre-existing global order but to redeem it. Hence, other countries needed to meet America's expectations of a new world order, or the US could legitimately retract its commitment. There was a 'deal' of sorts in operation: if 'the world', meaning most especially Europeans, failed to live up to its duty to reform, the United States would by implication be freed from any obligation to support the world order. Wilson was not shy about this conditionality:

> In coming into this war, the United States never for a moment thought that she was intervening in the politics of Europe ... Her thought was that all the world had now become conscious that there was a single cause which turned upon the issue of this war. That was the cause of justice and of liberty for men of every kind and place. Therefore, the United States should feel that its part in this war had been played in vain if there ensued upon it merely a body of European settlements. It would feel that it could not take part in guaranteeing those European settlements unless that guarantee involved the continuous superintendence of the peace of the world by the associated nations of the world.[80]

Wilson's predication of the new American internationalism on the abolition of the balance of power and the institution of a grand new cooperative order has been criticized by several analysts of Wilsonianism.[81] By tying American policy to the pursuit of such high objectives, they argue, he rendered American internationalism brittle: primed for disillusion as a consequence of pursuing ideals beyond the nation's power to achieve. Yet his reasons for constructing the new internationalism in this way are, on reflection, clearly understandable. America's history had left it ill-prepared in terms of ideological and political culture for entry into the global system as an active great power, even if its size and strength equipped it to play that role. It was perhaps only by arguing that the world order was changing to accommodate American principles that Wilson could hope to succeed in convincing the nation that the established taboo against entanglement in the balance of power had ceased to be relevant.

Interests, peoples and international cooperation

Wilsonianism asserted, contrary to balance-of-power thinking, that the self-interested pursuit of rivalry need not dominate international relations. If only states had the will, the international system could operate instead based on an underlying fundamental harmony to be found in states' deeper, truer interests. In his pursuit of the Monroe Doctrine, Wilson had insisted that his goal was 'to show our neighbours to the south ... that their interests are identical with our interests'.[82] When his policy turned to the European and global stages, he carried over the same approach.

The League, the centrepiece of the new order, was intended to abolish the alliance system based on the old, narrow conception of national interests. Thereafter, Wilson claimed, no 'special or separate interest of any single nation or group of nations' could be allowed to prevail which was not 'consistent with the common interest of all'. There could be 'no leagues or alliances or special covenants and understandings'.[83] The war meant that 'national purposes have fallen more and more into the background', replaced by 'the common purpose of enlightened mankind'.[84] Nations would be 'co-workers in tasks which, because they are common, will weave out of our sentiments a common conception of duty and a common conception of the rights of men of every race and of every clime'.[85] This faith in a new, cooperative order was founded in moral universalism:

> [W]hen we are seeking peace, we are seeking nothing else than this, that men should think the same thoughts, govern their conduct by the same ideals, entertain the same purposes, love their own people, but also love humanity, and above all else, love that great and indestructible thing which we call justice and right.[86]

European leaders, he claimed, had been compelled to embrace this new perspective by the epoch-defining events of the war. 'We sometimes think,' he noted on his return from Paris in 1919, ' ... that the experienced statesmen of European nations are an unusually hardheaded set of men, by which we generally mean ... they are a bit cynical ... that they do not believe things can be settled upon an ideal basis ... [I]f they used to be that way they are not that way now. They have been subdued.'[87]

Wilson's confidence that nations would come to interpret their interests in the more cooperative way he desired was based on two important sub-claims: first, that there was a crucial distinction to be made between 'peoples' and governments; and second, that the trend towards peoples acquiring control of their states, i.e. the spread of democracy, meant those states would *ipso facto* subscribe to the Wilsonian agenda. This first claim was key to the Wilsonianism attitude to foreign policy because it allowed Wilson to question other governments' assertions regarding their own national interests by claiming that their claims did not fit with 'real' interests, meaning those of 'the people'. This implicit limitation on Wilson's respect for other governments' legitimacy was on display in his statement, while on his pro-League speaking tour in America, that the peace settlement he had designed appealed to 'all statesmen who realized the real interests of their people'.[88] Whatever their governments might say, Wilson was always certain that 'the people' were in tune with his liberal vision, and this fuelled his unflagging optimism regarding the viability of the new world order.

The people/government distinction was not an invention of 1919. It had already been nurtured in Wilson's policy towards Latin America. And in wartime he invoked it as a central part of his narrative of the conflict with

Germany. Even as he asked for a declaration of war, he made a point of declaring: 'We have no quarrel with the German people ... It was not upon their impulse that their government acted in entering this war.'[89] Likewise, German espionage and intrigue during the United States' period of neutrality – culminating in the controversy over the co-called 'Zimmermann Telegram' seeking an anti-American alliance with Mexico – was attributed not to 'Germany' as a totality, but to the clique who controlled it: 'We knew that their sources lay not in any hostile feeling or purpose of the German people towards us ... but only in the selfish designs of a Government that did what it pleased and told its people nothing.'[90]

As Wilson saw it, the German people were controlled by, not in control of, their government, and thus could not be held responsible for its actions. In seeking to destroy the German government and the system that underpinned it, the United States was therefore fighting also 'for the liberation of ... the German peoples'.[91] It was, he argued, 'a People's War' for 'freedom and justice and self-government among the nations of the world ... the German people themselves included ...'.[92] Once peoples were empowered, he believed, the new order could flower. Speaking in Boston after his return from the peace conference, he declared that: '[W]hen I speak of the nations of the world, I do not speak of the governments of the world. I speak of the peoples who constitute the nations of the world. They are in the saddle, and they are going to see to it that if their present governments do not do their will some other governments shall.'[93]

Yet for all this talk of cooperation, it is striking that Wilsonianism was based on an intellectual approach not much less nationalistic than the more overt imperialism of Roosevelt. Most notably, it shared the assumption that the United States alone was entitled to identify authoritatively what the 'common interest' was, and what it mandated.[94] His unshakeable conviction that countries should be able to find mutually beneficial solutions to any conflict through reason and goodwill equipped Wilson poorly to deal with circumstances where nations insisted that their interests clashed with those of others, or with American preference. When this did happen, he was obliged by the logic of his ideological principles to tell other governments that they were simply mistaken in their reading of their own interests. Such was the case after the war, when the administration argued that Italian demands regarding control of Fiume were 'contrary to Italy's best interests'.[95] Such arguments went down poorly with the relevant leaders, for obvious reasons.

Universal liberal democracy as a necessary condition of Wilsonian order

Wilson's thinking about the new world order thus involved a series of interlocking, mutually supportive ideas, each essential to the overall vision: (1) the balance of power order was defective, as a matter of both morality and pragmatism, and had to go; (2) it could and should be replaced by a more cooperative international order; (3) bringing about a new cooperative spirit required states to accept that their true and fundamental national interests were in harmony, not in conflict; (4) this recognition would come about because the world's 'peoples', newly awakened, would oblige their governments to embrace the liberal Wilsonian agenda, because it was in line with their own values. The final link in the chain of ideas was therefore the universalization of liberal democracy within all states, for only if this occurred would peoples control governments effectively enough to insist on the requisite cooperative foreign policy. 'Self-determination' is well known as a Wilsonian phrase referring to the right of peoples within fragmenting empires to form separate nation-states, but the term also had meaning in reference to internal politics: the right of people to determine for themselves who should govern them.

In analysing the causes of the First World War, Wilson blamed not only the balance-of-power system as a whole, but also the nature of the German military autocracy, headed by the Kaiser's secretive, aristocratic establishment.[96] In an open society, he thought, the events that launched the war could never have occurred, and in a fully democratic world they would not be repeated:

> Cunningly contrived plans of deception and aggression ... can be worked out and kept from the light only within the privacy of courts or behind the carefully guarded conferences of a narrow and privileged class. They are happily impossible where public opinion commands and insists upon full information concerning all the nation's affairs.[97]

Autocratic government – i.e. the absence of popular control – was to blame for this and other wars, he argued: 'I am convinced that only governments institute such wars as the present, and that they are never brought on by peoples ... democracy is the best preventive of such jealousies and suspicions and secret intrigues as produce wars ...'.[98] Wilson was thus a subscriber to what would later be termed liberal or democratic peace theory, the idea that democratically constituted states do not fight one another. 'Power cannot be used with concentrated force against free peoples if it is used by free people,' as he put it in 1917.[99] His long-standing belief was that 'peace is going to come to the world only through Liberty ... One republic must love another just as one body of human beings must understand and sympathize with another body of human beings.' 'Great Democracies,' he asserted, with the United States in mind as the supreme example, 'are not belligerent. They do not seek or desire war ... Conquest and dominion are not in our reckoning; or agreeable to our principles.'[100]

From this he inferred that lasting peace could be achieved only through the absence of non-democratic states from the international system. As he urged the declaration of war in 1917, he told Congress: 'a steadfast concert for peace can never be maintained except by a partnership of democratic nations. No autocratic government could be trusted to keep faith within it or observe its covenants.' The world, he would argue later, could not be safe, 'so long as governments like that which ... drew Austria and Germany into this war are permitted to control the destinies ... of men and nations'.[101] The First World War, as he conceived of it, was not a war against one rogue nation and its allies, but a war against a system of government, 'a people's war ... waged against absolutism and militarism', 'not only a war between nations, but also a war between systems of culture'.[102] In making the argument that democracy was causally linked to peace, and dictatorship to war and aggression, Wilson laid the basis for an American concern with the domestic systems of others that would recur for generations.

It was universally true, Wilson insisted, that 'people have a right to live their own lives under the governments which they themselves choose to set up. That is the American principle and I was glad to fight for it.'[103] Fusing democratic universalism and 'Americanism' thus, Wilson justified the war as an American struggle for universal liberty: 'We wanted to destroy autocratic authority everywhere in the world.'[104] 'The object of the war was to destroy autocratic power ... There must not be men anywhere in any private place who can plot the mastery of civilization.'[105] 'There are not going to be many other kinds of Nations [than democracies] long, my fellow citizens,' he predicted. 'The people of this world – not merely the people of America, for they did the job long ago – have determined that there should be no more autocratic governments.'[106]

Wilson's objective, therefore, was not simply the creation of a new balance of power favouring America, but the alteration of the domestic systems of Germany and other states so as to allow a new order based on liberal theory. When armistice was agreed with Germany, it was on the condition that the Kaiser be deposed and his supporters expelled from the state apparatus. With that, Wilson told the American people, 'everything for which America fought has been accomplished. It will now be our fortunate duty to assist ... in the establishment of just democracy throughout the world'.[107]

The universal righteousness of liberal principles was central to the Wilsonian vision. He was certain that his ideas were in line with the progressive advance of history, reflecting not preoccupations particular to America but values of universal legitimacy. Of self-determination and government by consent, he declared:

> These are American principles ... [a]nd they are also the principles of progressive, forward-looking men and women everywhere, of every modern nation, of every enlightened community. They are the principles of mankind and must prevail.[108]

The values of liberty and democracy were ideologically contagious, Wilson explained. People everywhere, he said, had declared: 'It is not only in America that men want to govern themselves, it is not only in France that men mean to throw off this intolerable yoke. All men are of the same temper and of the same make and the same rights.'[109] The war had been 'a great cause which was not the peculiar cause of America but the cause of mankind and of civilization itself.'[110]

'Leader and umpire both': American primacy and destiny

For all the talk of freedom and equality, one of the most important of Wilson's numerous assumptions regarding future world order was that the United States would be pre-eminent in power and influence. No less than 'moral leadership' was being offered to the United States, he felt, and the nation had to decide 'whether we shall accept or reject the confidence of the world'.[111] This was partly based on the raw fact of America's material strength: 'If we are partners, we predict we will be the senior partner,' he told Americans, '... The other countries of the world are looking to us for leadership and direction.'[112] Yet he was reluctant to invoke the brute fact of America's economic advantage or military potential as the primary driver of American primacy; rather, he wanted to claim moral superiority. The most important source of US influence was the fact that 'the United States is the only nation in the world that has sufficient moral force with the rest of the world'.[113] To his mind, the 'whole moral force of right in the world depends upon the United States rather than upon any other nation'.[114]

Wilson's intense focus on the themes of cooperation and common interests clearly identify him on a rhetorical level as an opponent of nationalism, at least of a certain kind. Yet his certainty that it was America's place to exercise moral, even spiritual, leadership lent a nationalistic quality to his vision of the new world order that echoed Roosevelt's ambition to win a place for America in the history of the ages.[115] Of the 'distinction drawn between nationalism and internationalism', he observed:

> The greatest nationalist is the man who wants his nation to be the greatest nation, and the greatest nation is the nation which penetrates to the heart of its duty and mission among the nations of the world ... [T]he nation that has that vision is elevated to a place of influence and power which it cannot get by arms, which it cannot get by commercial rivalry, which it can get by no other way than by that spiritual leadership which comes from a profound understanding of the problems of humanity.[116]

This was the kind of leadership that he claimed was on offer to the United States, and he sought to insist that the rest of the US body politic embrace it. Whereas if America took up the baton of leadership and entered the League, he argued, it would be 'the determining factor in the development of civilization,' he argued, if it did not, then: 'the world would experience one of those reversals of sentiment, one of those penetrating chills of reaction, which would lead to a universal cynicism, for if America goes back upon mankind, mankind has no other place to turn'.[117]

The assumption of American primacy helped Wilson sustain his assumption that the institutions and norms of the new cooperative, multilateral world order would not clash with the interests or wishes of the United States, or force it into policies it would not otherwise adopt. In the same way as he had done in conceptualizing the Monroe Doctrine, he conflated the interests of the United States with the 'true' interests of other nations, and thus predicted that the future wishes of the United States and the collective will of the free world would perennially coincide. Universal democracy and cooperative international institutions would in and of themselves bring other nations into line with American positions on important matters, removing any foreseeable basis for clash. Ambrosius picks up on this theme in Wilson's thinking, noting that: 'Implicit in his conception of a league, as in the Monroe Doctrine, was the assumption that the United States would decide whether to guarantee the status quo or require changes. His approach to foreign policy was at once unilateral and universal.'[118] The kind of progress Wilson foresaw was towards general recognition of an objective 'right' into which the United States already had insight, while American global 'leadership' would allow the US a significant degree of control in managing that process. In the 'game' of managing the new world order, Wilson told Americans they would be 'trusted as leader and umpire both'.[119]

It did not seem conceivable to Wilson that the United States might in future find itself in conflict with the new order of international institutions and law that he had planned, because he conceived of the new order as the universalization of the standards of the United States itself. Axiomatically, therefore, America would be in the right; the purpose of a new system was to bring others into line with the United States, not vice versa. This underlying assumption was made explicit in Wilson's rejoinder to Senatorial critics who quibbled about the treaty terms providing for voluntary withdrawal from the League:

> I am inclined to ask: 'What are you worried about? Are you afraid that we will not have fulfilled our international obligations?' I am too proud an American to believe anything of the kind. We never have failed to fulfil our international obligations, and we never will, and our international obligations will always look toward the fulfilment of the highest purposes of civilization ... We have served mankind and we shall continue to serve mankind, for I believe, my fellow men, that we are the flower of mankind so far as civilization is concerned.[120]

Likewise, he had no fear that the provisions of the League that would subject US decisions to outside scrutiny might ever lead to justified criticism:

> There is only one conceivable reason for not liking [such provisions] ... and to me as an American it is not a conceivable reason; that is that we should wish to do some nation some great wrong. If there is any nation in the world that can afford to submit its purposes to discussion, it is the American Nation.[121]

Because he imagined that perceived American failure to meet international obligations could only arise from deliberate ethical deviancy on America's part, Wilson did not concern himself with the prospect. That an accusation of wrongdoing might result not from conscious malevolence but simply from differing national perceptions of obligation and interest did not, apparently, occur to him. He dismissed those who raised the spectre of the US being the recipient of critical judgements from any new international bodies as unpatriotic for even contemplating the prospect. League judgements could only be made against the US over its veto, he reminded them, if the US itself were party to the case under consideration. In that case, he asked: 'A party to what? A party to seizing somebody else's territory? A party to infringing some other country's political independence? Is any man willing to stand on this platform and say that the United States is likely to do either of these things?'[122] The Wilsonian worldview did not have room for the idea that judgements of international right and wrong might be subjective, likely to vary from nation to nation in accordance with interest and politics. Instead, it took it as read that so long as America intended to live up to its own standards, that fact alone would be sure to protect it from charges of malfeasance, because American standards themselves could be treated as the measure of objective right.

In making his case for the assumption of global leadership, Wilson also projected a vision of national destiny. America's 'isolation', he said, had ended 'not because we chose to go into the politics of the world, but because by the sheer genius of this people and the growth of our power we have become the determining factor in the history of mankind'. As a result, the nation no longer had a choice, because its influence was too decisive. Isolation had been ended, and thus the new internationalism brought about, by 'the processes of history'.[123] The emergence of the new order was 'a fulfilment of the destiny of the United States':

> At last ... the world has come to the vision that [America] had in that far year of 1776. Men in Europe laughed ... at this little handful of dreamers ... who talked dogmatically about liberty, and since then that fire which they started on that little coast has consumed every autocratic government in the world ... [124]

Now the only question left for America was: 'Shall we keep the primacy of the world or shall we abandon it?'[125] Even after it became apparent that he would have trouble securing the ratification of his peace plan at home, Wilson continued to frame his defence of it in the language of inevitability. Speaking to a sceptical Senate, he invoked divine imagery:

> The stage is set, the destiny disclosed. It has come about by no plan of our choosing, but by the hand of God who led us into this way. We cannot turn back. We can only go forward, with lifted eyes and freshened

spirit, to follow the vision. It was of this that we dreamed at our birth. America shall in truth show the way. The light streams upon the path ahead, and nowhere else.[126]

Wilson's divergence from Roosevelt: 'moral force' and the role of arms

Because he was convinced that his optimism regarding universal liberty would be vindicated, Wilson felt sure that the role of arms in international relations would greatly diminish under the new world order. This did not have its origins in outright pacifism, however – Wilson was assuredly no subscriber to that school. Once he finally gave up on neutrality in 1917, he exhorted the American people towards an almost orgiastic embrace of righteous violence:

> Germany has ... said that force, and force alone, shall decide whether Justice and peace shall reign in the affairs of men ... There is, therefore, but one response possible from us: Force, Force to the utmost, Force without stint or limit, the righteous and triumphant force which shall make Right the law of the world, and cast every selfish dominion down in the dust.[127]

But though he argued that a decisive fight with Germany was needed to clear the ground for righteous peace, he also anticipated that in the post-war order there could be significant global disarmament, and far less need for violence as a means of resolving international disputes. Disarmament was a key point in all his proposals for peace during the war, and he further advocated the nationalization of arms production to abolish any commercial incentives for war.

The key buttress supporting the new order, he forecast, would not be arms, but the mobilization of international opinion behind the Wilsonian worldview. 'It will be our high privilege,' he told an audience at Buckingham Palace in 1918, '... to organize the moral force of the world to preserve [the forthcoming] settlements, to steady the forces of mankind and make the right and the justice to which great nations like our own have devoted themselves the predominant and controlling force of the world.'[128] The Allied nations, 'temporarily together in a combination of physical force', would now be combined in exercising 'moral force that is irresistible'. The new order would place 'the conscience of the world ... upon the throne ...'.[129] He thus encouraged reliance, in effect, on moral peer pressure between nations as the ultimate guarantor of security. '[W]e are depending primarily upon one great force, and that is the moral force of the public opinion of the world,' he confessed with pride.[130] When he came to sell the League of Nations to Americans, he refused to acknowledge openly that a commitment to the use of armed force was required. Instead, he told Americans, the new order would ensure that 'instead of war there shall be arbitration ... discussion ... the closure of intercourse ... the irresistible pressure of the opinion of mankind'.[131]

Critics did challenge Wilson on this, noting that the Paris treaties appeared to commit the US to open-ended military intervention abroad. But he dismissed them with the paradoxical gambit that clear US commitment to act, as provided in the collective security pledge in Article X of the League Covenant, would in fact avert the need for future action. America could 'go into the great adventure of liberating hundreds of millions of human beings from the threat of foreign power,' Wilson argued '... without shedding a drop of human blood'. 'If you are squeamish,' he reassured Americans, 'I will tell you you will not have to fight. The only force that outlasts all others and is finally triumphant is the moral judgment of mankind.'[132] The League was not a trap for America leading to war, but through its deterrent power was 'a definite guarantee by word against aggression'.[133] The critics, he suggested, 'know physical force and do not understand moral force. Moral force is a great deal more powerful than physical force. Govern the sentiments of mankind and you govern mankind.'[134]

Wilson argued that in fact his opponents were the ones making military demands of Americans. His plan for League membership paved the way for minimal armament, he claimed, while rejection of it would necessitate building a sizeable military establishment to survive in a world collapsed back into balance-of-power rivalry.[135] This was therefore an area of clear divergence between Wilson and Roosevelt. Whereas TR felt pride and hope at the prospect of American physical might and devoted much of his public life to the cause of increased military appropriations, Wilson located himself in the opposite tradition, suspicious of efforts to turn the US permanently into a military titan. Their perspectives on post-war order differed accordingly: Roosevelt viewed the retention of armed strength by the US and its allies as key to the defence of civilization; Wilson meanwhile was confident that the power of moral force, with little role for arms, could make the new order work.

Mortality, personal and political

Wilson's peace settlement faced a swell of domestic opposition even before the Paris talks were concluded. Critics in the Republican-led Senate objected especially to the potentially open-ended commitment through Article X to defend all League members. Some, most famously Idaho's William Borah, were so-called 'irreconcilables', opposed to any movement away from the Founders' Era consensus. More numerous were centrist Republicans such as Henry Cabot Lodge and Elihu Root, who inherited status as the Republicans' weightiest spokesmen on foreign affairs when Roosevelt died. This latter group was willing to accept a watered-down League treaty, but insisted that a series of 'reservations' be attached diluting America's promises. But Wilson refused to compromise with the 'reservationists'. Accusing them of partisan opportunism, he noted bitterly that internationalist Republicans like Roosevelt and Lodge had supported the idea of a League only a few years before.[136]

For Wilson, amputating Article X from the treaty to gain ratification was unacceptable; it was 'the very backbone of the whole Covenant'.[137] His rationale for the end of American 'isolation' was the replacement of the balance-of-power alliance system with a new world order of universal and collective security. A more limited pact would amount not to a minor variation on his scheme, but to an attack on its ideological foundation. Rejecting compromise, he therefore sought to appeal over the heads of his Senate opponents by taking the case for unconditional ratification to the country in a great Western speaking tour beginning in September 1919. Often making several speeches in a single day, and intending to go on for several weeks, he hoped to stir the mass of the people to rise up in his support and force his Senate opponents to back down.

The choice before America, in Wilson's characteristically stark portrayal, was between his brand of internationalism, which assumed a radically reformed world order with America at its head, and the alternative of transforming America into a militarized and unilateral power within the old balance-of-power system, no better morally than the German state just defeated in war:

> [W]e are making a fundamental choice. You have either got to have the old system, of which Germany was the perfect flower, or you have got to have a new system ...[138]
>
> Is it possible ... that there is a group of individuals in this country who have conceived it as desirable that the United States should exercise its power alone, should arm for the purpose, should be ready for the enterprise, and should dominate the world by arms? ... Are we going to substitute for pan-Germanism a sinister pan-Americanism? The thing is inconceivable. It is hideous. No man dare propose that in plain words to any American audience anywhere. The heart of this people is pure ... It would rather have liberty and justice than wealth and power. It is the great idealistic force of history, and the idealism of America is what has made conquest of the spirits of men.[139]

His opponents, he said, offered only a return to the 'old and evil order ... that old and ugly plan of armed nations, of alliances, of watchful jealousies, of rabid antagonisms, of purposes concealed, running by the subtle channels of intrigue through the veins of people who do not dream what poison is being injected into their systems'.[140] Thus, he said, it was the reservationists who actually lay beyond the pale of America's ideological tolerance. They were the ones who wanted to take the United States into the world of the great powers without the radical transformation of the international system Wilsonianism thought essential to enabling such a change in policy. The choice, he argued, was extreme: 'We ought either to go in or to stay out. To stay out would be fatal to the influence and even to the commercial prospects of the United States, and to go in would be to give her leadership of the world.'[141]

During this battle Wilson's health broke. Exhausted and unwell, he returned to Washington on doctor's orders three weeks into the Western tour. On 2 October, he suffered a massive stroke. Though he recovered enough function – just – to continue in office, he was substantially incapacitated for the remainder of his presidency. Unable to convince enough senators to support the League treaty without amendments, he did retain sufficient support to block any version incorporating Lodge's reservations. This he chose to do. Thus, a coalition of 'irreconcilable' isolationists who sought no overseas commitments whatsoever, and those loyal to Wilson's absolutist demand for 'all or nothing', killed the prospect of any version of the treaty passing.

Even as defeat unfolded, Wilson maintained a sense of unwavering self-righteousness. As he had been happy to tell foreign governments in the past, he now told the US Government: 'the people' were behind his ideas; they, as representatives, were in error. 'Personally,' he wrote, in January 1920, 'I do not accept the action of the Senate of the United States as the decision of the Nation.' It was on this basis that he called for the 1920 elections to serve as 'a great and solemn referendum' on the Paris settlement.[142] His party was soundly beaten, and he slipped from office quietly in March 1921. He had been reduced, in less than four years, from perhaps the most politically dominant president in US history to a physically broken man in whose ideas the public seemed to have lost faith. Yet he retained belief in the ultimate triumph to come of what he had attempted. In the last public pronouncement of his life, delivered on Armistice Day of 1923, he addressed a group of veterans gathered outside his house, telling them:

> I am not one of those that have the least anxiety about the principles I have stood for. I have seen fools resist Providence before, and I have seen their destruction, as will come upon these again, utter destruction and contempt. That we shall prevail is as sure as that God reigns.[143]

Conclusion

Woodrow Wilson's presidency marked a key point of transition in American thinking about global entanglement. The spur for change lay in shifting national and international circumstances. The increased territory, economic size and potential military power of the United States since its foundation had made it likely, if not inevitable, that it would broaden the scope of its self-defined interests and adopt a more globally engaged policy. While a necessary condition, however, this was not of itself sufficient to prompt sudden, wholesale change. Huge growth in American power potential was already apparent by the time of Theodore Roosevelt's leadership, yet he remained constrained in his freedom of action by pre-existing principles embedded in American ideological culture regarding the separation of the

American and European/global spheres. What differed in Wilson's case was that the First World War brought about sudden upheaval in the international order. This generated pressure from the international system to complement the possibilities already created by increased American strength.

Following on the path established by Roosevelt, Wilson intervened widely in Latin America in the first years of his presidency. He supported this with an ideology of 'civilization' and self-determination under which the United States believed it could increase the 'freedom' of other peoples through interference in their national affairs, seeking to generate the proper conditions for them to enjoy liberty appropriately. This was rooted in the view that only certain forms of political order were compatible with progress, and that the US had a responsibility to guide other American nations in their exercise of freedom. Under the Wilsonian ideology, the interests of the US and the Latin American states were identical if properly conceived, and therefore it was legitimate to seek to build a cooperative system of states under a blanket of US hegemony. This conceptualization of the Monroe Doctrine would later serve as the basis of Wilson's global new world order.

Wilson's America was drawn into the First World War directly by German submarine attacks and indirectly by concern over the consequences of a German victory for US interests and broader geopolitical stability and security. But Wilson did not justify America's joining the war by arguing that it would achieve a more beneficial balance of power through it. Nor did he conceive of US internationalism in the post-war world as the entry of the United States into the system of international relations as it had existed prior to the war. Instead, he argued that the European balance-of-power system had been one of the causes of the war, and that that system must now been destroyed, to be replaced by a new world order based on cooperation and collective security. This would be made possible through the empowerment of 'peoples' by means of the imminent universalization of liberal democracy. Because 'peoples' correctly perceived their fundamental interests to be common and harmonious, Wilsonianism argued, democracy would produce peace. This intellectual separation of peoples from governments enabled Wilson to criticize foreign governments for incorrectly identifying their peoples' deeper wishes whenever they interpreted their national interests to be in conflict with American policy preferences. Wilson's vision of post-war order was further based on the belief that the United States would exercise leadership in the new system, and that the creation of new laws and institutions governing international behaviour would amount to the internationalization of American standards. Thus, it was not a consideration for Wilson that the US itself might ultimately be criticized or constrained in the pursuit of what it might consider its legitimate interests.

The emergence of Wilsonianism demonstrates one of the central claims of this book: that national strategy develops based on the interaction of circumstances with embedded ideological principles developed in the nation's past. Circumstances during Wilson's presidency called for a new level of international engagement. Established ideological principles, however, made the suggestion that the United States should enter into the European balance of power problematic within the context of US political culture. This led Wilson to craft the argument that the new internationalism into which he was leading the United States was predicated on the abolition of the old balance of power order and the creation of a new, liberal order under US leadership.

The new American internationalism was thus, via Wilsonian ideology, made conditional upon an imagined 'deal' whereby the United States agreed to be globally engaged only on the condition that it could legitimately demand from the world the universal liberal democracy upon which the new global order was to be founded. It is for this reason that realist critics have abhorred Wilsonianism, seeing it as the apotheosis of the moralistic strain that has plagued US foreign policy. As such, critics see it, the Wilsonian approach has fostered a damaging utopianism that binds the US national interest up with intrusive interventions aimed at perfecting foreign societies and encourages naïve faith in the capacity of international institutions to preserve global security. What both critics and defenders of Wilson can agree upon is that he sought to lead America into the global system not through adoption of that system's existing norms, but through reform of the world and its constituent nations in line with American preferences. The feasibility of such an enterprise, and therefore the 'realism' of making its pursuit the centrepiece of American objectives, has been the core debate of US foreign policy for almost a century since.

Though Wilsonianism fell into abeyance for a number of years after Wilson's personal political failure, this 'deal' would be a crucial component in the strategic thinking that followed the Second World War. After the Second World War, the United States at last made the strategic decision mandated by its size and strength: to accept status as a linchpin of the global order. It would do so, however, based not on the balance-of-power ideology of the old European order, but on a fusion of Wilsonian ideas regarding global international reform and Rooseveltian ones embracing the necessity of military might in the service of the good.

6 The Truman administration

'In the struggle for men's minds, the conflict is world-wide'[1]

Introduction

The United States' embrace of a new internationalism did not proceed uninterrupted after the First World War. In the 1920s and 1930s, after Wilson's departure from public life, the nation eschewed the level of entanglement he had envisioned. Though the US did play a significant role in European affairs through the provision of credit and economic advice, it refrained from firm military-political alliance commitments. Ideologically, there was an effort to recapture the spirit of well-intentioned but ultimately detached relations with Europe that had been the core of the Founders' Era consensus. The Kellogg–Briand Pact of 1928, a treaty that sought to prohibit the use of force as a tool of statecraft, was the most visible American commitment to European diplomatic affairs. It had more in common, however, with the pre-First World War tradition of arbitration treaties than with the firmer commitments to mutual defence represented by the League of Nations and, later, by the North Atlantic Treaty.

In fact, the direction of intellectual travel on America's part in the inter-war years was away from entanglement rather than towards it. In the 1930s, the Great Depression instilled pessimism and inward focus, while the rise of fascism and the worsening of diplomatic relations between the major European nations bred anxiety regarding the possibility of another major war. Rather than pre-emptive efforts to avert war through American commitment, the United States' chief response was Congress's passage of a series of Neutrality Acts in 1936, 1937 and 1939, prospectively limiting trade with belligerents in wartime so as to avoid a recurrence of 1917's *casus belli*. Ultimately, however, America did not stay out of the Second World War. This was due partly to the efforts of President Franklin Roosevelt to aid the Allied side, and partly to the decision of Japan to attack the United States at Pearl Harbor in December 1941, and that of Hitler's Germany to declare war immediately thereafter.[2]

This chapter focuses on the period after that conflict was won. It does so because it considers the years of the mid- and late 1940s, under the leadership of Harry Truman, to be a decisive moment in the history of US strategic thought and policy. It was in this period that the decision to embrace a fully engaged global internationalism took place. Certainly there had been internationalist individuals in the United States before, and a strand of national life given over to their way of thinking. But it was only after the Truman administration's period in office that a stable bipartisan consensus existed in favour of extensive American commitments to preserve global order and to maintain the military capability to meet such commitments. This chapter argues that the Truman administration made the case for, and commitment to, a new American internationalism on the basis of a revival of Wilsonian principles of liberal universalism and the Rooseveltian argument for accumulating armed strength in the defence of a righteous civilizational cause. In doing so, it broke decisively with the ideology of the Founders' Era consensus, which finally lost the last of its hold over the thinking of American political leaders. Simultaneously, however, it also rejected American entry into global affairs on the basis of seeking a stable balance of power between rival states with equivalently legitimate interests. This rejection had profound implications for the ideological basis of US strategic thinking in the decades to come.

This chapter first sets out the national and international context in which the Truman administration operated. It then discusses the decline in relations between the United States and the Soviet Union, i.e. the emergence of the 'Cold War', which demanded a coherent new global strategy. The remaining sections then examine in detail the strategic thinking that emerged in response to this conflict with the USSR. These cover President Truman's own conception of the Cold War, the vision of 'containment' advanced from within of the State Department by George Kennan, and the construction of a strategy of militarized confrontation in the Clifford–Elsey Report and NSC-68. In outlining the strategy formulated by the Truman administration, this chapter emphasizes the administration's Wilsonian attribution of the problems of global order to the domestic constitution of the Soviet state, and its insistence on the universalization of liberalism as the ultimate route to international peace and stability. It also notes the decisive adoption by US leaders of Rooseveltian beliefs concerning the necessity of a large standing military establishment on the part of the United States.

What follows is not an argument about whether the Cold War did or did not produce a balance of power 'on the ground'; clearly it did. The argument made here concerns America's own perception of what it was doing and why. The conclusion it reaches agrees with Macdonald that the Cold War should be viewed not as a simple balance of power, but as a clash of rival, frustrated universalisms: 'The irony,' as he notes, 'was that neither Leninism nor American-style liberalism accepted traditional balance of power politics philosophically, but structural realities meant that this was the most that could be hoped for in the short run.'[3]

National and international context

The Second World War profoundly altered the global distribution of power, leaving the traditional great powers of Western and Central Europe outside the top rank. By 1945, Germany lay in ruins economically, politically and ideologically. France had clearly been defeated and humiliated in the war even though it recovered its sovereignty, thanks to Allied victory. The United Kingdom, in spite of its central role in the defeat of Germany and Churchill's place alongside Stalin and FDR at the table of the 'Big Three', had seen its solvency and its grip on empire irreparably undermined, facts that would become painfully apparent soon after the end of hostilities. In Asia, Japan submitted to US occupation, while in China civil conflict raged.

The United States and the Soviet Union were the only powers to emerge from the war stronger. The USSR had endured enormous loss of life, and had suffered a political near-death experience immediately following Hitler's invasion. It had regrouped, however, and assembled titanic military capacity, the brutal effectiveness of which had been displayed in a fierce counter-onslaught across Europe to Berlin. The United States, meanwhile, suffered none of the carnage others endured on the home front, and under the demands of war its economy had demonstrated a productive capacity that towered over that of others. Before the Second World War the international system had been based around a multiplicity of significant powers. By 1945, there were only two in the top tier. As a result, unprecedented systemic pressure existed for the United States to play a central role in the management of international order.

Domestically, too, the war had changed the United States, through its impact on the views of American leaders. America's decision to turn away from Wilson's legacy in favour of defensive isolation looked in hindsight like an error of historic moment. It had allowed a war that might have been contained in size by early American commitment to engulf half the world before pulling the United States in anyway. Many, therefore, looked to Wilsonianism for inspiration in seeking to build a new peace. They hoped that peace might centre on a new world organization, a successor to the League of Nations.

Yet such aspirations for a new world order had been raised and then discarded in US politics only 25 years before. There remained, even among influential political leaders, a school of thought that believed a retraction of US commitments to within its own hemisphere could once again be workable and desirable.[4] It remained to be seen if a durable new internationalism could be constructed. That it did ultimately prove possible owed much to the pressures created by external circumstance: the desire of the Soviet Union to play the role of military and ideological superpower, and the inability of others to resist it without American assistance. The manner in which the United States reasoned its way to its new internationalism, however, was also significant.

From 'one world' to 'two ways of life': Truman's inheritance and the deterioration of US–Soviet relations

Precisely when and why US–Soviet relations passed the point of no return from alliance to enmity is a matter of debate.[5] The visible fracture came after the transition from President Franklin Roosevelt, who died in office in April 1945, to his successor, Harry Truman. Most historical accounts attribute importance to the shift from FDR's nuanced – some would say disingenuous – management of Big Three diplomacy to Truman's insistence on plainer speaking. Certainly, Truman was not kept well informed by FDR regarding the details of his Soviet policy.[6] There is an argument to be made that in adopting a confrontational approach and demanding the Soviet Union meet undertakings made at the Yalta Conference of February 1945, Truman's approach ran counter to reassurances informally given by FDR to Stalin regarding the meaning of those agreements.[7]

The Declaration on Liberated Europe made at Yalta did appear to commit the USSR to hold free elections and form representative governments in territories under its military control, but it is clear, with hindsight, that Stalin had no intention of living up to American conceptions of freedom and representation. FDR's priority, however, was to preserve friendly personal relations with Stalin, and thus he seems to have been willing to tolerate the emergence of an unspoken divergence of interpretation regarding what was agreed at Yalta.[8] Pierce terms this the 'Rooseveltian practice of disguising unprincipled agreements with the pretence of principle', arguing that it was a practice 'with which Truman never felt comfortable ... and which he would soon abandon. He would also abandon the idea that cooperation was to be valued in and of itself, even if principles had to be sacrificed for the sake of it.'[9] Others have suggested that the difference between FDR's trajectory just before his death and Truman's upon arrival in office may have been more a matter of timing and style than underlying substance. FDR, they suggest, hoped ultimately to use his powers of persuasion to iron out problems through personal diplomacy at a later stage, but by the last days of his life he had begun to see the need for a toughening of policy.[10] Access to the definitive truth on Roosevelt's thinking is impossible, however, as he left no record of his innermost thoughts and plans.

FDR also left a legacy of planning for a new world organization, the United Nations, which would be established by the San Francisco Conference of April–June 1945. The central plank of world order was to be concert between 'Four Policemen': the United States, the Soviet Union, Britain and China. FDR expressed the hope that the 'common denominator' of a desire for peace would bring together the dominant world powers in a 'common association of interest'. Reflecting on the failed experiment of Wilson's League, he observed that it had been 'based on magnificent idealism', but that 'good intentions alone' were inadequate defence against 'the predatory animals of this world'. Rather than subscribe to Wilson's faith in the controlling influence of 'moral force', therefore, FDR embraced his cousin Theodore's belief that a secure order must rest on proper acknowledgement of the role of hard power.[11]

Yet if FDR was 'realistic', then part of that realism involved recognizing the ideological constraints imposed by America's own politics. As one pair of close analysts notes, Roosevelt believed in 'rightful primacy of the strong' and 'trusteeship of the powerful'. But in dealing with the Soviet Union he also believed that explicit 'sphere-of-influence politics would produce a new wave of American isolationist recoil, rooted in moral disgust, and that this could fatally undermine prospects for American leadership – either in war or in a postwar effort to secure a lasting peace'.[12] Cordell Hull, FDR's Secretary of State, had promised Congress and the American people in November 1943 that in the settlement brought about after the war there would 'no longer be need for spheres of influence, for alliances, for balance of power, or any other of the special arrangements through which, in the unhappy past, the nations strove to safeguard their security or promote their interest'.[13] Such rhetoric reinforced American cultural resistance to thinking of international relations in terms of balance-of-power politics. As a matter of reality, Wilsonian ideas of universality had to be invoked to make new international commitments politically palatable.

At the outset of his presidency, Truman rhetorically summoned the combined spirits of Wilson and FDR to drive forward the plan for the UN, and continued to express the aspiration of a fundamentally cooperative world order. 'It is one world, as [Wendell] Willkie said,' he noted. 'It is a world in which we must all get along ... And it is my opinion that this great Republic ought to lead the way. My opinion is that this great Republic ought to carry out the ideals of Woodrow Wilson and Franklin D. Roosevelt.'[14] Echoing Wilson's call to the American people after the First World War, Truman emphasized that America's great power had bestowed upon it a 'duty to assume the leadership and accept responsibility'. The reality of American power as displayed in the war was 'the fact that underlies every phase of our relations with other countries', he warned. 'We cannot escape the responsibility which it thrusts upon us. What we think, plan, say and do is of profound significance to the future of every corner of the world.' As Wilson had done before him, Truman told Americans: 'the entire world is looking to America for enlightened leadership and progress'.[15]

At first, as Pierce puts it, the 'UN revived the internationalist hope that it was possible to universalize American principles'.[16] As with Wilson's new world order, however, the American plan for international cooperation implicitly depended upon the political character of the states within that order. Unfortunately for hopes of harmony, the Soviet Union was invested in political principles starkly at variance with American leaders' liberal assumptions. This manifested itself starkly in Europe, where areas under Soviet control were denied anything Americans could accept as democratic process. At the Potsdam Conference in the summer of 1945, Stalin responded sharply to criticism, declaring that 'if a government is not fascist, a government is democratic'. This was a blunt early demonstration of divergence between Soviet and American readings of Yalta.[17]

'Cold War' policy, as the term is usually understood, did not emerge fully in America until the outbreak of the Korean War in the summer of 1950, which secured political approval for a massive military build-up. The degeneration of US–Soviet diplomatic relations into hostility occurred before that, however, the result of a steady accumulation of confrontations. In 1946, the United States successfully forced the Soviets out of northern Iran and resisted a Soviet push for joint control (with Turkey) of the Dardanelles. In 1947, the Truman Doctrine and Marshall Plan were announced. The former promised American military aid to fight communist rebels in Greece and Turkey, the latter pledged stability-boosting economic support for Western Europe, crucial to undermining communism's advance on the political front. 1948 saw stand-off in the divided European theatre: a communist coup in Czechoslovakia and the Soviet blockade of Berlin, the latter prompting an American-led airlift of supplies to thwart Stalin's plan to strangle the city into submission. In 1949, the United States broke its taboo against military alliances with the North Atlantic Treaty, providing unprecedented commitment to the defence of Western Europe. Meanwhile, the Soviet Union gained new ability to threaten America and its allies with its acquisition of the atomic bomb. In Asia, the fall of China to Mao's communists underlined the global nature of the Cold War struggle. The militarization of US policy ushered in by Korea was thus the logical conclusion of a trend well established in the five years that preceded it.

Over the course of this period the Truman administration made the journey from a vague desire to 'get tough' with the Soviets to a comprehensive diagnosis of the nature of the Soviet threat and a programme to respond to it. The emergence of this programme had both a public and an internal dimension. In public, it took the form of an argument presented by the president and his top aides that the Soviet Union, because of its malign political nature, threatened freedom on a global basis, and the United States needed to respond. Internally, it took the form of a series of reports that fleshed out the same argument at more length. Both the public and the internal discussion arrived at the same conclusions: (1) that the source of the threat lay in the nature of the Soviet system itself, (2) that the United States must act to help others defend their freedom against Soviet/communist encroachment, and (3) that the long-term goal of US policy was to undermine the Soviet system itself. Reform of the Soviet state was necessary to the emergence of a lasting peace. Both publicly and privately, the administration rejected simple acceptance of a balance of power based on spheres of influence. Instead, it adopted a policy of containment aimed ultimately at engineering the collapse the Soviet system.

Truman's conception of the Cold War[18]

Truman's conception of the Cold War, and the argument he made to justify America's participation in a global struggle, rested on five key, interconnected principles. First, that the divergence of political values between the American-led 'free world' and the Soviet Union was the central feature of world politics. Second, that the United States had a responsibility to defend freedom against Soviet efforts to undermine the political systems of free states, and a duty to object to Soviet domination in the states where it was already established. Third, that a simple spheres-of-influence deal with the Soviet Union, requiring America to accept the USSR's actions in its own putative sphere as legitimate, was unacceptable. Fourth, that the values of 'freedom' were universally valid, and their spread was part of the historical destiny of the world; even the Soviet Union could not resist them for ever. Fifth, that military strength on the part of the United States would form an essential part of the defence and ultimate advance of freedom and the establishment of peace of the world. 'Freedom' in this system of thought was, as one would expect, defined as democratic capitalism. Thus, Truman subscribed to internationalist convictions that blended Wilsonianism and Rooseveltianism, universal civilizational moralism with, if not militarism, then at least a belief in the righteous necessity of military strength – and potentially physical force – in defence of the right.[19]

Pierce notes that Truman 'found it difficult to look at the divisions forming in Europe in terms of power alone', and this is reflected in a great many of his statements.[20] The 'Truman Doctrine', expounded in an address to Congress in March 1947, was the landmark statement that publicly signalled the United States' adoption of a mission to resist Soviet communism. In it, Truman described the world as divided between 'two ways of life', between which 'every nation' had to choose, but where the choice was 'too often not a free one'. One way of life, he said, was 'based upon the will of the majority, and ... distinguished by free institutions, representative government, free elections, guarantees of individual liberty, freedom of speech and religion, and freedom from political oppression'. This was, in idealized form, the American system. The second, embodied by the Soviet Union, was 'based upon the will of a minority forcibly imposed upon the majority. It relies upon terror and oppression, a controlled press and radio, fixed elections, and the suppression of personal freedoms.' With the world divided thus, Truman argued, 'it must be the policy of the United States to support free peoples who are resisting attempted subjugation by armed minorities or by outside pressures'.[21] The immediate practical purpose of the Doctrine's proclamation was to justify US aid to the Greek and Turkish resistance to domestic communist forces. Truman's argument reflected the Wilson–Roosevelt conception of self-determination, as played out in Latin America, in asserting that even substantial US intervention served to preserve the autonomous freedom of the affected states, not to impose American political preferences. Intervention was justified as necessary to protect the natural path of 'free' development from interruption by outside forces, but was not itself acknowledged to be a form of outside interference.

Communism, to Truman, was the cause only of 'a militant minority, exploiting human want and misery'. The 'seeds of totalitarian regimes', he argued, were 'spread and grown in the evil soil of poverty and strife. They reach their full growth when the hope of a people for a better life has died. We must keep that hope alive.' The purpose of US aid would be to 'restore internal order and security, so essential for economic and political recovery', which would in turn allow the aided states to 'build an economy in which a healthy democracy can flourish' and thus allow the country 'to become a self-supporting and self-respecting democracy'.[22] Thus, communism was not treated as one of the legitimate courses that might freely be taken by a people, even in reaction to poverty and disorder. Rather, it represented the destruction of freedom and, as such, had to be resisted. True freedom consisted in the establishment of the preconditions for democratic capitalism to flourish, even if that meant US interference. US policy sought the 'creation of conditions in which we and other nations will be able to work out a way of life free from coercion', Truman argued. This goal drew a line of continuity between the recent war and the new conflict with the Soviets. The Second World War had been a victory 'over countries which sought to impose their will, and their way of life, upon other nations'. Now, as then, he told Americans, the 'free peoples of the world look to us to us for support in maintaining their freedoms'.[23]

'We follow [our] policy for the purpose of securing the peace and wellbeing of the world,' he said in a radio address later the same year. 'It is sheer nonsense to say that we seek dominance over any other nation. We believe in freedom, and we are doing all we can to support free men and free governments throughout the world.'[24] In unmistakable echo of Wilson's desire for 'conquest of the spirits of men' rather than territory, Truman later told an audience at Berkeley: 'The only expansion we are interested in is the expansion of freedom ... The only realm in which we aspire to eminence exists in the minds of men.'[25] His narrative, like Wilson's, was that only the United States identified its national interests with those of the whole; American interventions were therefore uniquely righteous, preserving freedom and autonomy, even though the interventions of others undermined those values.

Yet though the pressing concern was to avert Soviet expansion, Truman did not set it as his strategic objective to simply hold the line against the Soviets in a perpetual balance of power. Instead, he argued explicitly that American principles had universal validity, and hence a universal appeal to peoples that would ensure their ultimate triumph, even in Russia. Speaking in Chicago in July 1949, he argued that the Soviet mindset of 'relying on force as a method of world organization', which called for 'the destruction of free governments', was doomed in the long run to either 'destroy itself, or abandon its attempt to force other nations into its pattern'. In contrast, 'the democratic principles which have been tried and tested in free nations' had 'superior attraction for men's minds and hearts', which was why they were 'now winning the allegiance of men throughout the world'. 'The world longs for the kind of tolerance and mutual adjustment which is represented by democratic principles,' he said.[26] America's role in advancing this was a special one, in Truman's view: 'We have always been a challenge to tyranny of any kind. We are such a challenge today,' he declared.[27]

In his farewell address in January 1953, he made it clear that the long-term strategy of the United States was the internal reform of the Soviet system:

> As the free world grows stronger, more united, more attractive to men on both sides of the Iron Curtain – as the Soviet hopes for easy expansion are blocked – then there will have to come a time of change in the Soviet World. Nobody can ever say for sure when that is going to be or exactly how it will come about, whether by revolution, or trouble in the satellite states, or by a change inside the Kremlin. Whether the Communist rulers shift their policies of their own free will – or whether change comes about in some other way – I have not a doubt in the world that a change will occur. I have a deep and abiding faith in the destiny of free men. With patience and courage, we shall one day move on into a new era.[28]

Thus Truman saw the long-term establishment of international peace as coming from the universalization of liberty and the extinction of the destabilizing influence of totalitarian government. This did not mean that he lacked pragmatism; he was well aware that the costs of war were too high to permit a military crusade to liberate those under Soviet domination immediately. A war with the Soviets, he warned in 1945, would be 'total war, and that means the end of our civilization as we know it'.[29] The hard fact that the United States was not in a position to overwhelm the Soviet Union militarily compelled Truman to tolerate a de facto division of the world into spheres of influence. But this element of common-sense realism did not imply acceptance that the division of the world into spheres was the natural and stable product of international relations as usual, an equilibrium between two states legitimately pursuing their competing interests. Rather, Truman combined grudging recognition that 'we have to operate in an imperfect world' with insistence that 'we shall not give our approval to any compromise with evil'.[30]

The Soviet Union had its sphere as a material fact, but that did not mean the US had to accept it in principle. In Pierce's formulation, Truman 'combined resignation to a Soviet sphere and the principled belief that the Soviets should not have been allowed a sphere in the first place ... [Although] the sphere might be tolerated, it would never be accepted.'[31] A balance of power thus emerged in practice as the Cold War distribution of power, but ideologically this reflected frustrated universalism rather than contentment with a theory of order based on balance-of-power rivalry. Of self-determination and self-government, Truman observed in 1945:

> It may not be put into effect tomorrow or the next day. But, nonetheless, it is our policy; and we shall seek to achieve it. It may take a long time, but it is worth waiting for, and worth striving to attain. The Ten Commandments themselves have not yet been universally achieved over these thousands of years. Yet we struggle constantly to achieve them ... [32]

Truman accepted the Wilsonian link drawn between the existence of illiberal government and international instability. In the Truman Doctrine address, he argued that America's objective of a cooperative and peaceful world order would be unattainable 'unless we are willing to help free peoples to maintain their free institutions and their national integrity against aggressive movements that seek to impose upon them totalitarian regimes'. This was essential because 'totalitarian regimes imposed upon free peoples, by direct or indirect aggression, undermine the foundations of the international peace, and hence the security of the United States'. Intervention now, to preserve governments against communism, was 'an investment in world freedom and world peace'.[33] In his 1949 inaugural address, he declared that 'the actions resulting from the Communist philosophy are a threat to the efforts of free nations to bring about ... lasting peace'.[34] Thus the problem was not merely Soviet behaviour, but the system of government from which that behaviour sprang forth.

In making this attack on the domestic ideological roots of Soviet behaviour, Truman opted to build his foreign policy around what Pierce calls 'a broad conception of national security – one in which he included the principles of democracy ...'.[35] 'In the long run,' he told Americans in early 1950, '... our security and the world's hopes for peace lie ... in the growth and expansion of freedom and self-government. As these ideals are accepted by more and more people ... they become the greatest force in the world for peace.'[36] This formulation became part of the bedrock of Cold War ideology. By the end of his presidency, it had become uncontroversial for Truman to assert that the objective of US foreign policy was universal liberty, telling Congress that America's goal was to 'bring peace to the world and to spread the democratic ideals of justice and self-government to all people'.[37]

Truman also adopted the Wilsonian intellectual distinction between 'peoples' and governments, essential to America's recurring claims to serve common interests even when faced with the opposition of other states. 'I believe men and women of every part of the globe intensely desire peace and freedom,' Truman explained in an address at Berkeley in 1948. 'I believe good people everywhere will not permit their rulers, no matter how powerful they may have made themselves, to lead them to destruction. America has faith in people. It knows that rulers rise and fall, but that the people live on.'[38] Thus, though his time in office witnessed the emergence of a world defined by conflict between the American and Soviet governments, Truman could argue with conviction that the true interests of the Russian and Soviet-dominated peoples were also best served by America's aspirations. Speaking from the floating transmitter of the Voice of America in 1952, he declared:

> There is a terrific struggle going on today to win the minds of people throughout the world ... We have no quarrel with the people of the Soviet Union or with any other country ... We know that you are suffering under oppression and persecution. We know that if you were free to say what you really believe, you would join with us to banish the fear of war, and bring peace on earth and good will towards all men.[39]

This statement was propagandistic, certainly, in the sense that it was intended to serve political ends. Yet it was not *ipso facto* insincere. As Wilson had been before him, Truman was acutely conscious that the new attitude he was demanding from the American people entailed a significant ideological shift. As a soldier in Europe after the armistice of November 1918, Truman had himself embodied Americans' habitual desire for non-entanglement, writing home that 'most of us don't give a whoop (to put it mildly) whether Russia has a Red Government or no Government and if the King of the Lollipops wants to slaughter his subjects or his Prime Minister then it's all the same to us'.[40] Such sentiments had overpowered Wilsonianism in the inter-war years. Now, in the 1940s, Truman sought to convince the next generation of Americans to think differently.

Like Wilson, he was aware of the scale of the political challenge. 'I knew that George Washington's spirit would be invoked against me, and Henry Clay's and all the other patron saints of isolationism,' he recalled. 'But I was convinced that the policy I was about to proclaim was indeed as much required by the conditions of my day as was Washington's by the situation in his era and Monroe's doctrine by the circumstances which he then faced.'[41] Truman sought change, spurred by changing circumstances, but knew that he had to be sensitive to his ideological inheritance in the process; he needed to bridge from the old consensus to a new internationalism without leaving a daunting gap. Like Wilson, he did this by avoiding the suggestion that America should join the great power balance of self-interested rivalry that it had shunned thus far. Instead, its new global engagement would be justified by the pursuit of a new world order based on liberty.

Regarding the role of armed strength, however, Truman clearly embraced the strategic perspective of Theodore Roosevelt rather than that of Wilson. For the United States to play the role he wished it to, and for world order to take the desired shape, America would have to embrace peacetime military build-up on a level not previously countenanced. In 1945, Truman drove forward unification of the armed forces, and began to nudge the nation towards accepting the need for increased military means to achieve America's broadened ends. 'The desire for peace is futile', he warned Congress,

> ... unless there is also enough strength ready and willing to enforce that desire in an emergency. Among the things that have encouraged aggression and the spread of war in the past have been the unwillingness of the United States realistically to face this fact, and her refusal to fortify her aims of peace before the force of aggression could gather in strength.[42]

Just as Roosevelt had called on Americans to set aside their suspicion of military establishments to meet the demands of a changing international environment, so Truman now took up the cause. In April 1946, on Army Day, he told the public that:

we must remain strong because only so long as we remain strong can we ensure peace in the world. Peace has to be built on power for good. Justice and good will and good deeds are not enough. We cannot on one day proclaim our intention to prevent unjust aggression and tyranny in the world, and on the next day call for the immediate scrapping of our military might.[43]

Military strength was no longer – as it had been for the bulk of American history – a necessary evil to be minimized, or a peripheral feature of American political life. It was to be instrumental to America's new global role. 'We must face the fact that peace must be built upon power, as well as upon good will and good deeds,' he admonished Congress in autumn 1945.[44] The translation of such rhetoric into reality took time. At first, Truman's achievements were limited to administrative reform of the armed forces, commitment to aid Greece and Turkey, and the ratification of the North Atlantic Treaty. These were considerable achievements when measured against the prior ideological consensus, but authorization for a large military build-up of the sort advocated in internal documents such as NSC-68 remained elusive, for reasons both budgetary and political. It was only at the turn of the decade, with the crisis atmosphere sparked by the outbreak of the Korean War, that proposals for a vast expansion of military expenditure were enacted. Nevertheless, in a way that had not been the case since Roosevelt – and with more lasting impact – Truman wove a narrative that combined America's duty to pursue a universalist liberal agenda with a commitment to a substantial peacetime military establishment. He had concluded early in his presidency that 'unless Russia is faced with an iron fist and strong language another war is in the making. Only one language do they understand, "How many divisions have you?".'[45]

Truman's feelings toward liberals who did not believe in military expansion, who placed their faith in diplomatic outreach to resolve tensions with the Soviet Union, resembled Roosevelt's irritation with the 'pacifist tendency'. In his diary in September 1946 Truman wrote of former Vice President Henry Wallace, who was pushing for a policy of accommodation towards the Soviet Union:

He wants to disband our armed forces, give Russia our atom bomb secrets, and trust a bunch of adventurers in the Kremlin Politburo. I do not understand a 'dreamer' like that ... The Reds, phonies and 'parlor pinks' seem to be banded together and are becoming a national danger. I am afraid they are a sabotage front for Uncle Joe Stalin. They can see no wrong in Russia's four-and-a-half million armed force, in Russia's loot of Poland, Austria, Hungary, Rumania, Manchuria. They can see no wrong in Russia's living off the occupied countries to support the military occupations.[46]

Truman was clear that he *could* see the wrong in it. The Soviet sphere might exist in practice, but it should be opposed in principle by the United States.

To do so credibly, and to defend free states against expansive Soviet tendencies, the United States would need to be armed, and heavily so.

George Kennan and the sources of Soviet conduct

The thinker associated more closely than any other individual with the policy of 'containment' of the Soviet Union – apart, arguably, from Truman himself – was George Kennan. Kennan had formulated his analysis of the Soviet system and strategy while serving at the US embassy in Moscow. He then returned to Washington to head the new Policy Planning Unit at the State Department, created to promote long-term thinking and strategic coherence in US policy. Kennan first registered as a major intellectual presence with his 'Long Telegram', a message transmitted from Moscow that delivered a pessimistic assessment regarding the Soviet Union's openness to US diplomacy.[47] Then, shortly after being installed in Washington, he published 'The Sources of Soviet Conduct' (under the pseudonym 'X') in the journal *Foreign Affairs*. The article offered a similar diagnosis, aimed this time at the American public, and proposed 'containment' as the best strategic response.[48]

In later years, Kennan would become a prominent realist critic of US policy, accusing others of interpreting containment too militaristically and invoking universal principles too readily and without effect.[49] Yet inspection of these two most influential pieces of writing, which coincided with the formulation and promulgation of the Truman Doctrine and Marshall Plan, reveals that despite being the 'realist in residence' of the Truman administration Kennan himself contributed to the development of two of the critical ideological pillars of American Cold War ideology. These were the beliefs that (1) the barrier to international peace lay in the nature of the Soviet system of government, and (2) the long-term objective of US strategy must be a change in that system. By helping to establish these principles in administration strategy, Kennan aided the embedding of the Wilsonian mindset of which he was later critical.

In both the Long Telegram and the X Article Kennan argued that the Soviet outlook was driven by a poisonous blend of traditional Russian security paranoia with the more recent phenomenon of Marxism–Leninism. The resulting worldview, he said, provided the rationale for the USSR's harsh policies at home and belligerent demeanour abroad. According to the Russian perspective, he explained, the Soviet Union existed 'in antagonistic "capitalistic encirclement" with which in the long run there can be no permanent peaceful coexistence'.[50] 'The truth', as Kennan saw it, was that '[i]f not provoked by forces of intolerance and subversion' the '"capitalist" world of today is quite capable of living at peace with itself and Russia'. The Soviet government, however, had convinced itself of the inevitability of conflict between capitalism and communism. Thus it viewed its relations with the outside world as necessarily founded on conflict.[51] 'Ideology', he argued, had taught Russians '... that the outside world was hostile and that it was their duty eventually to overthrow the political forces beyond their borders.'[52]

'[The] Soviet party line is not based on any objective analysis of [the] situation beyond Russia's borders,' he explained:

> At [the] bottom of [the] Kremlin's neurotic view of world affairs is [a] traditional and instinctive Russian sense of insecurity ... [T]hey have always feared foreign penetration, feared direct contact between [the] western world and their own ... [and] they have learned to seek security only in patient but deadly struggle for total destruction of rival power, never in compacts and compromises with it.[53]

This was the product of Russian history as well as communist doctrine, he noted, though the latter was well suited to the soil provided by the former. 'Only in this land which had never known a friendly neighbor or indeed any tolerant equilibrium of separate powers, either internal or international,' he suggested, 'could a doctrine thrive which viewed economic conflicts of society as insoluble by peaceful means.'[54]

This paranoid perspective, conjuring imagined enemies all around, had served to justify extraordinary repression within the Soviet political system, of which Kennan had caught glimpses while in Moscow. Seeking chiefly the 'security of their own rule', Kennan argued, Soviet leaders had been 'prepared to recognize no restrictions, either of God or man, on the character of their methods'.[55] The 'basic altruism of purpose' of the Bolshevik 'dogma', he observed, had served to provide 'justification for their instinctive fear of [the] outside world, for the dictatorship without which they did not know how to rule'. Now the Marxist ideology was the

> fig leaf of their moral and intellectual respectability. Without it they would stand before history, at best, as the last of that long succession of cruel and wasteful Russian rulers who have relentlessly forced [the] country on to ever new heights of military power in order to guarantee [the] external security of their internally weak regimes ...[56]

The Soviet attitude was the product of 'uneasy Russian nationalism, a centuries-old movement in which conceptions of offence and defence are inextricably confused'.[57] A prevailing ideology of 'hostile encirclement' served to prop up a vicious regime, allowing internal opposition to be:

> portrayed as the agents of foreign forces of reaction antagonistic to Soviet power ... [T]here is ample evidence that the stress laid in Moscow on the menace confronting Soviet society from the world outside its borders is founded not in the realities of foreign antagonism but in the necessity of explaining away the maintenance of dictatorial authority at home.[58]

The Soviet system was totalitarian, its politics shrouded in secrecy at home. Abroad, Kennan argued, it would seek to expand its power to the maximal extent unless prevented from doing so by the United States. At the moment, he said, Soviet expansionism was 'restricted to certain neighboring points conceived of as being of immediate strategic necessity ... However, other points may at any time come into question, if and as concealed Soviet political power is extended to new areas.'[59] Because the 'theory of the inevitability of the eventual fall of capitalism' had 'the fortunate connotation that there is no hurry about it', Soviet expansionism was less acute a threat than Hitler's had been.[60] Nevertheless, the long-term Soviet objective was clear, and needed to be resisted by force, or at least the ability to threaten it.

Key to Kennan's analysis was the idea that Soviet policy was 'impervious to logic of reason'. It was, however, 'highly sensitive to logic of force'. The Soviets could and would withdraw when 'strong resistance' was encountered. 'Thus,' he advised, 'if the adversary has sufficient force and makes clear his readiness to use it, he rarely has to do so. If situations are properly handled there need be no prestige engaging showdowns.'[61] This aspect of his analysis – emphasizing caution – reveals why Kennan was uncomfortable with the more confrontational stances advocated by later Cold War policy makers. It is also clear, however, that the necessity of military strength on the part of the United States *was* an essential component of Kennan's analysis, even if not in the one-dimensional way he felt others later misinterpreted him as having meant. Talking and goodwill would not resolve the issues on which the US and the USSR were in conflict, he advised; Soviet leaders were 'not likely to be swayed by any normal logic in the words of the bourgeois representative. Since there can be no appeal to common purposes, there can be no appeal to common mental approaches.'[62] In describing the role he saw for force, Kennan echoed Roosevelt's search for balance between strength and restraint. The United States needed to pursue 'a long-term, patient but firm and vigilant containment of Russian expansive tendencies', but should not confuse such a policy with 'outward histrionics: with threats or blustering or superfluous gestures of outward "toughness"'.[63] While seeking to avoid outright confrontation, containment was 'a policy ... designed to confront the Russians with unalterable counter-force at every point where they show signs of encroaching upon the interests of a peaceful and stable world'.[64]

Yet despite the realism of much of his advice, Kennan's analysis also tacitly accepted the Wilsonian agenda of intellectually separating peoples from governments and looking to the former to embrace liberal ideas. In the Long Telegram he reported that 'never since [the] termination of [the] civil war have mass of Russian people been emotionally farther removed from [the] doctrines of communist party than they are today'.[65] On an underlying level, he argued, the attitude of the Soviet leadership 'does not represent the natural outlook of the Russian people'. The people, he asserted, were 'by and large, friendly to [the] outside world, eager for experience of it, eager to measure against it talents they are conscious of possessing, eager above all to live in peace and enjoy [the] fruits of their own labor'. The Soviet leadership might push the party line with discipline, but Kennan felt that the public was 'often remarkably resistant in the stronghold of its innermost thoughts'.[66] Continuing this logic, he argued that if the United States could be successful in frustrating Kremlin plans to extend its power, the Soviet system itself would come under stress. This could prompt reform of that system, which should be the ultimate objective of American policy. '[T]he United States has it in its power to increase enormously the strains under which Soviet policy must operate,' he wrote, 'to force upon the Kremlin a far greater degree of moderation and circumspection than it has had to observe in recent years.' By so doing, he suggested, the United States would 'promote tendencies which must eventually find their outlet in either the break-up or the mellowing of Soviet power.'[67]

Once the United States had established a secure line against Soviet subversion of other societies, its objective should be to establish a functioning and prosperous free world, the attractiveness of which to all people would undermine the sustainability of the Soviet system. The 'health and vigor' of American society was essential, he said, as was advocacy of a positive alternative to communism as a global ideology. 'We must formulate and put forward for other nations a much more positive and constructive picture of [the] world we would like to see than we have put forward in [the] past.'[68] In the peroration of 'Sources', Kennan invoked the historic American sense of destiny and mission:

> To avoid destruction the United States need only measure up to its own best traditions and prove itself worthy of preservation as a great nation ...
> Providence ... by providing the American people with this implacable challenge, has made their entire security as a nation dependent on their pulling themselves together and accepting the responsibilities of moral and political leadership that history plainly intended them to bear.[69]

Though he was the most 'realistic' thinker in the Truman administration, Kennan thus in fact in his most famous documentary contributions aided the emergence of a strategic worldview that blended Wilsonianism with Rooseveltianism rather than embracing balance-of-power realism. He attributed some of the paranoia of Soviet policy to the prevailing attitudes bred by Russian historical experience, but also argued that a major cause of the problem lay in ideological perceptions without basis in the USSR's external environment. It was the need to preserve and justify a totalitarian domestic system of politics at home that drove Soviet policy.

If this was the origin of the problem, then it was logical that its ultimate solution must be the reform of the Soviet domestic system. This was likely the wish of the Soviet peoples anyway, according to Kennan, who were quite distinct in attitude from the Soviet government, and who were growing – and would continue to grow – increasingly disillusioned with the system. The key to attaining the peaceful international order sought by the United States lay, first, in amassing the physical power to defend liberal government where it currently existed, and then in putting pressure on the USSR in such a way as to hasten the ultimate breakdown of the Soviet system at home. Kennan was a cautious strategic thinker, who emphasized patience and restraint, and thus less bold and militaristic an advocate of 'regime change' than others who followed him. Yet the Wilsonian principle that to achieve lasting peace one needed to change the internal character of other states was still central to the strategy he sold to the administration and the nation.

Polarization and militarization: the Clifford–Elsey Report and NSC-68

Two of the most significant internal documents on US–Soviet relations produced by the Truman administration were the 'Clifford–Elsey Report' of September 1946, so known because compiled by White House counsellor Clark Clifford and aide George Elsey,[70] and the Report to the National Security Council of April 1950, generally known by the short-form title NSC-68.[71] As the dates suggest, Clifford–Elsey was a relatively early analysis, coming after the Long Telegram but predating the Truman Doctrine. Alongside Kennan's analysis, it contributed to the administration's initial decision that its approach to Soviet relations should toughen. NSC-68 was written and read significantly later, when the policy of containment was already established doctrine. Principally prepared by Paul Nitze, Kennan's successor as head of the planning unit, it was chiefly important for its advocacy of substantial military build-up to meet the Soviet threat. The effective adoption of NSC-68 as a guiding policy document after the outbreak of the Korean War in summer 1950 marked a decisive point in the American leadership's embrace of a 'Cold War' strategic perspective.

The two documents reflect the outset and conclusion of an intellectual journey: one was written as the US–Soviet conflict was still taking form; the other confirmed the Cold War's establishment, in militarized form, as the dominant paradigm for US policy making. Clifford–Elsey crystallized a growing sense that the desired cooperative world order would not prove possible, due to the pathologies of the Soviet system. It suggested that the US prepare for the fact that it might have to accept, in the short term, the division of the world into free and unfree spheres, and take the steps necessary to defend the free world. NSC-68, coming later, served to confirm the logic of ideas already expressed by Truman, Kennan and others: it argued explicitly that the long-term objective of US policy should be to apply counter-pressure leading ultimately to the reform of the Soviet system. It was also significant for its embrace of military build-up as an essential component in such a strategy.

The documents' classified status adds a further dimension to their interest-value when seen in parallel with the administration's public statements. Though government officials may sometimes write with the historical record in mind, such documents – for internal consumption only – serve to demonstrate at least that there was no wholesale divergence between the administration's public and private assessments. Certainly the reports were not designed for public propaganda purposes: Truman considered Clifford–Elsey sufficiently 'hot' that he ordered all copies kept under lock and key because of their potential to inflame the diplomatic situation.[72] Dean Acheson, Truman's Secretary of State, famously observed in his memoirs that NSC-68 was designed to serve a bureaucratic purpose: to 'bludgeon the mass mind of "top government"' so it would support Truman's intended policy of militarized containment. In such an enterprise, he observed '[q]ualification must give way to simplicity of statement, nicety and nuance to bluntness, almost brutality, in carrying home a point'. The result, he admitted, was that the administration may have made its points 'clearer than truth', though in that it 'did not differ from most other educators'. Yet even if it served to simplify, NSC-68 nevertheless accurately reflected the core of administration thinking.[73]

The Clifford–Elsey Report

Clifford–Elsey offered an analysis that laid the intellectual ground for the case later presented to the public. It diagnosed that the 'fundamental tenet of the communist philosophy embraced by Soviet leaders' was that 'the peaceful coexistence of communist and capitalist nations is impossible'. This explained the USSR's 'seizing every opportunity to expand the area, directly or indirectly, under Soviet control'.[74] Like Kennan's analysis, the report claimed that 'conventional diplomacy, goodwill gestures or acts of appeasement'[75] could have no hope of success when dealing with the Soviet Union. The only positive was that Soviet leaders wanted 'to postpone the conflict for many years' and would be 'flexible in proportion to the degree and nature of the resistance encountered'.[76]

The report provided a dispiriting catalogue of the accumulating disputes between the Soviet Union and the United States in Europe. Noting the Soviet government's formal subscription to the Declaration of the United Nations, the Declaration of Three Powers at Teheran and the Declaration on Liberated Europe at Yalta, the report observed that the USSR was therefore committed on paper to a host of liberal principles, including respecting 'the right of all peoples to choose the form of government under which they will live', commitment to 'the elimination of tyranny and slavery, oppression and intolerance', and aiding 'liberated' European nations 'in establishing internal peace, forming representative governments and holding free elections'.[77] The USSR had violated these understandings, the report argued, by imposing one-party communist rule, 'exploiting … the Soviet definitions of terms such as "democratic", "friendly", "fascist", et cetera, which are basically different from the non-communist understanding of these words'.[78] Governments created in the Soviet sphere were 'notoriously unrepresentative', the report said, but the Soviet Union was 'determined to maintain them by as much force as necessary inasmuch as no truly representative government would be reliable, from the Soviet point of view'.[79] That being the case, in Germany as elsewhere: 'Political life in the Soviet zone is not being reconstructed on a democratic basis. Democratic ideas, in our sense of the term, are not being fostered.'[80]

Following the Wilsonian tradition of separating 'people' and state, Clifford–Elsey argued that Soviet policy was 'based, not upon the interests and aspirations of the Russian people, but upon the prejudices, calculations and ambitions of the inner-directorate of the Communist Party in the Soviet Union'.[81] The diplomatic posture of the Soviet government could best be explained as a tool used to preserve the dictatorial state: '[V]erbal assaults on the United States are designed to justify to the Russian people the expense and hardships of maintaining a powerful military establishment and to insure the support of the Russian people for the aggressive actions of the Soviet Government.'[82] In essence, the USSR's aggressive foreign policy was the product of dictatorship at home.

At this early stage in the Cold War, before the public breakdown of relations signalled by the Truman Doctrine and the X Article, there still remained a degree of belief that the Soviet leadership might be talked into turning back from the precipice:

> The primary objective of United States policy toward the Soviet Union is to convince Soviet leaders that it is in their interest to participate in a system of world cooperation, that there are no fundamental causes for war between our two nations, and that the security and prosperity of the Soviet Union, and that of the rest of the world as well, is being jeopardised by aggressive militaristic imperialism such as that in which the Soviet Union is now engaged.[83]

Even in its peroration, the report expressed residual hope that Soviet leaders would 'change their minds and work out with us a fair and equitable settlement when they realize that we are too strong to be beaten and too determined to be frightened.'[84] The goal, as with Wilsonian thinking in the past, was to convince a hostile power that the United States had the 'true' interests of other nations' peoples at heart, and invite it to join it in furthering the agenda of harmonious interests that US policy sought to advance. Failure of this strategy, as per the Wilsonian formula, could be attributed to the illiberal nature of the government in question, which caused it to misperceive the true interests of its people.

In the absence of 'Soviet cooperation in the solution of world problems', the report concluded, the United States needed to be prepared for conflict. First, the US 'should be prepared to join with the British and other Western countries in an attempt to build up a world of our own which will pursue its own objectives …'.[85] Using this cooperative 'American system' as a base, it should resist Soviet efforts to 'expand into areas vital to American security'.[86] This meant that the US ought to 'support and assist all democratic countries which are in any way menaced or endangered by the USSR'. It should be the objective of US policy to 'ensure that economic opportunities, personal freedom and social equality are made possible in countries outside the Soviet sphere by generous financial assistance'.[87]

Prefiguring the military build-up to come, Clifford–Elsey argued that:

> The language of military power is the only language which disciples of power politics understand ... Compromise and concessions are considered, by the Soviets, to be evidences of weakness ... The mere fact of preparedness may be the only powerful deterrent to Soviet aggressive action and in this sense the only sure guaranty of peace.[88]

The Clifford–Elsey Report's historical significance lies in its early mapping out of the shape of the coming conflict between the United States and the Soviet Union. Also worth noting, however, is its reiteration of Wilsonian principles regarding the sources of conflict, the possibilities for cooperation and the reasons for Soviet unwillingness to cooperate. It also began the process of blending in the Rooseveltian argument for the necessity of military strength, not as a tool of expansion, but to provide the 'preparedness' required to preserve peace.

NSC-68

NSC-68 was more philosophical in tone than the Clifford–Elsey Report. It went beyond summarizing the facts of perceived Soviet agreement-breaking, offering an expansive portrait of global ideological struggle. It set the conflict between the superpowers in the context of international systemic factors: 'the international distribution of power', it argued, had been 'fundamentally altered' by the Second World War, producing a bipolar world. But it also focused on the character of the Soviet state, which rendered the situation particularly dangerous. The Soviet Union, 'unlike previous aspirants to hegemony,' it said, 'is animated by a new fanatic faith, antithetical to our own, which seeks to impose its absolute authority over the rest of the world'. As a result America faced choices 'involving the fulfilment or destruction not only of this Republic but of civilization itself'.[89]

The root of the conflict between the US and the Soviet 'slave state', the document argued, lay in their contrasting systems. The goal of America was 'to assure the integrity and vitality of our free society' and 'create conditions under which our free and democratic system can live and prosper'.[90] It was also the 'principal center of power in the non-Soviet world and the bulwark of opposition to Soviet expansion', making it 'the principal enemy whose integrity and vitality must be subverted or destroyed by one means or another if the Kremlin is to achieve its fundamental design'.[91] The reason for the USSR's particular hostility towards America, it argued, lay in the impossibility of coexistence between the states' rival systems. This was symptomatic of a centuries-old conflict of ideas: 'The idea of freedom,' it asserted, '... is peculiarly and intolerably subversive of the idea of slavery ... the most contagious idea in history, more contagious than the idea of submission to authority.'[92] As the nation that best embodied freedom, the United States could supposedly rely on others' natural attraction to the idea, feeling 'no compulsion ... to bring all societies into conformity with it'.[93] The Soviets, on the other hand, saw the idea of freedom as 'a permanent and continuous threat' to their society, and therefore regarded its continued existence as 'intolerable'.

This natural antipathy of ideologies, combined with the 'polarization of power', created a crisis in global affairs because it 'inescapably confronts the slave society with the free'.[94]

One of NSC-68's targets for attack was the supposition that Americans should consider it possible to return to the attitude of detachment from global affairs that had historically prevailed. The pursuit of such a policy, the report argued, would allow the Soviet Union to dominate Eurasia. This would leave the US facing the military threat of a USSR empowered with vast new resources, as well as burdening America with 'a deep sense of responsibility and guilt for having abandoned their former friends and allies'. At the other extreme, a pre-emptive attack on the USSR would be terribly risky militarily, and also 'morally corrosive'.[95] What NSC-68 proposed was the 'middle way': pressing ahead with the central concept of containment – seeking to frustrate the 'Kremlin design' by means short of war – but adding considerably greater investment in both military strength and foreign aid, in recognition that the scale of the challenge had grown.

NSC-68 was, on one level, a one-dimensional narrative of good versus evil.[96] Yet its reasoning was also, on close inspection, rather convoluted. Its argument centred on a contrast between America's lack of felt need to force others to embrace its system of 'freedom', and the Soviet Union's alleged compulsion to seek domination and conversion. Yet in attributing the source of this Soviet compulsion to its system of government, the effect of NSC-68's argument was to set it as America's strategic objective to bring about a change of regime type in the USSR. Thus, in seeming to argue that totalitarian regimes inherently threatened US interests, NSC-68 pushed an essentially Wilsonian conclusion: that only conversion of others to liberal systems of government could ultimately guarantee international peace.

NSC-68 argued that the short-term goal of the United States should be to 'create a situation which will induce the Soviet Union to accommodate itself, with or without conscious abandonment of its design, to coexistence on tolerable terms with the non-Soviet world'.[97] Yet that strategy involved threatening the survival of the Soviet regime itself. The purpose of containment, the report argued, was to 'in general, so foster the seeds of destruction within the Soviet system that the Kremlin is brought at least to the point of modifying its behavior to conform to generally accepted international standards'.[98] And in sowing 'the seeds of destruction', there was clearly hope for a harvest. '[O]ur policy and actions,' the report stated, 'must be such as to foster a fundamental change in the nature of the Soviet system ...'. The aspiration was that this be achieved 'to a maximum extent as a result of internal forces in Soviet society'.[99] But the 'intensifying struggle,' it observed, 'requires us to face the fact that we can expect no lasting abatement of the crisis unless and until a change occurs in the nature of the Soviet system'.[100] Thus, America's goal must be 'to change the world situation by means short of war in such a way as to frustrate the Kremlin design and hasten the decay of the Soviet system'.[101] In its conclusion, the document emphasized that:

> The only sure victory lies in the frustration of the Kremlin design by the steady development of the moral and material strength of the free world and its projection into the Soviet world in such a way as to bring about an internal change in the Soviet system.[102]

NSC-68 thus recommended a strategy that did not respect the Soviet Union's claim to its own sphere of influence as a legitimate component in a balance-of-power rivalry. On the contrary, the course it recommended was to

> take dynamic steps to reduce the power and influence of the Kremlin inside the Soviet Union and other areas under its control. The objective would be the establishment of friendly regimes not under Kremlin domination. Such action is essential to engage the Kremlin's attention, keep it off balance and force an increased expenditure of Soviet resources in counteraction. In other words, it would be the current Soviet cold war technique used against the Soviet Union.[103]

Reprising the now-familiar distinction between the people and the state, the report argued that the United States should try to 'make the Russian people our allies in this enterprise'. The measures taken by the US must be 'not so excessive or misdirected as to make us enemies of the people instead of the evil men who have enslaved them'.[104] The United States, therefore, had to be careful to wield force carefully, so that 'the Russian people can perceive that our effort is directed against the regime and its power for aggression, and not against their own interests ...'.[105] The Cold War was not simply a conflict between governments over power or territory, the report argued: 'at the ideological or psychological level, in the struggle for men's minds, the conflict is world-wide'.[106] 'It may even be said that the capabilities of the Soviet world, specifically the capabilities of the masses who have nothing to lose but their Soviet chains, are a potential which can be enlisted on our side,' the report advised.[107] This analysis reflected the Wilsonian universalist tradition of thinking about international order. The 'greatest vulnerability' of the Soviet Government lay 'in the basic nature of its relations with the Soviet people', because 'Soviet ideas and practices run counter to the best and potentially the strongest instincts of men, and deny their most fundamental aspirations.' Faced with an adversary such as the United States whose ideology could affirm the 'constructive and hopeful instincts of men' and was 'capable of fulfilling their aspirations, the Soviet system might prove to be fatally weak'.[108]

Unlike Wilson's hopeful anticipation of a new world order, however, NSC-68 argued that the United States would need to acquire greatly increased military strength in order to advance its international agenda. In this regard it injected the strongest dose yet of Rooseveltian thinking into Truman administration strategy. The United States, it warned, 'cannot afford in the face of the totalitarian challenge to operate on a narrow margin of strength. A democracy can compensate for its natural vulnerability only if it maintains clearly superior overall power in its most inclusive sense.'[109] Clearly, a step change was needed; the report warned that 'the programs now planned will not meet the requirements of the free nations'.[110] 'A building up of the military capabilities of the United States and the free world is a precondition to the achievement of the objectives outlined in this report and to the protection of the United States against disaster,' it noted.[111] Sounding like Roosevelt in his pomp, the report warned that 'no people in history have preserved their freedom who thought that by not being strong enough to protect themselves they might prove inoffensive to their enemies'.[112]

As in its contrast of alleged American pluralism with Soviet ideological universalism, NSC-68 displayed a degree of solipsism in its justification of American military build-up. It unequivocally attributed aggressive intent and 'excessive strength' to the USSR because of its assessment that the Soviet Union possessed 'armed forces far in excess of those necessary to defend its national territory'.[113] Yet the facts presented by the report itself made it clear that the underlying resources of the United States and its allies were far greater than those of the Soviet Union. The report's recommendations for an American build-up would therefore produce an even more 'excessive' military capacity if the standard for acceptability was indeed the means 'necessary to defend its national territory'. Though this apparent contradiction was not explicitly articulated, it is not difficult to imagine how it was resolved in the minds of the authors: via an implicit assessment of intentions. The assumption was that the intentions of the United States were axiomatically pacific, and that whatever strength it accrued in response to perceived threats would be used to preserve the conditions of freedom, not to impose a self-centred new order. But from the Soviet perspective, of course, an American pledge to defend and spread the 'conditions necessary for freedom' *was* a threat to impose an order advantageous to America's own interests and antithetical to the Soviet Union's interests as it defined them. Inability or unwillingness to appreciate this potential for divergence of perspectives regarding the benign quality of American intentions reflected a line of ideological continuity from the Wilson–Roosevelt approach to order and intervention. For better and for worse, the same perceptual blind spot lay at the heart of the American perspective in the Cold War as during the first decades of the century.

Conclusion

The Truman administration governed during a crucial period of change in American strategic thinking. As a result of shifts in the international distribution of power following the Second World War, systemic pressure called for the engagement of the United States with the management of global order on an unprecedented level. During these years, a new internationalism was crafted which accepted a vastly increased role for the United States. From this point onwards, the Founders' Era consensus would no longer be the reference point for policy, and the United States would be 'entangled' in Europe and all the globe's other theatres.

Yet the manner in which that engagement took shape was the product of interaction between new national circumstances and existing ideological dispositions. The new internationalism did not entail an acceptance by American policy makers that the United States should participate in a balance-of-power system of order based on rival interests of equivalent legitimacy. That is to say, it would not join the international system as already existent. Instead, the new internationalism was based on a weaving together of Wilsonian and Rooseveltian ideas. This meant that the US saw its ultimate objective as an American-led international order based on the supposedly fundamentally harmonious interests of all peoples. The refusal of the Soviet Union to cooperate with this plan for world order was attributed, in the Wilsonian style, to its flawed system of illiberal government, and reform of that system was thus a key US objective. This objective, and the defence of 'freedom' to the extent that it was already established, would require America to develop its military might on an unprecedented scale. The nation needed to prepare for the manly defence and expansion of civilization that Roosevelt had argued must be the United States' destiny.

In the Cold War mindset, interweaving Wilsonianism and Rooseveltianism, intervention was not considered real intervention if it was American intervention, because America sought only to establish the basis for 'true' autonomy and freedom. The interests of other nations could not truly be in conflict with those of the United States, though it was possible that illegitimate governments might have a warped understanding their country's national interest. Ultimately, the peoples of the world, if they could only control their governments, would support the American agenda. Uniquely equipped with insight into the true interests of peoples and nations, the United States could exercise legitimate global leadership as it pursued its liberal universalist objectives. Most crucially of all, the new internationalism was contingent on the pursuit of these objectives. To attempt less would be for the US to accept membership of the old, rivalrous balance-of-power order. Only the pursuit of the new world order, with all the reform on the part of other nations that would be required for that order to function, could justify the abrogation of the Founders' Era consensus. Wilson's 'deal' was still thought valid.

The actual international order that was brought about by Cold War policy was a de facto balance of power between the United States and the Soviet Union. Ideologically, however, this was not the result of balance-of-power philosophy on the part of the United States. Rather, it was the result of frustrated universalism, an important distinction. As Walter Lippmann, arguably more of a realist thinker than Kennan or any others at the core of administration policy, observed after hearing the Truman Doctrine declared, the administration's strategy was 'a vague global policy which sounds like the tocsin of an ideological crusade, has no limits. It cannot be controlled. Its effects cannot be predicted.'[114] Whereas balance-of-power philosophy positively desires limits and shudders at the prospect of hegemonic quests, the United States clearly set it as its Cold War objective to attain military and ideological supremacy.

7 The George W. Bush administration
'A balance of power that favours freedom'

Introduction

The Cold War defined world order from the 1940s until the collapse of the Soviet Union in 1991, and the strategy pursued by the United States throughout that period was based on the principles established under Truman. When it ended, it did so on something close to the basis that the Truman administration had hoped: the USSR, contained over decades by US pressure, struggled to maintain the vitality of its political and economic ideology in the eyes of its own people. Ultimately, even those at the top of the system came to favour a limited degree of liberalizing reform, beginning a chain of events that led to the revolutionary overthrow of the Soviet regime.

This chapter focuses not on the immediate years of the 'post-Cold War era', as it is often termed, but on the first administration of the twenty-first century: that of George W. Bush. Like many of his predecessors, including Theodore Roosevelt and Woodrow Wilson, Bush was a state governor when he ran for national office. He was also the son of a president and grandson of a US Senator. Despite this combination of experience and pedigree, however, he came to the presidency with extremely limited knowledge of foreign affairs. Despite this fact – perhaps because of it – he went on to embrace a foreign policy during his first term of office that all analysts thought bold, and some considered revolutionary.[1] Especially noted was the administration's combination of ambitious activism abroad with a disposition favouring unilateral action.

The chapter begins, as usual, by discussing national and international context, before providing a brief survey of the way in which the Bush administration was assessed by its critics. It goes on to set out the central thrust of the administration's strategic vision, headlined in the National Security Strategy of 2002 as the quest for a 'balance of power that favours freedom'. This is then followed by a number of sections describing the key ideological elements of that strategy, namely: proclaiming the universal validity of liberal political values; linking international security to the spread of liberal democracy; asserting a fundamental commonality of interest between the world's nations; distinguishing conceptually between peoples and governments; arguing that historical destiny mandated the triumph of the United States and its ideas; and claiming US military hegemony as a virtuous objective. Having thus distilled the key features of the Bush strategy, drawing out in the process the evident parallels between Bush and the Wilson–Roosevelt–Truman tradition, the chapter then spells out point by point the alternative realist 'road not taken'. In so doing, it makes clear that US policy under Bush has not been a simple cause-and-effect response to external circumstances, but a chosen course influenced by the embedded ideological traditions guiding America's engagement with the international system.

The purpose of the chapter, adding the final major component to the thesis of the book as a whole, is to demonstrate the intellectual linkages that rooted the strategy pursued by Bush in the evolving tradition of America's evolving internationalism. The argument is *not* that Bush's strategy was indistinguishable from that of earlier presidents. His administration dealt with circumstances quite changed from those his predecessors faced, and consequently one would expect some change in policy. The argument, as in previous chapters, is that changing national and international circumstances called for a degree of change in American thinking about international order and the US global role. But the administration could only carry forward that change on the basis of some connection to the pre-existing ideological framework of US foreign policy making. Though it may have appeared radical – and in some ways it was – Bush administration policy in these years was in fact grounded in established principles of the American internationalist ideology, as evolved during the transition to global engagement via Roosevelt, Wilson and Truman. What emerged under Bush was in a sense new, but it was also the product of interaction between circumstances and ideological inheritance.

National and international context

At the turn of the twenty-first century, the international order was defined by unipolar distribution of hard power. Though by no means omnipotent, the United States combined the world's largest economy with a level of military spending that bested that of the other major powers combined.[2] Beyond its ability to coerce, the appeal of American culture and of the ideals underlying its political system – America's 'soft power', in Joseph Nye's terminology – had outstripped all rivals since the demise of the communist threat.[3] In the decade since the end of the Cold War, no power had managed to assemble the resources required to challenge America's preponderance of power. Thus US leaders were called upon to strategize in an international environment defined by their own nation's primacy.

Simultaneously, the international distribution of power had also 'globalized' further. Europe remained a significant region, but European great powers were no longer pre-eminent actors constituting the core of the international system. Demographically gigantic powers such as China and India had risen in significance, and continued to rise, thanks to economic growth and relatively stable government. In Latin America and Africa, functional and autonomous states existed to an extent that they had not in previous eras. In short, though the United States was the sole superpower, the number of significant powers in the next-highest tier had become larger and more widely geographically scattered. Economic globalization had also impacted upon the international system, with the range, depth and complexity of economic interdependence reaching levels unprecedented in previous centuries.

Perhaps the most significant change confronting American leaders was the increased consideration given to non-state actors in matters of national and international security. The terrorist attacks of 11 September 2001, during which hijacked aeroplanes were flown into the twin towers of the World Trade Center in Manhattan and the Pentagon in Virginia, compelled the US government to think with renewed intensity about the significance for national security of stateless terrorist movements. This bred a new concern regarding the militant *jihadist* ideologies which mandated terrorist assaults on the United States, and the political, economic and social problems of the societies in which those ideas had taken root. This problem dovetailed with fear of proliferation of weapons of mass destruction. Such weapons had been a central feature of international life since the end of the Second World War, and the prospect of their spread created problems for American security that extended beyond the traditional and best-understood threat occupying the thoughts of statesmen, i.e. military assault by a hostile great power.

The Bush administration was therefore obliged to try to construct a coherent strategy for the advance of American interests that paid due attention to the key themes of US primacy, diffusion of global power, radical Islamist terrorism and the potential spread of lethal weapons technology. The need for such a strategy was dictated by the realities of the international environment and the position of the United States within the global system. The particular form that strategy took, however, was also shaped by the intellectual legacy of the past, meaning not only that of the Cold War, but also the earlier ideological principles whose evolution had in turn preceded and shaped Cold War strategy.

'A balance of power that favours freedom': the National Security Strategy

The central document setting forth the Bush administration's approach was the National Security Strategy, published in September 2002.[4] The NSS was a public document, and as such aimed to explain the administration's guiding worldview to the outside world in as persuasive a manner as possible, with the interested segment of the general population in mind. It also sought to provide a guiding framework to which the administration itself could refer, bringing coherence to the different strands of day-to-day policy. The process of preparing the NSS began prior to the 9/11 terrorist attacks, but by the time of its publication the final document was inevitably and justifiably seen as a response to the strategic environment thrown up by those events.

Much immediate reportage focused on the concept of 'pre-emption', which as a result became the signature concept of the strategy in the popular mind. The NSS warned of the potential for connection between the threats of terrorism and weapons of mass destruction (WMD), with the president warning in his foreword that 'the gravest danger' faced by the nation lay 'at the crossroads of radicalism and technology'. The consequences of terrorists acquiring WMD being dire, the strategy declared that to 'forestall or prevent such attacks by our adversaries, the United States will, if necessary, act pre-emptively'.[5] The NSS was published after the administration had already successfully overthrown the Taliban government of Afghanistan, which had harboured al-Qaeda terrorists, and at a time when many considered an invasion of Iraq a strong likelihood. In such a political context, 'pre-emption' was widely interpreted as the administration's strategic centrepiece, even though it was mentioned relatively few times in the document and not emphasized in the introduction or conclusion.[6]

Those who saw in the NSS a forewarning of regime change in Iraq had their suspicions borne out, of course, by the invasion of March 2003. Yet despite the discursive tornado that arose in response to the doctrine of pre-emption alone, a conceptual worldview of greater breadth and depth was also set out in the NSS – an outline of the administration's vision of the nature of international order, present and future. The emphasis chosen by accompanying and follow-up texts published by National Security Advisor Condoleezza Rice and Secretary of State Colin Powell suggested that both considered the most significant concept to be something they termed 'a balance of power that favours freedom'.[7] In contrast to pre-emption, this phrase was used twice in the president's foreword, and on several occasions in the opening paragraphs of sections within the document itself. It was also the headline of the article and lecture delivered by Rice to coincide with the strategy's official publication.

Before it began, there was some expectation that a Bush presidency would embrace a more realist worldview, placing emphasis on a narrowly defined national interest and traditional great power diplomacy, in contrast to the liberal interventionism of the preceding Clinton years. This was encouraged by a widely read article published by Rice in *Foreign Affairs* during the presidential campaign of 2000, which criticized nation-building and liberal ideas of 'international community'.[8] The events of 9/11, however, forced some change of focus, obliging the administration to address more centrally the problem of non-state actors and the ideological dimension introduced into international security by the militant Islamist threat. What emerged was a worldview that retained some emphasis on military power and relations with great powers, but also injected powerful elements of ideological universalism and moralism. In short, what emerged was something that bore significant resemblance to the Roosevelt–Wilson–Truman internationalist ideology, but adapted for the threats of a new era.

The NSS contained several key planks. First, it underlined the perceived importance of tackling rogue regimes, which provided the link between the threats of terrorism and WMD proliferation. Second, it reaffirmed with force the US Government's belief in the absolute and universal righteousness of basic American values and practices: in its interaction with the rest of the world, the nation should be committed to the universal realization of both liberal democracy and capitalism. Third, it asserted that there was at present unprecedented potential, which should be seized upon, for all great powers in the international system to cooperate.[9] These three interconnected principles formed the spine of logic supporting the administration's worldview.

The most essential fact to be noted regarding the NSS was that its central concept, the 'balance of power that favours freedom', was not what it at first appeared. The invocation of the phrase 'balance of power' seemed to send the signal that a new realism had emerged in US policy. On inspection, however, the concept and the ideology underlying it were deeply liberal in their assumptions regarding international order. Contrary to conventional usage in international relations discourse, this 'balance of power' did not really describe a 'balance' at all. Rather, it envisioned a vast preponderance of hard power on a single side – that of the United States – and a world defined by the triumphant universalization of liberal ideological values.

The administration's vision of international order was thus not of power balancing power, but of a concerted coalition of all major powers in furtherance of what it purported to be common interests and universal values. Cooperation between major powers and the emergence of concord around foundational political values were viewed as mutually reinforcing trends, based on a dynamic of historical inevitability, and together, it was supposed, they would support the emergence of a lasting world peace. The concept of a balance of power need not necessarily imply absolute equality of capabilities on each side, but it does entail respect for the legitimacy and inevitability of the fact that significant forces and interests will be opposed to one another. On the basis of this belief, those of a realistic disposition seek a sustained equilibrium that might enable peaceful coexistence. If this is the definition of 'balance', then the Bush administration sought nothing of the sort.[10]

'Universal, human hopes': the universal legitimacy of liberal values

A fundamental feature of Bush's strategic approach was stridency in asserting the universal validity of liberal political values. The National Security Strategy contended that only the model of society based on such values remained viable, having triumphed in the contest of historical evolution:

> The great struggles of the twentieth century between liberty and totalitarianism ended with a decisive victory for the forces of freedom – and a single sustainable model for national success: freedom, democracy, and free enterprise. ... [The] values of freedom are right and true for every person in every society ...[11]

Such sentiments are common in American political discourse, but the Bush administration was especially regular and vocal in expressing them. Even in his first inaugural address, before the post-9/11 surge in foreign policy activism, Bush told Americans that the nation's 'democratic faith' was 'more than the creed of our country, it is the inborn hope of our humanity, an ideal we carry but do not own, a trust we bear and pass along'.[12] In the post-9/11 environment, with focus on the terrorist threat, this perspective hardened and deepened. In his State of the Union address of 2002, best known for the identification of the 'axis of evil', the president was also strident in identifying 'liberty' as a universal value. '[L]iberty and justice ... are right and true and unchanging for all people everywhere. No nation owns these aspirations, and no nation is exempt from them,' he declared. He denied that the United States had any intention of 'imposing our culture', but nevertheless insisted it would 'stand firm for the non-negotiable demands of human dignity: the rule of law; limits on the power of the state; respect for women; private property; free speech; equal justice; and religious tolerance'.[13]

Arguing for the applicability of such principles even in the world's most politically troubled regions, he insisted: 'Prosperity and freedom and dignity are not just American hopes, or Western hopes. They are universal, human hopes. And even in the violence and turmoil of the Middle East, America believes those hopes have the power to transform lives and nations.'[14] In January 2003, as the final order to topple the government of Iraq drew closer, he told Congress and the nation that 'Americans are a free people, who know that freedom is the right of every person and the future of every nation. The liberty we prize is not America's gift to the world, it is God's gift to humanity.'[15]

In a widely reported speech to graduates at the military academy at West Point in 2002, he declared that:

> The 20th century ended with a single surviving model of human progress, based on non-negotiable demands of human dignity, the rule of law, limits on the power of the state, respect for women and private property and free speech and equal justice and religious tolerance. ... When it comes to the common rights and needs of men and women, there is no clash of civilizations. The requirements of freedom apply fully to Africa and Latin America and the entire Islamic world. The peoples of the Islamic nations want and deserve the same freedoms and opportunities as people in every nation. And their governments should listen to their hopes.[16]

This sentiment was repeated in the radio address delivered after the commencement of Operation Iraqi Freedom, the invasion to overthrow Saddam Hussein's government. In it, he reassured Americans that 'Iraqis, like all people ... welcome their own freedom. It should surprise no one that in every nation and every culture, the human heart desires the same good things ... As people throughout Iraq celebrate the arrival of freedom, America celebrates with them.'[17] 'The desire for freedom is not the property of one culture, it is the universal hope of human beings in every culture,' he observed again a fortnight later.[18]

The administration was intolerant of those who expressed doubt regarding the suitability or readiness of certain societies for the establishment of democratic processes. Sometimes this could be blunt, coming close to accusing the administration's critics of sectarianism, or even racism. 'There's a lot of people in the world who don't believe that people whose skin color may not be the same as ours can be free and self-govern,' the president told a press conference in April 2003. 'I reject that. I reject that strongly. I believe that people who practice the Muslim faith can self-govern. I believe that people whose skins aren't necessarily – are a different color than white can self-govern.'[19]

The administration's sensitivity to the accusation that 'promoting' the American conception of freedom amounted to a form of cultural imperialism was reflected in strenuous efforts to pre-emptively deny any such equivalence. The president repeatedly used public pronouncements to disavow any desire to impose American standards upon others, while simultaneously asserting that liberal principles were synonymous with universal human aspirations. This was a message replete with internal tension. Key to the American self-image and the president's vision of his own policy was the idea that the US was not imposing its own ideas but merely facilitating others in obtaining what they naturally, on some underlying level, wanted for themselves. This desire to reconcile insistence on universal principles with a parallel craving to be seen as respectful of others' autonomy contained clear echoes of the tensions within Wilsonianism generations before.

Sensing this insoluble dilemma, the administration tried to insist that it did not expect all societies to replicate American methods. In discussing the US-led efforts to reconstruct Afghan and Iraqi society as part of the 'forward strategy of freedom in the Middle East', Bush stated: 'we are mindful that modernization is not the same as Westernization. Representative governments in the Middle East will reflect their own cultures. They will not, and should not, look like us.' Possible alternatives he conceded might include 'constitutional monarchies, federal republics, or parliamentary systems'. He also conceded that 'working democracies always need time to develop – as did our own'.[20] In his Second Inaugural Address, he would claim to be prepared for the fact that new democracies might 'reflect customs and traditions very different from our own'. 'America', he insisted, 'will not impose our own style of government on the unwilling. Our goal instead is to help others find their own voice, attain their own freedom, and make their own way.'[21]

Yet although he denied the need for wholesale transposition of institutions, Bush still insisted on an extensive foundation of commonality that all societies should share – what he termed the 'essential principles common to every successful society, in every culture'. 'Successful societies,' he argued:

limit the power of the state and the power of the military – so that governments respond to the will of the people, and not the will of an elite. Successful societies protect freedom with the consistent and impartial rule of law, instead of ... selectively applying the law to punish political opponents. Successful societies allow room for healthy civic institutions – for political parties and labor unions and independent newspapers and broadcast media. Successful societies guarantee religious liberty – the right to serve and honor God without fear of persecution. Successful societies privatize their economies, and secure the rights of property. They prohibit and punish official corruption, and invest in the health and education of their people. They recognize the rights of women. And instead of directing hatred and resentment against others, successful societies appeal to the hopes of their own people.[22]

If this list of principles was to be taken at face value, it was clear that the administration's claim to be at ease with cultural pluralism was not credible. The prescriptions for other societies put forward by the administration encompassed pretty much the full range of liberal civil and political rights, as well as insisting upon not only private property but privatization. Essentially, Bush asserted an idealized conception of America's own political and economic liberalism as universally valid, with only cosmetic variation from that model considered legitimate.

Democratic peace: 'This advance of freedom will bring greater security'

Bush's assertive declaration of the supremacy of liberal values was not purely a moral imperative. Central to the logic of his administration's strategy was a direct link drawn between the progress of liberal values and the defence of American national security. This intellectual connection was established from the earliest days of the post-9/11 'war' against terrorism, but was made much more explicit in the years that followed. In the first months after 9/11, the administration was obliged to focus on dealing with the groups and governments most directly involved in the attack on America, chiefly using the armed forces and intelligence service. But a somewhat grander longer-term strategy also emerged. In his 2002 State of the Union address, the president told Congress that America had 'a greater objective than eliminating threats and containing resentment ... [A] just and peaceful world beyond the war on terror.'[23] What this meant became clearer as the administration steadily expanded its public agenda to encompass Iraq. In his West Point speech, in June 2002, Bush defended the concept of pre-emption, arguing that it was now impossible to trust the Iraqi government. In making this argument, he drew special attention to that government's undemocratic and illiberal nature. 'We cannot put our faith in the word of tyrants, who solemnly sign non-proliferation treaties, and then systemically break them,' he warned. 'If we wait for threats to fully materialize, we will have waited too long.'[24]

In theory, the administration held open the possibility that Saddam Hussein might remove the need for war by opening up the country for inspection and disarmament and ceasing to 'destabilize' the region. But, displaying thinking reminiscent of NSC-68, the administration made it clear that it was aware that root-and-branch changes of the sort demanded of Hussein would inexorably undermine the very characteristics – secretiveness, militarism and resistance to the US agenda – that made his regime's existence viable. As such, US demands were almost certain to be rejected. Meeting America's demands, the president declared, would 'change the nature of the Iraqi regime itself', and while one might hope for this, there was 'little reason to expect it'. Hence 'regime change' was 'the only certain means of removing a great danger to our nation'.[25]

With invasion imminent, the ideological horizons of the American argument expanded. Saddam Hussein's government had, Bush said 'shown the power of tyranny to spread discord and violence in the Middle East'. 'A liberated Iraq', by contrast – meaning one governed in accordance with liberal/universal values – would 'show the power of freedom to transform that vital region, by bringing hope and progress into the lives of millions'. This set the stage for broadening the issue beyond the contribution of Hussein alone, to regional problems, making the far more general link between regional instability and 'tyranny', an entire category of government encompassing potentially any non-democratic regime disapproved of by the United States. Thus, the demands of security and ideals had become, in the administration's formula, mutually supportive: 'America's interest in security, and America's belief in liberty, both lead in the same direction: to a free and peaceful Iraq. The first to benefit from a free Iraq would be the Iraqi people themselves.'[26]

Bush rejected the argument that seeking to spread freedom might undermine peace and stability. On the contrary, he argued, it would further it, by getting at the roots of terrorism. 'The world has a clear interest in the spread of democratic values,' he argued, 'because stable and free nations do not breed the ideologies of murder. They encourage the peaceful pursuit of a better life.'[27] The United States and its allies should work 'to create the conditions for peace'. This would be best achieved

> by seeking the advance of freedom. Free societies do not nurture bitterness, or the ideologies of terror and murder ... American interests and American founding beliefs lead in the same direction: We stand for human liberty.[28]

The 'advance of freedom is the surest strategy to undermine the appeal of terror in the world', he asserted after military operations had succeeded in taking Baghdad. 'Where freedom takes hold, hatred gives way to hope. When freedom takes hold, men and women turn to the peaceful pursuit of a better life.'[29]

Condoleezza Rice, a one-time realist seemingly converted to the president's mindset, pressed home the same arguments. Bringing a much-used analogy to bear, she declared of terrorists that 'the fever swamps in which they grow can be drained'. The war on terror was 'as much a war of ideas as a war of force', she told an audience in Los Angeles in June 2003, and it could only be won

> by appealing to the just aspirations and decent hopes of people throughout the world – giving them cause to hope for a better life and a brighter future, and reason to reject the false and destructive comforts of bitterness and grievance and hate. Terror grows in the absence of progress and development. It thrives in the airless space where new ideas, new hopes and new aspirations are forbidden. Terror lives where freedom dies.[30]

This ideological expansion of the regional agenda reached its full bloom in the latter half of 2003, as the administration reacted to perceived success in Iraq by outlining a bold agenda for the whole of the 'Greater Middle East'. In November, Bush set out what he termed his 'forward strategy of freedom in the Middle East'. The intention, he said, was for the United States henceforth to adopt a direct and muscular approach to promoting liberal democracy. 'Sixty years of Western nations excusing and accommodating the lack of freedom in the Middle East did nothing to make us safe – because in the long run, stability cannot be purchased at the expense of liberty,' he lamented. 'As long as the Middle East remains a place where freedom does not flourish, it will remain a place of stagnation, resentment, and violence ready for export. And with the spread of weapons that can bring catastrophic harm to our country and to our friends, it would be reckless to accept the status quo.'[31]

Shortly thereafter, the president reaffirmed the message on a state visit to London, telling his audience that

> by advancing freedom in the greater Middle East, we help end a cycle of dictatorship and radicalism that brings millions of people to misery and brings danger to our own people … As recent history has shown, we cannot turn a blind eye to oppression just because the oppression is not in our own backyard. No longer should we think tyranny is benign because it is temporarily convenient.[32]

Iraq, the case in which the administration had most directly intervened to topple a 'tyranny' and open space for 'freedom', was a vital symbol of this new policy era, because 'a free and democratic nation, at the heart of the Middle East' would 'send a message … from Damascus to Tehran, that democracy can bring hope to lives in every culture. And this advance of freedom will bring greater security to America and to the world.'[33]

Having broadened its 'freedom agenda' from Iraq to the Middle East, this process of expansion reached its logical conclusion in the Second Inaugural

Address's call for an eradication of tyranny across the globe. In that speech, Bush proclaimed that America faced a 'mortal threat' which could not be resolved without the liberation of the entire world from 'resentment and tyranny'. The United States, the president argued, had to accept that the 'survival of liberty in our land increasingly depends on the success of liberty in other lands. The best hope for peace in our world is the expansion of freedom in all the world.'[34] 'America's vital interests and our deepest beliefs are now one,' he noted. It must be 'the policy of the United States to seek and support the growth of democratic movements and institutions in every nation and culture, with the ultimate goal of ending tyranny in our world'.[35]

Thus, the administration's strategy placed the idea of 'freedom' at the heart of its national security policy, and argued that applied liberal-democratic peace theory could serve as the basis of the nation's global strategy. Its strategic objective was not to attain or preserve peace by prudent manipulation of relations between the states of the world as presently constituted. Rather, it was to reconstitute that world and the states within it along liberal lines, thus enabling the birth of a new international order and the ultimate world peace. As an academic with a background in international relations as well as a practitioner who had served closely under Brent Scowcroft (National Security Advisor to President Bush's father), Rice was surely aware what the central realist criticism of such strategy would be. Any vision of peace requiring the universal acceptance of America's preferred values was transparently – to realist eyes – utopian foolishness. Yet despite her own prior reputation as a realist, she rejected this realist analysis.

'The statecraft that America is called to practice in today's world is ambitious, even revolutionary, but it is not imprudent,' she wrote in the *Washington Post* in 2005, setting out the intellectual case for a strategy based on 'democratic peace':

> If the school of thought called 'realism' is to be truly realistic, it must recognize that stability without democracy will prove to be false stability. ... Our experience of this new world leads us to conclude that the fundamental character of regimes matters more today than the international distribution of power. Insisting otherwise is imprudent and impractical. The goal of our statecraft is to help create a world of democratic, well-governed states that can meet the needs of their citizens and conduct themselves responsibly in the international system. Attempting to draw neat, clean lines between our security interests and our democratic ideals does not reflect the reality of today's world. Supporting the growth of democratic institutions in all nations is not some moralistic flight of fancy; it is the only realistic response to our present challenges.[36]

As Arthur Link had written of Woodrow Wilson, so others could now write of Rice and Bush: they aspired to craft a 'higher realism'.

'Common interests and ... common values'

The Bush administration acquired a reputation early for confrontational antidiplomacy and unilateralism. But seen through its own ideological lenses its position was more complex. Its attitude reflected the tendency on the part of American leaders, discussed in earlier chapters, to regard even unilateral American action as leadership in the pursuit of common interests beneficial to all. Bush imagined that as other states came to accept the universal validity of America's domestic political values, they would necessarily also come to see that their interests lay in common with America's. In the meantime, the United States could presume to have an insight into the common interest that others lacked.

The National Security Strategy was premised on the idea that an awakening of common aspirations across the peoples of the world, combined with the common threats of the post-9/11 environment, could lay the basis for cooperation between all the world's major powers.[37] The assumption was ever-present, if only partially articulated, that the 'progress' in the world of which the document spoke would consist of movement on the part of other powers towards the values and practices identified by the United States as desirable. Convergence of values was decidedly not anticipated to be a process involving mutual movement towards some compromise point. It also appeared implicit that it would be America's prerogative to determine the specific courses of action supposed to arise from the 'common interests' mandating great power cooperation.

The picture of world order painted by the NSS was of a concert of powers cooperating peacefully under US leadership, facilitated in their perception that they shared interests in common by an increasing confluence of values. The administration's worldview was thus notable not so much for its lack of interest in international cooperation as for the presumptuous conviction that a new era of such cooperation could coalesce around its own agenda. Certainly this feature of the NSS's message seems to have been more important to Rice and Powell than the more widely discussed 'pre-emption' doctrine, which both sought to play down.[38] Both went out of their way to emphasize the importance of the idea of great power concert, arguing that now was the time to realize at last the long-standing American dream of an international system based on cooperation and common interest rather than competitive power-balancing. As Rice framed it:

> This confluence of common interests and increasingly common values creates a moment of enormous opportunities. Instead of repeating the historic pattern where great power rivalry exacerbates local conflicts, we can use great power cooperation to solve local conflicts ... Great power cooperation also creates an opportunity for multilateral institutions to prove their worth ... And great power cooperation can be the basis for moving forward on problems that require multilateral solutions – from terror to the environment.[39]

The centrepiece of the NSS, Rice asserted, was the administration's marriage of US interests to the unstoppable spread of liberal political values, a process that served to undercut the now-obsolete dichotomy between 'realists' and 'idealists'. In Powell's *Foreign Affairs* article of early 2004 he sought to herald a new era of cooperation between nations:

> [I]t is revolutionary news ... An insight of the Enlightenment and a deep belief of the American Founders – that politics need not always be a zero-sum competition – has at last been adopted by enough people worldwide to promise a qualitative difference in the character of international relations. If, instead of wasting lives and treasure by opposing each other as in the past, today's powers can pull in the same direction to solve problems common to all, we will begin to redeem history from much human folly.[40]

Both Powell's article and the NSS referred to Bush's West Point speech, which was the first to set out this argument, that there had been some sort of historic 'paradigm shift' ushering in a more cooperative international order. In that speech Bush claimed that America presently had its 'best chance since the rise of the nation state in the 17th century to build a world where the great powers compete in peace instead of prepare for war'.[41] Such a new order could tolerate 'competition' within agreed parameters, but only limited competition, based on shared regard for the values of freedom and progress. Mutual respect for these values would avert the perceived fundamental divergences of interests that had in the past fed a 'series of destructive national rivalries that left battlefields and graveyards across the Earth'. Competition between great nations was inevitable, he declared, but armed conflict was not:

> More and more, civilized nations find ourselves on the same side – united by common dangers of terrorist violence and chaos. Today the great powers are also increasingly united by common values, instead of divided by conflicting ideologies. The United States, Japan and our Pacific friends, and now all of Europe, share a deep commitment to human freedom, embodied in strong alliances such as NATO. And the tide of liberty is rising in many other nations ...[42]

Russia, he suggested, was 'now a country reaching toward democracy', while 'in China, leaders are discovering that economic freedom is the only lasting source of national wealth. In time, they will find that social and political freedom is the only true source of national greatness.' Hence, the long-standing American dream of cooperation rather than balance-of-power rivalry could become reality: 'When the great powers share common values, we are better able to confront serious regional conflicts together, better able to cooperate in preventing the spread of violence or economic chaos.'[43]

The 2003 effort to assemble global support for regime change in Iraq was a potential testing ground for the plausibility of this vision of cooperation in response to new threats. The United States argued that its proposed invasion was aimed at addressing the intertwined threats to global order posed by rogue states, WMD and terrorism. By Bush's account, overthrowing Hussein would further the common interests of all the world's major powers, and indeed of the world as a whole. In practice, however, a large number of governments mobilized to obstruct US efforts to assemble a coalition for invasion. The fact that concert on Iraq proved elusive serves to highlight an inherent problem at the heart of Bush's hope to base policy on the pursuit of common interests: subjectivity. National interests, while they can in the language of generalities be asserted to be common, cannot be defined with sufficient objectivity to guarantee agreement on policy in concrete cases. A reasonable case can almost always be made, based upon identical assertions of national interest in the abstract, that a given action either is or is not desirable. As a result, an actor, if it insists on pressing ahead unilaterally to advance what it considers to be the interests of all, can easily find itself executing policies which many of the alleged beneficiaries oppose. This was the precarious ideological posture into which US policy twisted itself during the Iraq debate. A powerful nation may very well claim insight into common interests, but in the face of disagreement from others this takes on the appearance of pure presumptuousness.

As Bob Woodward, the outsider with closest access to the administration, wrote in 2002:

> When it came to fighting terrorism, the president ... wanted world leaders to equate their national interests with American interests. Some would go along with him when their interests and goals coincided roughly with his, but go their own way when they did not. Bush didn't like that when it happened and at times he took it personally.[44]

The president's speeches from the outset of the war on terror reflect this conflation between the American national interest and the global, or even civilizational, interest. On the day after 9/11, Bush made clear his hopeful expectation that the United States would 'rally the world', because the terrorists had 'attacked not just our people, but all freedom-loving people everywhere in the world'.[45] Addressing Congress later that same month, he characterized the coming American campaign as 'the world's fight. This is civilization's fight. This is the fight of all who believe in progress and pluralism, tolerance and freedom. We ask every nation to join us.' Confidently, he claimed that the 'civilized world' was already 'rallying to America's side'.[46] A refusal to acknowledge that national, religious or cultural differences might provide the basis for divergence in perception of national interests led the administration to cultivate what might be termed a 'rhetoric of expectation': others were not merely hoped or desired but *expected* to support America, because its cause was that of 'civilization'. To do otherwise was to commit an act of moral failure.

Condoleezza Rice, first as National Security Advisor and later as Secretary of State, shadowed these arguments that some higher collective interest was being served by US actions, even as it might appear to some that US national interests were clashing with those of others. The Iraq war was not simply about pushing US interests, she said in the summer of 2003: 'The world has a vital interest in seeing these efforts succeed, and a responsibility to help.' America's campaign, she argued, was against 'the common enemies of man', making advancing it 'not only the right thing to do, it is the clear, vital interest of the world to do so'.[47]

Peoples and governments

The explanation for the Bush administration's expectation of cooperation from all other free societies, and its contempt for non-democracies, was rooted in the Wilsonian intellectual distinction between peoples and governments. Like Wilson, the administration believed the route to a new world order of concord with American desires was through the empowerment of peoples. During the effort to build support for an attack on Iraq, the distinction between people and regime could be used to support the ideological claim that America acted in a higher universal interest, capable of encompassing a nation's people even as it clashed violently with the same nation's government. Upon receiving authorization from Congress to use force in Iraq if he thought it necessary, Bush assured Americans that in accepting the 'responsibility' to confront Saddam Hussein's government 'we also serve the interests and the hopes of the Iraqi people', who would be the first to benefit when 'the world's' demands were met. 'Americans believe all men and women deserve to be free,' he observed. 'And as we saw in the fall of the Taliban, men and women celebrate freedom's arrival.'[48] 'America is a friend to the people of Iraq,' he told Americans in a public address a few days later. 'Our demands are directed only at the regime that enslaves them and threatens us.'[49]

In those tyrannous nations that fomented disorder – something they did, of course, by virtue of their very nature, according to the administration – the president claimed to find encouragement in the support of 'the people' for America's objectives. Though Iran, for instance, had 'a government that represses its people, pursues weapons of mass destruction, and supports terror', it was possible also to see 'Iranian citizens risking intimidation and death as they speak out for liberty and human rights and democracy. Iranians, like all people, have a right to choose their own government and determine their own destiny – and the United States supports their aspirations to live in freedom.'[50] Bush emphasized to Americans that with the toppling of the Hussein government the Iraqi people would feel that 'their country is finally returned to them'.[51] In her summer 2003 remarks in Los Angeles, Rice echoed the point, proposing that the Iraq campaign was 'about building a better future for all of the people of the region. Iraq's people, for sure, will be the first to benefit.' Success, she noted, would also 'add to the momentum for reform that is already touching lives, from Morocco to Bahrain and beyond'.[52]

His Second Inaugural Address allowed the president to underline his support for people's interests over those of their oppressors. As he spoke of the 'transformational power of liberty', he predicted admiringly that 'citizens of Afghanistan and Iraq' would 'seize the moment' and that their 'example' would 'send a message of hope throughout a vital region'. 'I believe that millions in the Middle East plead in silence for their liberty,' he proclaimed. 'I believe that given the chance, they will embrace the most honorable form of government ever devised by man.'[53] In assuming the posture of freedom's champion, Bush believed that the United States was aligning itself more closely with the interests of the peoples of other nations than were their own governments:

> All who live in tyranny and hopelessness can know: the United States will not ignore your oppression, or excuse your oppressors. When you stand for your liberty, we will stand with you. Democratic reformers facing repression, prison, or exile can know: America sees you for who you are: the future leaders of your free country ... The leaders of governments with long habits of control need to know: To serve your people you must learn to trust them. Start on this journey of progress and justice, and America will walk at your side.[54]

The dynamic of historical inevitability

The Bush administration's rhetoric, and the strategy underlying it, asserted that it was historically inevitable that American objectives would be realized. Much as Truman and Wilson had painted the alternatives to liberal democracy as unsustainable, so the Bush administration took ideological comfort from the same thought. Even if long struggles lay ahead, and temporary setbacks might intrude, America's desired destination – universal liberty – lay at the end of history's ordained road.

Immediately after 9/11, Bush offered a narrative that fitted America's attackers into the pattern of the nation's many past, defeated opponents. The terrorists were 'the heirs of all the murderous ideologies of the twentieth century', being guilty of 'sacrificing human life to serve their radical visions ... abandoning every value except the will to power'. They followed 'in the path of fascism, and Nazism, and totalitarianism'. Though those threats were grave, the comparison was reassuring: it meant that they would assuredly 'follow that path all the way, to where it ends: in history's unmarked grave of discarded lies'. 'The course of this conflict is not known,' Bush told Congress, 'yet its outcome is certain. Freedom and fear, justice and cruelty, have always been at war, and we know that God is not neutral between them.'[55] He revisited this theme in a speech before the United Nations a month later:

> There is a current in history and it runs toward freedom. Our enemies resent it and dismiss it, but the dreams of mankind are defined by liberty ... We're confident ... that history has an author who fills time and eternity with his purpose. We know that evil is real, but good will prevail against it. This is the teaching of many faiths, and in that assurance we gain strength for a long journey.[56]

This claim to insight into global destiny blended with a Wilsonian sense of American mission to create an argument that America had a duty to submit to service as a global leader, inspiring the world towards the fulfilment of its destiny. 'We did not ask for this mission,' he declared, 'yet there is honor in history's call. We have a chance to write the story of our times, a story of courage defeating cruelty and light overcoming darkness. This calling is worthy of any life, and worthy of every nation.'[57]

Later, with the 'freedom agenda' in the Middle East proclaimed, the president expanded on these ideas as part of his advocacy of the liberal democratic peace. The forces of history, he argued, lay behind the expansion of liberal and democratic forms of organization. 'We've witnessed, in little over a generation, the swiftest advance of freedom in the 2,500 year story of democracy,' he said in November 2003. Noting that historians would no doubt present a variety of explanations for this phenomenon, he highlighted two that particularly convinced him. First, he believed, it was 'no accident that the rise of so many democracies took place in a time when the world's most influential nation was itself a democracy'. In other words, America's rise to power had been crucial to the spread of freedom. Second, he added, future historians would 'reflect on an extraordinary, undeniable fact: Over time, free nations grow stronger and dictatorships grow weaker.' Thus America's primacy combined with the self-sabotaging flaws of other systems of government to ensure liberty's success. 'The advance of freedom is the calling of our time,' he declared in the same speech. 'It is the calling of our country ... We believe that liberty is the design of nature; we believe that liberty is the direction of history.'[58]

Such faith in progressive history did not equate at all with passivity or fatalism. Indeed, in the less triumphalist moments of his speech, Bush argued that while he was clear that while 'the progress of liberty is a powerful trend', it was also the case that 'liberty, if not defended, can be lost'. 'The success of freedom,' he argued, 'is not determined by some dialectic of history. By definition, the success of freedom rests upon the choices and the courage of free peoples, and upon their willingness to sacrifice.'[59] The worldview advanced by the president thus contained an internal tension, no doubt the result of his desire to assure Americans of the righteous ultimate victory awaiting the liberal cause without undermining their sense of urgency in fighting for it. Still, the worldview itself was not necessarily inconsistent, or at least its contradictions were not unique in the realm of universalizing ideologies; after all, Bolsheviks believed in the inevitability of communism's ultimate victory – or professed to – yet they joined that faith to a powerful imperative for action in order to precipitate their desired revolution. The Bush administration's attitude towards history thus had a Leninist character: the process of its unfolding entailed a single inevitable path, but human action could affect the speed at which it was followed.

Bush's ideology sought to interweave a narrative regarding the pressures of history with one allowing for the belief in human free will that was essential to liberal democracy's *raison d'être*. He explored this complex balance of ideas in the visionary rhetoric of the second inaugural when he declared that:

> We go forward with complete confidence in the eventual triumph of freedom. Not because history runs on the wheels of inevitability; it is human choices that move events. Not because we consider ourselves a chosen nation; God moves and chooses as He wills. We have confidence because freedom is the permanent hope of mankind, the hunger in dark places, the longing of the soul. When our Founders declared a new order of the ages; when soldiers died in wave upon wave for a union based on liberty; when citizens marched in peaceful outrage under the banner 'Freedom Now' – they were acting on an ancient hope that is meant to be fulfilled. History has an ebb and flow of justice, but history also has a visible direction, set by liberty and the Author of Liberty.[60]

'Military forces that are beyond challenge': hegemonic US hard power

Bush combined these multiple Wilsonian features of policy with an absolute commitment to the importance of military power. As well as refusing to accept the sort of political pluralism necessary for a world order genuinely oriented around the idea of a balance of power, the administration's worldview was equally incompatible with the balance-of-power sensibility when it came to material considerations, in that it refused to countenance having the military power of the United States counterbalanced in any way. It was central to the Bush administration's vision that the world's hard power should not be widely distributed, and certainly never used to place any kind of check on the actions of the United States. Rather, it should be heavily concentrated in the hands of America. 'We will build our defenses beyond challenge, lest weakness invite challenge,' Bush proclaimed at the moment of taking office.[61] The preservation of strength beyond challenge, and the disposition to act on the assumption that such strength presently existed, were arguably the most consistent features of the Bush administration.

The National Security Strategy declared explicitly that the United States would seek to maintain an unassailable military predominance over other powers. It envisioned a cooperative system of order, perhaps, but one predicated upon overwhelming – and perpetual – superiority on the part of the United States. In her accompanying lecture, Rice announced that:

the United States will build and maintain twenty-first century military forces that are beyond challenge. We will seek to dissuade any potential adversary from pursuing a military build-up in the hope of surpassing, or equalling, the power of the United States and our allies.[62]

Given the NSS's supposition that all the great powers would be America's 'allies', this might be interpreted as less bold than it first appears. Yet notwithstanding mild encouragement for friendly countries, such as those in Europe, to increase their ability to share burdens, the strategy in practice entailed keeping the United States itself alone at the global pinnacle of military strength. This supposition was reflected in the administration's military planning, reflected in the Quadrennial Defence Reviews published under the Bush presidency.[63]

Such a strategy showed no appreciation of the realist sensibility's desire to base world order on a balance of power. America instead aspired to overwhelming hard-power hegemony, complemented by ideological supremacy. In contrast to the restrained perspective commended by realism, the administration adopted a view of hard power resembling Theodore Roosevelt's civilizational imperialism, updated to be even more thrusting in light of unipolarity. Vast resources of hard power concentrated in one nation's hands, under this ideology, represent a positive feature of world order so long as the hands in question are those of a 'civilized' power disposed to use them for the extension of civilization's writ. The United States being the ultimate civilized power, a near-monopoly on force on its part is not a threat to order, but serves as the ultimate guarantor of civilization and progress. Indeed, it was the American near-monopoly on force – in other words, the massive *imbalance* of power in the international system – that, according to Bush's ideology, would enable the inauguration of the new era of cooperation. 'America has, and intends to keep, military strengths beyond challenge,' he declared in his West Point speech, 'thereby, making the destabilizing arms races of other eras pointless, and limiting rivalries to trade and other pursuits of peace.'[64] Such beliefs, if translated into practice, would amount to the attainment of what Roosevelt had speculated upon and Wilson had promised: the extension of the Monroe Doctrine to encompass the globe.

Critiques of Bush

The Bush administration was chiefly associated with unilateralism, interventionism, militarism and an extremely forceful rhetoric of universalist democracy promotion. As a result, each of the major schools of thought in international relations has found cause to criticize it for going against at least one of the principles each considers central to good policy. In the case of realism, the Bush administration might almost have been conceived as a case study for its preferred points of attack. Structural realists could point to the administration's abrasive self-assertion, and the response it has produced in others, as evidence of the tendency of aspirant hegemons to overreach and other powers to seek to pull them back.[65] Classical realists could argue that Bush's preference for moralistic talk and universalist objectives betrayed insufficient regard for the limits imposed on US power by external reality.

Bush pursued grand objectives, namely military-led regime change in Iraq, nation building in Afghanistan, and the universal 'end of tyranny' as proclaimed in his Second Inaugural Address. He did so, however, without adequate calculation of the costs of such a project were it to be seriously attempted.[66] As a result of setting unattainable goals, realists argue, the United States simultaneously over-extended itself and provoked justifiable charges of hypocrisy.[67] He also neglected the pursuit of tactically necessary support from other powers, failing to show due regard for established allies and institutions.[68] And he alienated strategically useful non-democratic nations through the use of extremist rhetoric in favour of democratization.[69] In short, the Bush administration represented the apotheosis of the unrealistic 'messianic' strain of US foreign policy making which it is realism's founding purpose to oppose.[70] In giving vent to these impulses, realists believe, Bush's administration neglected to pursue, and ultimately did grave damage to, the true national interest.

Bush has also been the target of substantial liberal criticism. For liberal critics, his major crime was undermining the liberal international order and the institutions underpinning it. Having constructed a world order broadly in line with its own principles in the post-Second World War era, liberals believe that the US continues to be a leading beneficiary of that order, which serves to preserve and legitimize its influence. Bush's policies provoked arguments with allies and undermined international law by bypassing institutional approval mechanisms (at the UN and within NATO) and neglecting diplomacy, especially during the launch of the Iraq War. From the liberal perspective, these were profound strategic errors, draining the legitimacy of a world order that the United States should be striving to sustain.[71]

Many writers of a realist[72] disposition, and some liberals,[73] have accepted the proposition that Bush's America was gripped by a version of imperialist ideology, fuelled by the nation's immense hard power and universalistic impulses. Both schools, for their own reasons, question the wisdom, practicality, sustainability and legitimacy of the United States seeking an imperial status in the world. Critics have also approached from a constructivist and/or post-structuralist perspective, seeking to deconstruct the administration's use of the concepts of 'terrorism' and 'war' to justify its policies. Such analysts by and large regard the Iraq conflict and the 'war on terror' as components in an imperialistic project enabled by a false rhetoric of liberation.[74]

The administration's doctrine also had its defenders, who should not be forgotten. The most obvious of these are neoconservatives, from whose ideas Bush was perceived by many to have taken his inspiration.[75] The strong element of idealism and universalism in his rhetoric also drew support from left-wing 'hawks', however.[76] As his policies ran into practical difficulty and bled popularity over the course of his two terms, support for 'Bush Doctrine' became rarer, but there are those who argue that its essential points represent a core of ideas from which there cannot realistically be much divergence in years to come.[77] This argument is based on the view – counter to the arguments of Daalder and Lindsay or Ikenberry that the Bush strategy represented a sharp break with the past – that there are thick strands of continuity from American history running through Bush.[78]

The argument made here in this chapter and in the conclusion that follows sides with those who argue for continuity, at least in the descriptive sense that the Bush administration's strategy evidently does represent the continuation of themes from the past, to a degree greater than is commonly acknowledged. Bearing in mind its overarching argument regarding embedded ideological culture, it also endorses the view that radical short-term change in the substance of strategy is unlikely. Whether or not this is desirable is of course another matter; the argument here is that change is unlikely, mostly because of the historically evolved national character of the United States, not because no other strategy is conceivable or workable in principle. As made clear at the outset, this book does not seek to arbitrate in the prescriptive debates of the discipline regarding the optimal foreign policy for America's future. In its diagnosis of the ideological character of America's predominant strategic worldview, it is sympathetic to the classical realist perspective. It is agnostic, however, regarding the feasibility of that school's proposed solution, which is in effect to call for a revolution in America's collective mindset – no modest objective. This book attempts to make it apparent that Bush's strategy emerged out of long-standing patterns in the historical evolution of the culture of US foreign policy. Whether that serves to commend, excuse or condemn his presidential tenure is a judgement for another place.

The road not taken: ideological choice and the Bush administration

The quotation and analysis provided in earlier sections has set out clearly the pillars of the Bush administration's ideological worldview. Its key beliefs and principles, which might usefully be enumerated at this point, were:

1 That an international order based on any genuine balance of power was not desirable;
2 That a historic opportunity existed to create a new world order based on cooperation rather than rivalry;
3 That only one set of values, and one system of social organization was legitimate: liberal democracy and capitalism;
4 That the universalization of that system was essential to American security, under the logic of democratic peace theory;
5 That shared values and democratic systems would lead to the acceptance by all states that their interests were fundamentally common or harmonious, not in conflict;

160 *The George W. Bush administration*

6 That the United States, being the natural leader among nations, could claim to have special insight into the common interest, and thus legitimately expect others to support its agenda;
7 That 'peoples' should be distinguished from governments. Peoples could be expected to embrace the American agenda because of their sympathy for the universal human values for which it stood. Governments who perceived their interests to be in conflict with the American agenda could *ipso facto* be said to lack insight into their people's true interests, and be accused of failing to represent them properly;
8 That a progressive narrative underlay history, driving the ultimate triumph of liberal forms of social organization;
9 That unchallengeable military supremacy on the part of the United States could and should serve as the foundation of international peace, and the defence of 'civilization'.

These principles did not stand disconnected from one another, but were mutually supportive components in a cohesive ideological edifice. Together, they formed an ideological network of support for administration policy. The reason that bringing about an unprecedented cooperative new world order was thought to be possible, for example, was because of the irresistibility of liberal values to awakening peoples throughout the world. And American leadership in promotion of the spread of universal values could be justified by reference to the implications of democratic peace theory for US national security. Military hegemony on the part of the United States, meanwhile, could be considered compatible with seeking world peace because of the exceptional role accorded the United States in terms of civilizational advancement and its special insight into the common interest. This rendered its possession of such force benign, when in other hands the same disproportionate means might be seen to threaten order.

There was nothing inevitable about the US government's adoption of these principles as the basis of its worldview, at least not as a matter of simple logic. In principle, it would have been perfectly possible for American leaders to adopt a quite different perspective. Among the possible alternatives was a true balance-of-power approach based on realist principles. Such an approach would have emphasized the following principles, running counter to those embraced by Bush:

1 That the international order, being essentially anarchic, is defined by the competitive pursuit by states of their mutually antagonistic interests. The only stable world order is one based on a balance of power between these competing entities, and sound US policy should pursue such a balance.
2 That an international order based fundamentally on cooperation and identity of interests is inherently unfeasible. States' interests are incompatible, due to the very nature of the system: gains in power and security for some translate into losses for others.

3 That liberal values are the historically contingent product of social development spurred by events in particular places in particular periods, and no more. While societies based on them do have apparent strengths, they also have weaknesses, and there is no sound basis for assuming all other societies will eventually be based on liberal values of the sort embodied in the West. They may never be.
4 That there is no necessary reason why universalizing liberal social structures should be required for America's own security. Armed strength and a strategy aimed at balancing threats against one another is the best strategy to gain security.
5 That there is no such thing as a 'common interest' in the broad sense that liberals use the term, and the interests of the world's powers are far from identical. In the absence of detailed agreement on what such an interest is and what policies would serve it, declarations of the existence of a 'common interest' merely advance an empty concept.
6 That the United States has no basis for claiming special insight into others' interests, nor does it have any entitlement to world leadership beyond what its coercive power can compel or its persuasive power can elicit. A nation that presumes to lecture others on their 'true' interests is engaging only in ideological assertion, and is guilty of conflating its own interests with those of others. Given the tendency of states to prize autonomy, this is more likely to generate resentment than procure cooperation.
7 That 'peoples' may well be distinct from governments, but projecting American preferences onto the populations of dictatorships only serves to foster illusions regarding the prospect of global harmony. Peoples with different histories and present contexts may desire social structures quite different from the 'liberty' favoured by the Bush administration. Even if all nations did embrace something approaching liberal democracy, the theory that this would ameliorate all disputes over national interests remains highly debatable.
8 That history has no progressive narrative. Perhaps it is cyclical, with phases of creation and destruction and no ultimate destination. Perhaps there is no discernable trend at all, save the interpretation imposed by men's minds.
9 That an effort by the United States to sustain unchallengeable military hegemony runs counter to the logic of the international system and the lessons of the ages. Others are discontented by such extreme imbalance, and it also tempts the hegemonic power to overreach and exhaust itself.

The real-world implications of a shift from the Bush administration's worldview to one based on this latter set of principles would likely be substantial. An approach based on the second set of principles would emphasize the capabilities and intentions of other states, not their domestic political character. It would tend to attribute other states' intentions and actions to their leaders' interpretation of their national interests rather than to shortcomings in their embrace of liberal values. This would have an impact on policy towards 'rogue states', with blame for their behaviour no longer being attributed primarily to defects in their domestic order. It would not necessarily mean a reduction in interventionism, but it would assuredly change the character of that intervention, reducing the importance of democratizing regimes in pursuit of utopian harmony. The character of American relations with other major powers would also change, with a new acceptance of the pursuit of compromise between rival ideas of national interest rather than a narrative of struggle between the common civilizational interest represented in the US agenda and the recalcitrance of others. Maximization of America's power with a view to defending its interests would become a narrower objective, conceived in less messianic terms.

Examining the major actions and pronouncements of the Bush administration, one can clearly identify ways in which such an alternative worldview might have resulted in different outcomes. The decision to occupy Iraq with a light touch, based on the conviction that a democratic successor state would 'emerge' after only a brief period, is far less comprehensible if one strips out Bush's optimistic assumptions regarding the universality of liberal values among peoples. The administration's pursuit of the 'forward strategy for freedom' in the Greater Middle East would have been unsustainable without faith in the democratic peace theory's claim that the solution to terrorism lay in liberalizing and democratizing other nations. Contrary to the relevant statements by Bush, Rice and Powell, under this alternative worldview the international system would not appear poised for unprecedented cooperation and peace. Instead, the rise of major new powers and the shrinking of American influence and popularity due to failing interventionism in the Middle East might suggest the opposite: the dawn of a new era of conflict. And without the Bush administration's faith in the inevitable triumph of democracy and the moral righteousness of American efforts to hasten its onset, policy towards such non-democratic great powers as Russia and China would likely be quite different, in terms of both the issues discussed and the manner of their discussion.

The Bush administration approached its policy decisions on the basis of a liberal universalist worldview. It is important to note that this does not mean that its particular policies were the only ones that could possibly have been pursued on the basis of such a worldview. All ideologies exist on a spectrum ranging from the fundamentalist pursuit of principle to the pragmatic pursuit of compromise; one can imagine without much difficulty an administration wedded to the idea of the democratic peace but which was more cautious in its pursuit of that end.[79] Nevertheless, though tactical decisions played a role in determining events, the overarching ideological assumptions held by the Bush administration still played a role, leading to strategic conclusions that in turn impacted upon the way it perceived its tactical choices.

One way to assess foreign policy choices made by a state is to look simply to the 'national interest' as the determining variable: to say that the United

States did as it did in order to maximize its power and security. In the case of the Bush administration's choices, however, such an analysis does not take us far, if anywhere. The administration explicitly argued that its policies served the national interest by neutralizing the threat of WMD proliferation while spreading the model of democracy. Yet this portrayal could easily be – and was – criticized by taking issue with the liberal universalist assumptions underlying the administration's definition of the national interest. It is clear that it is in the ideological territory related to *defining* national interests that the argument between Bush and his critics took place; the dispute was not over whether or not to pursue the national interest, but over what it meant to do so.

Yet in examining the 'alternative principles' outlined above, which might have directed US policy otherwise, one is somehow struck – whatever their objective merits – by the implausibility of a US president declaring them, either to the political elite or to the mass public, as the essential principles guiding his foreign policy. Such principles are of course not unknown in the elite foreign policy discourse: they resemble postures adopted by European statesmen in certain periods, or described by tragedian historians of the classical world, or sometimes admired by the most self-consciously realist thinkers in the modern foreign policy arena. But there is an intuitively 'un-American' quality to them. This sense of contradiction between true balance-of-power realism and American identity highlights an important truth regarding the formation of foreign policy strategy: that the national ideological history of the United States has shaped its political culture in such a way that the Bush administration's conception of international affairs fits well within the mainstream of its evolution. The balance-of-power alternative, meanwhile, would be profoundly at odds with the course of that stream.

As the first chapter of this book noted, ideology serves to provide policy makers with simplifications by which to understand the world, and a vision of some end-state they aspire to bring into being. It also provides them with a language in which to speak to their national audience when seeking to mobilize political support. It provides terms that capture shared conceptual understandings as to how the world operates, and should operate, and a sense of the role of the nation within that international context. The Bush administration formulated its version of the national interest and how it should be pursued, its vision of the international system and the American world role, in the context of a set of ideological concepts and understandings that preceded the administration itself in their existence and influence. This ideological framework affected the administration internally, through the intellectual formation of the president and his advisers themselves, and also externally, through the expectations of the public – elite and mass – to which it needed to communicate its ideas in order to mobilize support for its exercise of power. It would be bold to insist that national ideology was the primary determining factor in the policies of the Bush administration, and ludicrous to suggest that it was the only factor. National and international circumstances played a significant role. But it is impossible to adequately explain the administration's translation of those circumstances into policy without reference to ideology and its role in the formation of strategy. And it is impossible, in turn, to understand ideology's impact in this specific case without reference to national history.

Conclusion

The Bush administration came to office in the context of a unipolar world order resulting from the end of the Cold War. The nature of the future world order and the appropriate role for the United States within it were matters of ongoing uncertainty. The terrorist attacks of 11 September 2001 then presented it with an even more pressing imperative to contemplate the appropriate strategy for the United States in such a world. The strategy that it formulated centred on liberal universalism combined with insistence on the importance of military strength. In this, it blended the core elements of Wilsonianism and Rooseveltianism, following in the tradition of the Truman administration's management of the United States' ideological transition to global engagement.

Bush's National Security Strategy described its desired new world order as 'a balance of power that favours freedom'. It did not, however, truly reflect a balance-of-power mindset regarding order. In fact, it set forth an argument in favour of American military hegemony. It also asserted vigorously the universal validity of liberal political and economic values. Its objective was a fundamentally cooperative international order under American leadership, based on common acceptance of liberal principles. To be clear: 'balance-of-power thinking', in the sense in which this book has used the term, is a state of mind or philosophy that leads one to approach any scenario – be it one of weakness, equality or even unipolar strength – by thinking in terms of material power, its manipulation and its limits. There were thus ways of approaching even the post-Cold War and post-9/11 strategic scenarios with a genuinely deep realist mindset, the principles of which were spelled out in the last section of this chapter. Bush's approach, however, was to think not in these terms, but in terms of a universally beneficial order that could be brought about by altering the internal nature of other states, and to blame the dictatorial character of other nations' regimes for the failure of an internationalist utopia to be realized.

The administration's foreign policy strategy was dominated by its assertion of the democratic peace theory, which linked American security to the spread of liberal democratic capitalism. In Iraq and beyond, this conceit served as the centrepiece of the administration's strategic thought. In making his case, Bush relied on a variety of Wilsonian principles, including the distinction between governments and peoples, and the claim of special insight on the part of the United States into the common interests mandated by the universality of liberal values. Similarly to Wilson, Bush claimed that the new world order he sought, predicated on the reform of other states' domestic systems, was in line with the progressive direction of history, and that US leadership of the advance of progress was destiny. Similarly to Roosevelt, his strategy linked US military power with the defence and advance of civilization. His vision of world order resembled Wilson's desire to globalize the Monroe Doctrine. In a sense, this was the realization of the objectives set by the Truman administration, whose strategy emerged in response to the Soviet Union's frustration of America's universalist objectives.

Intellectually, there were alternative principles upon which the Bush administration might have based its strategy, perhaps focusing instead on a realist understanding of national interests and the pursuit of an order based on a balance of power. That it refused to engage with such an alternative had significant policy consequences. Yet it is difficult to conceive of the United States embracing such alternative principles, because those of the Bush administration fit so well within the mainstream of American internationalism as it has evolved from the Founders' Era through Roosevelt, Wilson and Truman. The Bush administration conceived of its strategy while operating in an ideological environment and political culture shaped by the particular national history of the United States. This made it far more likely that it would embrace certain ideological principles than others, which in turn had major consequences for policy. The Bush administration, while its strategies appeared radical to some, was also in important ways the natural flower of its national history. The nature of this relationship between history, ideology and strategy is discussed in the concluding chapter.

8 Conclusion
The Bush strategy and national ideology

This book has sought to draw together international relations and history, while focusing on national ideology. It has argued that the Bush administration's often controversial worldview cannot be fully understood without placing it in the context of the historical evolution of American internationalism. In part, the historical narrative of ideological evolution presented here serves to endorse one of realism's core principles: as the underlying economic and military potential of the United States has grown, and as international circumstances have called for it, America's strategic horizons have expanded. This is not the full story, however. The trajectory of steady expansion, involving enormous increases in global diplomatic and military commitment, necessitated the development of an ideological structure to support it. In noting the importance of this element, the book's analysis finds itself in sympathy both with classical realism and with those varieties of constructivism that have sought to use domestic factors, especially national character and political culture, as an explanatory factor in state behaviour.

It is crucial to note that the argument here is not that there is simple historical continuity, though this is to an extent true. It is about change in response to circumstances, but as shaped and constrained by the intellectual legacy of the past. The George W. Bush administration's strategic worldview displayed continuity from the objectives and assumptions of the Cold War strategy crafted by the Truman administration. That Cold War strategy in turn represented a blending of the Wilsonian and Rooseveltian ideas that formed the foundation of America's first embrace of global engagement. And going back still further, the incipient internationalism constructed by Wilson and Roosevelt was itself the indirect product of America's history, though not in the sense of straight continuity of thought: rather, it was an ideological bridge resulting from the need to carry the United States from the Founders' Era ideology of hemispheric separatism to one of global entanglement. Viewed as a series of interlocking steps, therefore, the argument of the book is that the ideological posture of the United States in the twenty-first century can be linked explanatorily to the nation's circumstances – and its ideas – during its earliest years.

The national and international context of the United States in the years of the Founders' Era, and the choices its leaders made in those years, led it to shun conscious involvement with the global balance-of-power order based upon competing national interests. Instead, it sought separation from the global system, while pursuing a steadily expanding benevolent hegemony in the Western Hemisphere. When circumstances – in the form of its own growing latent power as well as turbulence in the international system – subsequently pushed the United States to accept the status of a global power, it was not prepared politically simply to join the pre-existing balance-of-power order. The nation was culturally predisposed to resist such a move because it would require an outright break with the consensus ideology on foreign policy that had been dominant for several generations. America's history had rendered the nation ideologically averse to explicit balance-of-power thinking about international order, and unwilling to openly participate in it.

The policies called for by changed circumstances were ultimately reconciled with the ideological principles of the past by making the new American internationalism conditional on the pursuit of radical reform of the international order in accordance with Wilsonian and Rooseveltian principles. This reformist agenda, however, meant not only demanding a more cooperative system of relations between states, but also the pursuit of the internal reconstruction of other nations. The strong causal connection drawn in American minds between liberal democracy *within* states and the emergence of a new world order *between* them lent to US foreign policy a prominent universalistic quality with which it has since become inextricably associated. Experienced in relating to other nations only by seeking either ideological detachment or the benign domination of the Monroe Doctrine, the United States sought in its new internationalism to extend the logic of the Monroe Doctrine to the global level. Its engagement with the world was predicated upon the spread of liberal values in an environment of American 'leadership'.

Though the Bush strategy of course represented a response to the particular demands of contemporary circumstances, it also reflected continuing commitment to this evolved American worldview. As such, knowledge of the national ideological history of the United States is a significant help when seeking to understand the Bush administration's mindset. The intended contribution of this book lies not merely in observing that an aversion to balance-of-power ideology is a feature of US foreign policy, but in offering this suggested explanation as to why that might be. It also serves to point out that while the Bush strategy's efforts to address contemporary circumstances gave it qualities specific to the moment of its construction, in its more general propositions that strategy sat comfortably within a very American tradition of thinking about world order.

The historical evolution of American internationalism

As set out in Chapter 3, the founding of the United States under the Constitution took place with foreign policy and international order in mind. Indeed, the operation of the European balance of power played a significant role in the birth of the nation. The growth of the American colonies was part and parcel of imperial rivalry between Europeans, and America's successful fight for independence owed much to the support of Britain's enemies, support with motives traceable to the global balance of power. The desire for a stronger union, which took concrete form in the new constitution, was based in rejection of Europe's balance-of-power order: the new American order was explicitly intended to avoid replicating the European system, and to exclude European interference from intra-American relations.

The relatively weak power position of the United States in its earliest years influenced its strategic choices, though it did not strictly determine them. With different leaders it might have chosen to align itself with one of the sides in Europe's struggle. The major foreign policy arguments in the early politics of the United States centred on whether the United States should tilt towards either Britain or France in their lengthy war, for reasons of either commercial interest or political sympathy. Ultimately, these questions were answered with a strategic worldview outlined first and best in Washington's Farewell Address and later accepted by opposition leader Thomas Jefferson upon his inauguration to the presidency in 1801. With Jefferson's embrace of Washington's principles, what this author has termed the Founders' Era consensus was forged, and this served as the spine of US ideology for the rest of the nineteenth century.

The consensus asserted that the United States existed in a separate sphere of interests from the European order, and on the basis of an incompatible set of values, and should thus reject playing a part in the European balance of power. As the material strength of the United States grew sufficiently to make it possible, and with European colonial control collapsing in Latin America, this ideology expanded into one of hemispheric separatism with the proclamation of the Monroe Doctrine. Within the Americas, the United States would pursue an 'American system' of order, based upon its own hegemonic strength, and cooperation founded on the supposed identity of interests between the US and its southern neighbours. The Europe-centred global balance of power would not be allowed to entangle the United States through military or political commitments, and, reciprocally, European powers would be expected to refrain from interference in the Americas beyond their diminished colonial holdings.

The United States was not as disconnected in practice from the global balance of power as it was in its own mind. The Monroe Doctrine was feasible only because of the support of British naval power. Further, the proclamation of a division of the globe into American and non-American sectors amounted to a de facto spheres-of-influence vision with a realist undertone. Importantly, however, the strategy was ideologized – that is to say, constructed intellectually – not as an extension of realist power balancing, but as a strategic and intellectual separation of the United States, morally and in terms of its interests, from the global balance of power. The US conceived of itself as overseer of a peaceful and cooperative new order in the Americas, while the European-dominated global order would continue to operate, separately, on the basis of rivalry and war.

America's strategic decisions in this period made sense in the context of its national and international circumstances. While the choices made were not the only ones that could have been, they were compatible with an easily appreciable conception of US national interest. Yet they also had ideological consequences beyond their effect on contemporary policy. By conceptualizing the international order and America's role within it in the way they did, the leaders of the Founders' Era laid the basis for a mode of thinking about these issues that was not compatible with the European balance-of-power system. Conceiving of relations only in terms either of benign hegemony or of separation, the United States was thus not 'socialized' into thinking about global order in balance-of-power terms, as the competitive interaction of rival states with divergent interests of equivalent legitimacy.

Chapters 4 and 5 describe the beginning of the United States' transition from this consensus to a new strategic global engagement. This was again in part driven by circumstances. The expanded territory, economic size and military potential of the US pressed for an increase in its world role. Likewise, the destabilization of the Europe-centred international order, and its eventual collapse during the First World War, provided external imperatives for a more expansive foreign policy. Any move towards international engagement, however, required change not merely in policy but in thinking – a shift in the ideology used by leaders both to understand and to explain policy. Both Theodore Roosevelt and Woodrow Wilson, each in his own way, sought to facilitate the necessary mental transition on the part of the nation.

Neither Roosevelt nor Wilson succeeded fully in leading the United States to accept its place as a great power in the existing global order. Indeed, and with certainty in the latter case, it can be argued that they did not seek to achieve such an objective, at least not if framed in that way. Yet these two leaders did lay the basis for a new American attitude towards the world. The new internationalism that resulted was made contingent, however, on the reform of the international order to bring it into line with American principles. As such, it reflected the importance of the nation's ideological inheritance: America refused to engage with international affairs on the basis of the balance-of-power philosophy precluded by the Founders' Era consensus.

Roosevelt was, to a limited extent, a realist thinker regarding international affairs. He believed in the expansion of America's hard power and its world role; he envisioned the nation as competing with others, past and present, for greatness. He inserted the United States into global great power diplomacy, from Africa to the Far East, in a way that his predecessors had not. Yet there was also a romantic, moralistic quality to his thought. In the Western Hemisphere, he extended the scope of the Monroe Doctrine to legitimize an open-ended right of hegemonic intervention on the part of the US, and justified this by reference to a fundamental identity of national interests and a civilizing mission on the part of the United States. He subscribed to a brand of liberal imperialism that asserted an objectively correct path for progress, with the United States possessed of the superior insight required to educate others, willingly or unwillingly, in the proper use of their freedom. In his attitude to global affairs, he was similarly inclined to think in terms of 'civilization' and progress, conceiving of the First World War in moralistic terms as a conflict between civilization and its enemies. Looking ahead to its conclusion, he advocated schemes not dissimilar to the idea of a 'concert of all powers' that was the basis of Wilson's League of Nations.

Roosevelt's chief divergence from Wilsonianism was his certainty that a predominance of armed strength on the side of the United States and other civilized nations would be essential to the preservation of a just order. To tweak the Bush administration's later phrase, Roosevelt sought 'a balance of power that favours civilization'. He was not altogether successful in his own lifetime. Though he did succeed in expanding the navy significantly as president, he largely failed in his pursuit of the goal of 'educating' the nation as to the need for a new attitude to large military establishments, which it continued to regard with suspicion even after the First World War.

Wilson held office during a period when external events produced a level of turbulence in international affairs more amenable to mobilizing support for radical change. In presiding over America's participation in the First World War and its settlement, he had the opportunity to make bolder strides than Roosevelt ever could. In the pre-war years of his presidency, Wilson's foreign policy served to expand and deepen the interventionism in the Western Hemisphere that had been legitimated by Roosevelt's corollary to the Monroe Doctrine. In so doing, he nurtured the ideological paradox at the heart of Wilsonianism: insistence on the necessity and legitimacy of regular, deep intervention into the internal affairs of other nations combined with sincerely meant and strenuous denial that American policy constituted interference. As with Roosevelt's civilizing mission, Wilsonianism conceived of political freedom as possessed of inherent limits. Liberty, it was thought, had an obligation to result in liberalism and capitalism, or else the nation under scrutiny could be said to have departed from the proper path of progress. US intervention was intended to create the preconditions for genuine 'freedom', even as it served to constrain the political and economic choices open to the nations it affected.

In entering the war in 1917, and seeking leadership in the agreement of a peace settlement, Wilson transplanted this agenda to the global level, with his vision of a new world order. Seeking to overcome the taboo against global entanglements imposed by the Founders' Era consensus, he was obliged to construct an ideological case for change. Crucially, he did not do this by arguing that changed circumstances required America to change its principles. Instead, he argued that the world was changing to bring international order into line with American ideals. The United States had been hostile to entanglement, Wilsonianism argued, because of the European balance-of-power system. After the war, there would be a new world order, based not on a competitive balance of power, but on cooperation founded in harmonious interests. This would be enabled by the universalization of liberal democratic government. He blamed Germany's autocratic system for the outbreak of the war, and for the nature of the international order that had preceded it. With Germany and its allies defeated, Wilson believed that the autocratic model of government had been discredited, and the tide had turned towards liberty. This would allow a cooperative system of international order, supported by a League of Nations.

This Wilsonian worldview was supported by a crucial intellectual distinction between governments and 'peoples'. The peoples of all nations were imagined to share common interests, and to support the Wilsonian agenda. As such, their obtaining 'self-determination' in the form of democratic control of their states would allow the new world order to be born. This distinction also allowed Wilson to accuse those governments who claimed that their interests clashed with American preferences of failing to represent their people properly; if they only looked in good faith, he felt, they would see that their true interests, and their peoples' wishes, lay in following American prescriptions. Wilson concerned himself little with the prospect of clashes between democratic nations, or indeed between the United States and the new body of international laws and institutions he sought to build. This was because he viewed the new order as an internationalization of American principles. He seemed to believe that the mechanics of liberal democracy would, by their operation, bring others into agreement with the American perspective. Thus there would be no conflict. Further, the superiority of the United States – 'leader and umpire both' – was built in to the Wilsonian vision, and he thought US leadership necessary to the new order.

In essence, and he said so explicitly, Wilson saw his new order as the transposition of his version of the Monroe Doctrine to the global level. As such, his new order would be an American-led system wherein other societies could pursue their interests within parameters set by American conceptions of appropriate liberty. This order would be cooperative and mutually beneficial, just as American leaders believed the Monroe Doctrine had been. In effect, Wilson brokered an imagined ideological 'deal' between America and the world: the United States would depart from its ideology of separation, but only on the condition that it could pursue a cooperative international order founded on the spread of liberal democracy. As Wilson put it, there should be an order based on an American-led 'community of power' rather than the pre-existing 'balance of power'.

The ideas of Wilson and Roosevelt fell into abeyance during the inter-war years. In a further illustration of the importance of national and international circumstances to policy change, this remained the case until the Second World War obliged the US to become embroiled once more in European affairs, and to think in global terms regarding the post-war peace. By 1945, now at the head of a superpower – one of only two – and with the great-power dominance of Europe broken, American leaders were obliged to countenance unprecedented levels of international entanglement, and to mobilize support for it politically, necessitating justificatory ideology. On one level, the

Cold War that emerged under the Truman administration represents a 'hard case' for the argument that the United States was resistant to thinking about international order in balance-of-power terms. Looking at the facts on the ground, after all, the result of the administration's strategy was a stand-off between two power blocs with conflicting interests: a classic bipolar balance of power. Yet ideologically the Cold War was not simply the balancing of two states competing for power: it was a clash of frustrated rival universalisms.

America's leaders sought to bring the post-war world into line with rediscovered Wilsonian principles of cooperation. This would involve the 'liberation' of peoples, in accordance with the American understanding of liberty. This, however, was rendered impossible by Soviet control of Eastern Europe and the USSR's desire to spread a political and economic system incompatible with American aims. All the major reports of the period, discussed in Chapter 6, including the Clifford–Elsey Report, George Kennan's Long Telegram and 'X' Article, and NSC-68, emphasized that the source of the conflict lay in the domestic system of the Soviet Union, which by its very nature could not coexist with 'freedom'. As they constructed this argument, the US leadership in effect demonstrated mirror-image ideological tendencies on its own part: it constructed a worldview in which the security and prosperity of the United States could not be secured until the Soviet system was compelled to accept a baseline of liberal principles that Americans insisted were essential to supporting a peaceful world order.

The policy of containment, though often celebrated for its realism – not altogether unjustly when compared with more extreme notions like 'rollback' – thus, perhaps surprisingly, originated in a reprise of Wilsonian thinking. It was believed that the ultimate peace would have to rest on the creation of a cooperative order that could only stand on the basis of universal liberty. There was to be no explicit spheres-of-influence deal with the Soviet Union – the obvious alternative course. Policymakers did not themselves believe in, nor could they readily justify to the American people, a policy based on the acceptance of Soviet actions as legitimate, even in the putative 'Soviet sphere'. According to the 'deal' at the heart of Wilsonianism, America's new global engagement was conditional on the pursuit of a cooperative order of harmonized interests via the universalization of liberty. During the Cold War, this was precisely the long-range strategic and ideological vision adopted by the United States.

In addition, the Truman administration and its successors, blending the ideas of Roosevelt and Wilson, pursued their objective by means of unprecedented military build-up. As both a moral and a practical question, the need to accept a large, standing military establishment was accepted for the first time in American history, based on the Rooseveltian moral insistence that 'right be backed with might', in the service of civilization. This blend of universalism and militarism served as the foundation of American internationalism through the Cold War.

The influence of national ideological history on the Bush worldview

The continuing effects of American internationalism's ideological evolution are evident in the Bush strategy described in Chapter 7. The Bush administration operated in the context of a unipolar world order, obliged to respond to an apparently shifting environment of threats. The strategy that emerged pursued the objective a 'balance of power that favours freedom', as set out in the National Security Strategy of 2002. As the last chapter argued, this concept is misleadingly named. In fact, the administration rejected anything resembling a true balance-of-power approach to international relations. It did not pursue a world organized by competitive equilibrium between rival nations, each nation recognized to have opposed but legitimate interests. Rather, the NSS described instead a system wherein all the major powers should be in concert, pursuing common interests on the basis of common values. This system would operate under US leadership, resting in part on American military hegemony. This power pre-eminence of the United States was envisaged as continuing indefinitely into the future.

Though sometimes perceived as radical, and though undeniably cast at times in blunt language, this worldview was consistent with the established ideological principles of American internationalism. The worldview of the Bush administration was based on the nine principles outlined in Chapter 7. The administration's advocacy of these principles was one rational response to its international context, based on a particular conception of the national interest. Certainly, understanding the power capabilities of the nation and its place in the international system is important to understanding the Bush worldview. However, this course was not the only possible response. In principle, the Bush administration could have responded to the challenges posed by its circumstances through the application of realist principles of the sort outlined in the 'alternative approach' also set out in the last chapter. That it did not do so, this author would contend, owes something to the ideological traditions of American internationalism.

The Bush perspective blended Wilsonian and Rooseveltian ideas about international order. In this it was similar in important regards to the worldview developed by the Truman administration when it established for the first time a durable basis for American global engagement. Bush's worldview, like the mainstream of American internationalism, was founded on the Wilsonian 'deal': the United States agreed to engage with global affairs in a way previously prohibited by the Founders' Era consensus, and in exchange perceived an entitlement to pursue the agenda of global reform contained in Wilsonian ideology. Unaccustomed, as a result of its national history, to dealing with international order on a consciously realist basis, US leaders have continually considered themselves to be faced with a choice between detachment from the global order or the pursuit of its reform.

This book has *not* presented an argument that there is stasis in American foreign policy thought. It does not mean to suggest that Bush's foreign policy was identical to Truman's or Wilson's, any more than that Wilson's or Roosevelt's were the same as that of George Washington. On the contrary, while pointing to aspects of underlying continuity, the argument of this book also concerns *change* and the manner of its occurrence. Ideological change, it has argued, does not manifest itself in a sharp break between all that has gone before and that which circumstances demand must now be. Rather, it takes the form of ideological elision: a narrative must be offered – for the benefit of leaders themselves as much as for the public – of how the policies of the 'new way' can be reconciled with the principles to which the nation and its leaders were committed up to that point. Roosevelt, Wilson and Truman reshaped existing ideological formulations for new purposes; they did not cut a new American ideology from whole cloth.

The principles on which the Bush administration based its strategy, like those of its internationalist forerunners, had some admirable features. They were idealistic and optimistic. They sought, in principle at least, to be inclusive rather than divisive regarding the future world order. They were morally concerned with the interests of other peoples, eschewing the language of American self-interest and zero-sum competition. In seeking a 'democratic peace', they proposed a comprehensive effort to address global problems, identifying a supposed root cause of global insecurity and seeking to address it. These very virtues, however, reveal on their reverse side the vices with which the administration became irrevocably associated. The objective of universal liberal capitalist democracy may be utopian and thus unattainable. Its pursuit may therefore be at best naïve, at worst irresponsible, inviting open-ended commitments beyond the means of any nation to fulfil. The presumed right of the United States to identify others' interests on their behalf and, in the event of disagreement, to question the legitimacy of others' definition of their own interests – even the legitimacy of their domestic systems – could not but be perceived as presumptuous arrogance. In pursuing global leadership, the Bush administration displayed an assumption of American superiority and omnipotence that would inevitably alienate others.

To understand US foreign policy today, it is essential to understand its deepest ideological assumptions and how they derive from the historical evolution of American internationalism. This book has sought to make a significant contribution to clarifying both. The Bush administration was defined not only by its brusque, unilateral anti-diplomacy, but also by its sincere calls for others to follow and its ultimately disappointed expectation that they would. It was notable for its assertion of the American national interest, yet also for placing universal political values and the quest for a liberal-democratic world peace at the heart of its strategy. These apparent tensions make most sense when seen as the ideological consequence of America's emergence from strategic detachment to the status of global power. The manner of that emergence meant that the Bush administration, like others since the establishment of American internationalism as the ideology of the mainstream, viewed unilateralism as compatible with serving the common interest, viewed armed intervention in other nations' domestic politics as compatible with furthering their freedom and independence, and viewed unparalleled US military armament as the cornerstone of a more peaceful world.

Most fundamentally, American leaders saw – and perhaps even after all that has happened still see – the engagement of the United States with global politics as conditional on its right to pursue a demanding programme of global reform. They crave a cooperative order of all nations under American leadership, and hope to realize it through the adoption by all nations of an idealized version of America's own political principles. Woodrow Wilson argued in 1919 that the modern United States sought not territorial expansion, but 'conquest of the spirits of men'. This remains the case today. The attainability of such a bold objective remains a matter of dispute and uncertainty. The historic consequences of its pursuit lie all around us.

Notes

1 Introduction

1 White House, 'The National Security Strategy of the United States of America', September 2002. Available online at http://georgewbush-whitehouse.archives.gov/nsc/nss.pdf (accessed 17 Mar 2009).
2 I use the word 'idealized' because the United States clearly has not always acted in line with liberal ideals, either at home or abroad. Nevertheless, the nation is still assumed to embody those values in American political discourse.
3 G. F. Kennan, *American Diplomacy*, expanded edition, Chicago: University of Chicago Press, 1984; H. J. Morgenthau, *American Foreign Policy: A Critical Examination*, London: Methuen & Co., 1952; Henry Kissinger, *Diplomacy*, New York: Touchstone, 1995.
4 C. Dueck, *Reluctant Crusaders: Power, Culture and Change in American Grand Strategy*, Princeton: Princeton University Press, 2006.
5 'X' [George Kennan], 'The Sources of Soviet Conduct', *Foreign Affairs*, 25:4, July 1947, pp. 566–82.

2 International relations, history and national ideology

1 For my taxonomy of American historiography I am in part indebted to F. G. Couvares, M. Saxton, G.N. Grob, and G.A. Billias (eds), *Interpretations of American History*, 7th edn, New York: The Free Press, 2000, vols 1 and 2, as well as the specific texts cited below.
2 K. Waltz, *Theory of International Politics*, Reading, MA: Addison-Wesley, 1979. For a flavour of the debate surrounding Waltz's ideas, see R. Keohane (ed.), *Neorealism and Its Critics*, New York: Columbia University Press, 1986. It is important not to overstate neorealism's claims concerning the overriding influence of systemic pressures in 'causing' state action. Waltz alleges that international pressures work in the manner of a 'market mechanism', in that they can in principle be ignored by individual states, though with dire consequences which deter such defiance and provide general rules for behaviour. See Kenneth Waltz, 'Reflections on *Theory of International Politics*: A Response to my Critics', in Keohane (ed.), op. cit., pp. 322–45. See also discussion in Martin Hollis and Steve Smith, *Explaining and Understanding International Relations*, Oxford: Clarendon, 1991, pp. 92–118.
3 S. G. Brooks and W. C. Wohlforth, 'American Primacy in Perspective', *Foreign Affairs*, 81:4, Jul/Aug 2002, pp. 20–33; William C. Wohlforth, 'The Stability of a Unipolar World', *International Security*, 29:1, Summer 1999, pp. 5–41; and 'US Strategy in a Unipolar World' in G. J. Ikenberry, *America Unrivaled: The Future of the Balance of Power*, New York: Cornell University Press, 2002, pp. 98–118.

In response, Waltz would say that balancing is not 'inevitable' per se, merely highly probable because the systemic imperative supports it. For Waltz's thoughts on unipolarity, see 'Structural Realism after the Cold War', in Ikenberry, op. cit., pp. 29–67.
4 J. J. Mearsheimer, 'The Future of the American Pacifier', *Foreign Affairs*, Sep/Oct 2001, 80:5, pp. 46–61; *The Tragedy of Great Power Politics*, New York: W. W. Norton & Co., 2001. Mearsheimer has shifted somewhat over time to embrace explanations emphasizing the capacity of national decision makers to err and the importance of domestic political influences on policy making, potentially drawing into question his credentials as a fully 'structuralist' thinker. See J. J. Mearsheimer and S. M. Walt, 'An Unnecessary War', *Foreign Policy*, Jan/Feb 2003, 134, pp. 51–61 and *The Israel Lobby and US Foreign Policy*, London: Penguin, 2008.
5 H. J. Morgenthau, *American Foreign Policy: A Critical Examination*, London: Methuen & Co., 1952; G. F. Kennan, *American Diplomacy*, expanded edition, Chicago: University of Chicago Press, 1984; H. Kissinger, *Diplomacy*, New York: Touchstone, 1995. There are, of course, many other Classical Realist analysts of the same period with names less well known: particularly excellent is R. E. Osgood, *Ideals and Self-Interest in American Foreign Relations* Chicago: University of Chicago Press, 1953.
6 F. Zakaria, *From Wealth to Power: The Unusual Origins of America's World Role*, Princeton, NJ: Princeton University Press, 1998.
7 This is not to say that structural realists are necessarily so bold as to deny that such factors exist, merely to note that their theories are by definition not keen to use them as components in their explanations.
8 C. Dueck, *Reluctant Crusaders: Power, Culture and Change in American Grand Strategy*, Princeton: Princeton University Press, 2006; C. Layne, *The Peace of Illusions: American Grand Strategy from 1940 to the Present*, Ithaca and London: Cornell University Press, 2006.
9 This is a prominent feature in Morgenthau, though there are also elements of the more structural sense of balance in his thought. For discussion see R. Little, 'The Balance of Power in *Politics Among Nations*', in M. C. Williams (ed.), *Realism Reconsidered: The Legacy of Hans J. Morgenthau in International Relations*, Oxford: Oxford University Press, 2007.
10 All realists make this point one way or another, but for example see W. Lippmann, *The Cold War: A Study in US Foreign Policy*, New York: Harper & Row, 1972.
11 Kennan argued that the dominance of 'legalism' and 'moralism' in US foreign policy thought were a serious barrier to its effectiveness.
12 This is perhaps unsurprising given the coincidence in timing between the rise of realism and the entrenchment of the Cold War. It could be argued that realism owed its early disciplinary supremacy to its 'fit' with the Cold War arrangement of international affairs.
13 See J. L. Gaddis, *The United States and the Origins of the Cold War*, New York: Columbia University Press, 2000; *Strategies of Containment: A Critical Appraisal of Postwar American National Security Policy*, Oxford: Oxford University Press, 1982.
14 To suggest that it can is to replace the Wilsonian discourse of objective interests in harmony – to which realists vehemently object – with a realist discourse of objective interests in intractable conflict. It is debatable whether this is an improvement.
15 H. J. Morgenthau, *Politics Among Nations: The Struggle for Power and Peace*, 6th edn, New York: McGraw-Hill, 1985.
16 For discussion of liberal/democratic peace see M. W. Doyle, 'A More Perfect Union? The liberal peace and the challenge of globalization', *Review of*

International Studies, 26 (suppl.) December 2000, pp. 81–94; 'Three Pillars of the Liberal Peace', *American Political Science Review*, 99:3, August 2005, pp. 463–66; Doyle, 'Kant, Liberal Legacies, and Foreign Affairs', *Philosophy and Public Affairs*, 12:3, Summer 1983, pp. 205–35. J. M. Owen, 'Democratic Peace Research: Whence and Whither', *International Politics*, 41:4, December 2004, pp. 605–17; 'How Liberalism Produces Democratic Peace', *International Security*, 19:2, Fall 1994, pp. 87–125.

17 R. O. Keohane and J. S. Nye, *Power and Interdependence: World Politics in Transition*, Boston: Little, Brown & Co., 1977. The 'English School' of IR, though not necessarily 'liberal' in all regards, likewise places emphasis on norms and institutions – in the broad sense of accepted patterns of behaviour – which move interstate relations away from pure *machtpolitik* and towards an 'international society'. H. Bull, *The Anarchical Society: A Study of Order in World Politics*, 3rd edn, New York: Columbia University Press, 1977.

18 For example, see J. M. Owen, 'Transnational Liberalism and American Primacy', in Ikenberry, *America Unrivaled*, pp. 239–59; T. Risse, 'US Power in a Liberal Security Community', in Ikenberry, *America Unrivalled*, pp. 260–83.

19 G. J. Ikenberry, *After Victory: Institutions, Strategic Restraint and the Rebuilding of Order after Major Wars*, Princeton: Princeton University Press, 2001; 'Democracy, Institutions and Strategic Restraint' in Ikenberry, *America Unrivaled*, pp. 213–38.

20 J. S. Nye, *The Paradox of American Power: Why the World's Only Superpower Can't Go It Alone*, New York: Oxford University Press, 2002; Nye, "The American National Interest and Global Public Goods", *International Affairs*, 78:2, April 2002, pp. 233–44.

21 An outstanding example of traditional diplomatic history is the work of Samuel Flagg Bemis. See his *A Diplomatic History of the United States*, 5th edn, New York: Holt, Rinehart and Winston, 1965; *John Quincy Adams and the Foundations of American Foreign Policy*, New York: Alfred A. Knopf, 1949. For an example of more recent work of the orthodox school see J. L. Gaddis, *We Now Know: Rethinking Cold War History*, Oxford: Oxford University Press, 1997.

22 The dean of progressive history was C. A. Beard, *An Economic Interpretation of the Constitution of the United States*, New York: Macmillan, 1913; *The Idea of National Interest: An Analytical Study in American Foreign Policy*, New York: Macmillan, 1934. Beard was noted in the 1930s and 1940s for his isolationist sentiment and opposition to entering the Second World War. A sample book from recent years that displays similarities of approach, in that it gives much play to the driving force of economic factors, but which differentiates itself by emphasizing regionalism below the level of the national unit, is P. Trubowitz, *Defining the National Interest: Conflict and Change in American Foreign Policy*, Chicago: Chicago University Press, 1998.

23 Kennan, for instance, treats the long-standing policy of the 'Open Door' in Asia as an example of ineffectual 'legalistic-moralistic' thinking, while progressives view it as a core component in a determined, somewhat malign master plan.

24 Probably the two most notable standard-bearers of this approach are William Appleman Williams and Walter LaFeber. W. A. Williams, *The Tragedy of American Diplomacy*, New York: Dell, 1972; *The Contours of American History*, New York: W.W. Norton, 1989. W. LaFeber, *The New Empire: An Interpretation of American Expansionism 1860–1898*, London: Cornell University Press, 1963; *Inevitable Revolutions: The United States in Central America*, New York: W.W. Norton, 1993; *America, Russia, and the Cold War, 1945–2000*, 9th edn, London: McGraw-Hill, 2002.

25 R. Kagan, *Dangerous Nation: America's Place in the World from its Earliest Days to the Dawn of the Twentieth Century*, New York: Alfred A. Knopf, 2006.

26 It is worth noting, however, that classical realists can do this too. Kennan, for one, was outspoken regarding his concern that democratic control hinders the implementation of an effective, i.e. 'realistic', foreign policy.
27 See M. Cox, "The Empire's Back in Town: Or America's Imperial Temptation – Again", *Millennium*, 32:1, 2003, pp. 1–29, which provides a useful survey of the re-emergence of 'empire' as a term in the policy discourse as well as an explicit defence of the concept's relevance. See also Cox, 'Empire by Denial: The Strange Case of the United States', *International Affairs*, Jan 2005, 81:1, pp. 15–30; 'Empire, Imperialism and the Bush Doctrine', *Review of International Studies*, 30:4, 2004, pp. 585–608.
28 N. Ferguson, *Colossus: The Rise and Fall of the American Empire*, London: Allen Lane, 2004; M. Ignatieff, *Empire Lite: Nation-Building in Bosnia, Kosovo and Afghanistan*, London: Vintage, 2003; M. Boot, 'The Case for American Empire', *Weekly Standard*, October 15, 2001; S. Mallaby, 'The Reluctant Imperialist', *Foreign Affairs*, 81:2, Mar/Apr 2002, pp. 2–7.
29 M. Mann, *Incoherent Empire*, London: Verso, 2003; 'The First Failed Empire of the 21st Century', *Review of International Studies*, 30:4, 2004, pp. 631–53; John Newhouse, *Imperial America: The Bush Assault on the World Order*, New York: Alfred A. Knopf, 2003.
30 Ferguson, op. cit.; P. Kennedy, *The Rise and Fall of the Great Powers*, London: Vintage, 1989.
31 G. Kolko, *The Politics of War: Allied Diplomacy and the World Crisis of 1943–45*, London: Weidenfeld & Nicolson, 1969; *Confronting the Third World: United States Foreign Policy, 1945–1980*, New York: Pantheon Books, 1988; *Another Century of War*, New York: The New Press, 2002. J. Kolko and G. Kolko, *The Limits of Power: the World and United States Foreign Policy*, New York, Harper & Row, 1972; N. Chomsky, *Deterring Democracy*, London: Vintage, 1992; *The New Military Humanism: Lessons from Kosovo*, London: Pluto Press, 1999; *A New Generation Draws the Line: Kosovo, East Timor and the Standards of the West*, London: Verso, 2000; *Hegemony or Survival: America's Quest for Global Dominance*, London: Penguin, 2004. Chomsky's aggressive deconstruction and attack is linked to detailed argument concerning the manipulation of public opinion on foreign policy within ostensibly free and democratic societies. See E. S. Herman and N. Chomsky, *Manufacturing Consent: The Political Economy of the Mass Media*, London: Vintage, 1994.
32 The best known recent scholar of exceptionalism is S. M. Lipset, *American Exceptionalism: A Double-Edged Sword*, New York: W.W. Norton & Co., 1996, but in modern academia the theme goes back as far as Frederick Jackson Turner's 'Frontier Thesis' in the late nineteenth century. Turner argued that the unique American environment, characterized as plentiful cheap land and a rugged, ever-receding frontier, had a formative influence on the American mind. This argument was conceived in opposition to the prevailing 'germ' theory, which attributed US political culture to an intellectual inheritance from Europe. F. J. Turner, *The Frontier in American History*, New York: Henry Holt & Co., 1920. As a concept, the notion of America's exceptional status goes back a good deal further, at least as far as John Winthrop's 'City on a Hill' sermon, and was later brought to social scientific prominence by de Tocqueville: A. de Tocquevcille, *Democracy in America*, New York: Library of America, 2004.
33 For some recent discussion of America's uniqueness, see J. Micklethwaite and A. Woolridge, *The Right Nation: Why America is Different*, London: Allen Lane, 2004.
34 For criticism of this sort of exceptionalism see William Pfaff, 'Manifest Destiny: A New Direction for America', *New York Review*, 54:2, 15 Feb 2007, pp. 54–9.
35 A. Wendt, *Social Theory of International Politics*, Cambridge: Cambridge University Press, 1999.

36 David Campbell, *Writing Security: United States Foreign Policy and the Politics of Identity*, Manchester: Manchester University Press, 1998.
37 M. H. Hunt, *Ideology and US Foreign Policy*, New Haven: Yale University Press, 1987.
38 W. A. McDougall, *Promised Land, Crusader State: The American Encounter with the World since 1776*, Boston: Mariner Books, 1997; A. Lieven, *America Right or Wrong: An Anatomy of American Nationalism*, London: HarperCollins, 2004.
39 R. E. Osgood, *Ideals and Self-Interest in American Foreign Relations*, Chicago: University of Chicago Press, 1953.
40 F. L. Klingberg, *Cyclical Trends in American Foreign Policy Moods: The Unfolding of America's World Role* London: University Press of America, 1983.
41 J. Monten, 'The Roots of the Bush Doctrine: Power, Nationalism and Democracy Promotion in US Strategy', *International Security*, 29:4, Spring 2005, pp. 112–56.
42 H. W. Brands, *What America Owes the World*, Cambridge: Cambridge University Press, 1998.
43 The themes identified by Hunt are national greatness, racial hierarchy, and conservative hostility to revolution. Lieven, who looks at American nationalism as a whole and not just in regard to foreign policy, identifies a tense duality in American thought between a universalistic and inviting civic nationalism and a more bellicose 'private club' sense of Americanism, the struggle between which can produce confused and confusing policy. McDougall, Klingberg and Osgood are closer in their enterprises to what this book attempts, focusing in a similar way on America's 'terms of engagement' in dealing with the international system. In their own ways, all conclude that America has struggled to find a golden mean between over-commitment and excessive self-restraint.
44 Hunt, p. xi. The explanation of ideology and culture adopted here owes something to Hunt's own theoretical arguments, see esp. pp. 11–18.
45 D. J. Macdonald, 'Formal Ideologies in the Cold War: Toward a Framework for Empirical Analysis', in O. A. Westad (ed.), *Reviewing the Cold War: Approaches, Interpretations and Theory*, London: Frank Cass Publishers, 2000, pp. 180–204. Quotation p. 191.
46 J. Goldstein and R. O. Keohane (eds), *Ideas and Foreign Policy: Beliefs, Institutions and Political Change*, Ithaca, NY: Cornell University Press, 1993.
47 Wendt, *Social Theory*, esp. pp. 224–45.
48 Campbell, *Writing Security*.
49 For an interesting effort at the taxonomy of different ideological subgroups concerned with American foreign policy, see for instance W. R. Mead, *Special Providence: American Foreign Policy and How it Changed the World*, New York: Routledge, 2002. His categories of Hamiltonian, Jeffersonian, Wilsonian and Jacksonian have since become widely used in the field.
50 Many of the schools of history described earlier in the chapter seek to do just this. Beard, for example, argues that American foreign policy from the late nineteenth century onward reflected the domination of a Hamiltonian conception of 'interest' over a Jeffersonian one of 'nation'. Beard, *Idea of National Interest*.
51 Such theories, it is often said, for example that of Waltz, posit that states are interchangeable units, with no relevant behavioural consequences arising from differences in domestic politics or governmental philosophy. Whether any theorist actually does defend such a stark position – except in the manner that, say, an economist defends the notions of 'rational man' and 'perfect information' as factually inaccurate but useful modelling assumptions – is a matter for debate.
52 See A. Giddens, *The Constitution of Society: Outline of the Theory of Structuration*, Cambridge: Polity Press, 1986. Giddens is a cited influence on the theory of Wendt.
53 To take one example, the historical field is divided over whether the end of the Cold War, with the fall of the Soviet Union, was the product of ideational change

or material collapse. To the extent that this is an interpretive debate over relative importance, this is of course legitimate. Explanation based on unidirectional causality, however, is not fruitful: by far the most plausible explanation is that the two intertwined inextricably. That is to say, that the Soviet Union opened up to new ideas because it was faltering in its material strength, and it was faltering materially in large part because of the determined implementation of ideas at odds with reality.

54 Vis-à-vis US foreign policy, this is true of someone such as Wilson in a way that it would not be true of, to choose a random example, Plutarch, without expending considerably greater effort to prove the reality of the alleged influence. It is intuitively obvious that a suggestion of influence through culture and tradition becomes increasingly tenuous the more distant the figure in question lies in time, place and topic of focus from the actors they are alleged to have influenced.

55 The distinction between public and private letters is blurred in the case of early American political leaders, as letter-writing was often a means for a politician to disseminate his thoughts more widely than the named addressee.

56 Hunt, pp. 15–17.

57 For example, Draper's relatively critical biography of George W. Bush suggests that there is no great discrepancy between what the president personally believed and what he said in his speeches. Robert Draper, *Dead Certain: The Presidency of George W. Bush*, London: Simon & Schuster, 2007.

58 Witness the immense political costs to the Bush administration of sustaining the practices of detention without trial and 'harsh interrogation' of prisoners while simultaneously pursuing a rhetorical strategy that emphasized liberty and condemned 'torture'.

59 Lieven, p. 2.

3 The Founders' Era consensus

1 Phrase from Alexander Hamilton, 'To George Washington', Apr 1794, in A. Hamilton, *Writings*, New York: Library of America, 2001, p. 813.

2 The basic historical narrative providing background for this chapter comes most notably from M. A. Jones, *The Limits of Liberty: American History 1607–1980*, Oxford: Oxford University Press, 1983; A. DeConde, *A History of American Foreign Policy*, New York: Scribner, 1963.

3 For detailed interpretive discussion of the international dimension of America's early politics, see J. Winik, *The Great Upheaval: America and the Birth of the Modern World, 1788–1800*, New York: Harper, 2007; R. Kagan, *Dangerous Nation: America's Place in the World from its Earliest Days to the Dawn of the Twentieth Century*, New York: Alfred A. Knopf, 2006, pp. 1–180; Michael Lind, *The American Way of Strategy*, Oxford: Oxford University Press, 2006. The latter two authors both take an interest in the ideological issues, but they disagree on the importance of moralistic interventionism. Lind considers Kagan's work to be neoconservative propaganda. See Lind, 'Dangerous History', *Prospect*, 140, Nov 2007, available online at www.newamerica.net/publications/articles/2007/danger ous_history_6238 (accessed 30 March 2009).

4 Morgenthau, among others, has made a plausible case that the Founders pursued a policy that was, in its essentials at least, realistic, meaning a rational course given American material capabilities and international context. See H. J. Morgenthau, *American Foreign Policy: A Critical Examination*, London: Methuen & Co. Ltd, 1952, pp. 1–39. See also J. J. Ellis, *Founding Brothers: The Revolutionary Generation*, New York: Vintage, 2002, esp. pp. 120–60.

5 John Dickinson of Pennsylvania, quoted in Jones, p. 64.

6 For biographical information on Hamilton and his ideas I base myself on: R. Chernow, *Alexander Hamilton*, New York, Penguin Press, 2004; B. Mitchell, *Alexander Hamilton: A Concise Biography*, New York: Oxford University Press, 1976; M. B. Hecht, *Odd Destiny: The Life of Alexander Hamilton*, New York: Macmillan, 1982. On foreign policy specifically: G. Lycan, *Alexander Hamilton and American Foreign Policy*, Norman: University of Oklahoma Press, 1970; J. L. Harper, *American Machiavelli: Alexander Hamilton and the Origins of U.S. Foreign Policy*, Cambridge: Cambridge University Press, 2004. My representation of his views is also based on primary sources, namely Alexander Hamilton, *Writings*, New York: Library of America, 2001. The above are on the whole sympathetic to Hamilton; for a harsher critical perspective see especially the biographers of Jefferson. Hamilton is often cast in dichotomous contrast with Jefferson as a defender of elitism and moneyed capitalism, notably in C. G. Bowers, *Jefferson and Hamilton: the Struggle for Democracy in America* Cambridge, MA: Riverside Press, 1925.

7 See Irving Brant, *The Fourth President: A Life of James Madison*, London: Eyre and Spottiswood, 1970, and, for primary materials, James Madison, *Writings*, New York: Library of America, 1999.

8 See Kagan, *Dangerous Nation*, pp. 7–38 for dissent from this national self-image.

9 Jefferson 'The Anas, 1791–1806', 4 Feb 1818, in Thomas Jefferson, *Writings*, New York: Library of America, 1984, p. 663.

10 Hamilton, 'The Continentalist No. III', 9 Aug 1781, in Hamilton, pp. 101–2.

11 Madison, 'Speech in the Continental Congress on Revenue', 21 Feb 1783, in Madison, pp. 19–20, footnote.

12 Madison, 'To Edmund Pendleton', 24 Feb 1787, in Madison, pp. 62–3.

13 Madison, 'Speech in the Federal Convention on Relations Among the States', 28 Jun 1787, in Madison, pp. 113–14.

14 Indeed, Morgenthau quotes Hamilton approvingly and at length in his seminal realist critique of US foreign policy. See Morgenthau, *American Foreign Policy*, pp. 14–18.

15 Hamilton, 'Federalist No. 6', 14 Nov 1787, in Hamilton, pp. 176–7.

16 Ibid.

17 Hamilton, 'Federalist No. 7', 17 Nov 1787, in Hamilton, p. 183.

18 Hamilton, 'Federalist No. 15', 1 Dec 1787, in Hamilton, p. 221–22.

19 Hamilton, 'Federalist No. 15', 1 Dec 1787, in Hamilton, pp. 223, 224.

20 Hamilton, 'Federalist No. 7', 17 Nov 1787, in Hamilton, p. 189.

21 Hamilton, 'Federalist No. 8', 20 Nov 1787, in Hamilton, p. 194–5.

22 Madison, 'Federalist No. 41', 19 Jan 1788, in Madison, p. 229.

23 Hamilton, 'To George Clinton', 13 Feb 1778, in Hamilton, p. 50.

24 Hamilton, 'The Continentalist No. VI', 4 July 1782, in Hamilton, p. 118.

25 Hamilton, 'Federalist No. 11', 28 Nov 1787, Hamilton, p. 208.

26 His Farewell Address notwithstanding, Washington's own ideas are not as much of a focus in this chapter as are those of Hamilton, Madison and Jefferson, though of course the events of his administration are under scrutiny. That fact notwithstanding, some biographical sources focusing on Washington have been consulted, including especially J. T. Flexner, *Washington: The Indispensable Man*, London: Purnell Book Services, 1976; J. J. Ellis, *His Excellency: George Washington*, New York: Alfred A. Knopf, 2004. This playing down of Washington's role as an ideologist is not intended to diminish his importance as a political actor: he was crucial in steering the ship of state in its first years. His chief contribution was to moderate policy, denying controlling sway to either Jefferson or Hamilton, the most intellectually forceful members of his Cabinet.

27 For sources on Jefferson, see M. D. Peterson, *Thomas Jefferson and the New Nation*, New York: Oxford University Press, 1970; M. Lerner, *Thomas Jefferson:*

America's Philosopher-King, New Brunswick: Transaction Publishers, 1996; L. S. Kaplan, *Jefferson and France: An Essay on Politics and Political Ideas*, New Haven: Yale University Press, 1967; J. J. Ellis, *American Sphinx: The Character of Thomas Jefferson*, New York: Vintage, 1998. For primary sources, see Thomas Jefferson, *Writings*, New York: Library of America, 1984.
28 Examples of his affectedly breezy indifference to expectations of formality would include the abolition of formal seating plans at presidential dinners and, on at least one occasion, meeting with a business caller to the White House while wearing slippers.
29 It was these measures – the bank and funding of the wartime debt at face value – that sparked the first conflict between Hamilton and Jefferson. Jefferson believed the former to be unconstitutional and the latter to be a gift to speculators, who had voraciously accumulated debt certificates at bargain prices from their original holders.
30 Madison, 'To Edmund Randolph', May 1783, in Madison, p. 21. Hamilton later developed such ideas in his legislatively ignored but politically seminal 'Report on Manufactures', 5 Dec 1791, in Hamilton, pp. 647–734.
31 Jefferson, 'To John Banister Jr.', 15 Oct 1785, in Jefferson, pp. 836–7.
32 Jefferson, 'To George Washington', 15 Mar 1784, in Jefferson, pp. 788–9.
33 See Madison, 'Letter to James Monroe', 7 Aug 1785, in Madison, p. 37.
34 These issues are discussed in J. A. Combs, *The Jay Treaty: Battleground of the Founding Fathers*, Berkeley: University of California Press, 1970; C. S. Campbell, *From Revolution to Rapprochement: The United States and Great Britain, 1783–1900*, New York: John Wiley & Sons, 1974.
35 Jefferson, 'Report on the Privileges and Restrictions on the Commerce of the United States in Foreign Countries', 16 Dec 1793, in Jefferson, pp. 445, 447.
36 Hamilton was upset – and surprised – by what he saw as Madison's political abandonment of him. See Hamilton, 'To Edward Carrington', 26 May 1792, in Hamilton, p. 745.
37 There is debate over how accurately Hamilton represented Washington's views as opposed to serving his own agenda in these undeniably devious back-channel negotiations. For discussion of the issue see Harper, *American Machiavelli*, pp. 49–87; Julian Boyd, *Number 7: Alexander Hamilton's Secret Efforts to Control American Foreign Policy*, Princeton: Princeton University Press, 1964. Harper rejects Boyd's analysis that Hamilton's actions amounted to treason.
38 'Memorandum by George Beckwith on a Conversation with Hamilton', Oct 1789, in Hamilton, p. 527.
39 Jefferson, 'Opinion on the French Treaties', 28 April 1793, in Jefferson, p. 423.
40 Jefferson, 'To Diodati', 3 Aug 1789, in Jefferson, p. 958.
41 Jefferson, 'To Madame d'Enville', 2 April 1790, in Jefferson, p. 965.
42 Jefferson, 'To William Short', 3 Jan 1793, in Jefferson, p. 1004; phrases such as this seem to justify Madison's later noting 'a habit in Mr Jefferson as in others of great genius of expressing in strong and round terms, impressions of the moment'. Madison, 'To Nicholas P. Trist', 23 Dec 1832, in Madison, p. 860.
43 Jefferson, 'The Autobiography', 6 Jan 1821, in Jefferson, pp. 85–6, 97.
44 Jefferson, 'To John Adams', 4 Sep 1823, in Jefferson, p. 1478.
45 Lafayette was involved in the reformism of the early Revolution, and would suffer at its hands – though not fatally – in its more radical phase.
46 Hamilton, 'To Lafayette', 6 Oct 1789, in Hamilton, p. 521. We can see in this the conservative anti-revolutionary strain in American thought noted by Michael Hunt, though this instance challenges any supposition that such instincts are always inappropriate.
47 Hamilton, 'To Edward Carrington', 26 May 1792, in Hamilton, p. 746. Italics are Hamilton's.

48 Hamilton, 'Memorandum on the French Revolution', 1794, in Hamilton, pp. 834, 836.
49 Hamilton, 'Draft of a Defense of the Neutrality Proclamation', c. May 1793, in Hamilton, pp. 797, 798.
50 Hamilton, 'To George Washington', 18 Aug 1792, in Hamilton, p. 761.
51 Madison, 'To Jefferson', 13 June 1793, in Madison, pp. 534–7. Hamilton offered a rebuttal of their arguments in his 'Draft of a Defense of the Neutrality Proclamation', c. May 1793, Hamilton, p. 797.
52 He denied to Washington that his efforts to impose commercial sanctions on Britain reflected a pro-French or anti-British bias: '[M]y system was to give some satisfactory distinctions to [France], of little cost to us, in return for the solid advantages yielded us by them; & to have met the English with some restrictions which might induce them to abate their severities against our commerce.' 'To GW', 23 May 1792, in Jefferson, p. 995.
53 The limits of Jefferson's position were brought into focus when Edmond Genêt, representative to the US appointed by the Girondist regime in Paris, embarrassed the Secretary of State by presuming his support for exhorting private American naval operations against the British. Jefferson was compelled to perform a difficult balancing act to keep the Frenchman under control without alienating his own pro-French supporters.
54 Like Jefferson, Hamilton always denied bias, and he painted himself as the champion of the national interest against an irresponsibly pro-French faction, though one can question this as readily as one might query Jefferson's self-perception. In any case, his version of the national interest clearly did lie in good relations with Britain at almost any price. See Hamilton, 'Letter Concerning John Adams', 24 Oct 1800, in Hamilton, p. 936.
55 Both were clear when writing in the mid-1780s that conducting commerce overseas inherently risked war, and that only a strong America could hope to defend its neutral rights. See Madison, 'Speech in the Virginia Ratifying Convention', 11 Jun 1788, in Madison, pp. 367–6. See also Jefferson, 'To John Jay', 23 Aug 1785, in Jefferson, p. 819.
56 Jefferson, 'To James Madison', 24 Mar 1793, in Jefferson, p. 1006–7.
57 Hamilton, 'To George Washington', Apr 1794, in Hamilton, p. 813.
58 Ibid., pp. 816–17.
59 Ibid., p. 820.
60 For discussion of the treaty and its political context, see Combs, *The Jay Treaty*; S. F. Bemis, *Jay's Treaty: A Study in Commerce and Diplomacy*, New Haven: Yale University Press, 1962.
61 For analysis of the Farewell Address, see the cited biographies of Washington and Hamilton, and also Ellis, *Founding Brothers*, pp. 120–61; F. Gilbert, *To the Farewell Address: Ideas of Early American Foreign Policy*, Princeton: Princeton University Press, 1961. For Hamilton's draft of the Address, somewhat different in language from Washington's final draft but evidently the core of the final text, see Hamilton, 'To George Washington (enclosing draft of the Farewell Address)', 20 July 1796, in Hamilton, p. 856.
62 For the Address as finalized by Washington, see 'The Farewell Address' in the George Washington papers. Available online at http://gwpapers.virginia.edu/documents/farewell/transcript.html (accessed 1 April 2009).
63 See Hamilton, 'The Defence, No. 1', 2 Jul 1795, in Hamilton, p. 845.
64 He was ultimately recalled by Washington amid much rancour.
65 The scandal surrounding these negotiations, known as the 'XYZ affair' stemmed from French foreign minister Talleyrand's representative's demand for bribes from America's envoys in exchange for access. Though apparently such practices were not altogether unusual in Europe in this period, public reporting of the event outraged American opinion and generated an anti-French backlash that gave the

Federalist party its last burst of national popularity before its ultimate fall from power in 1800.
66 It has been suggested that Hamilton intended to use this army as the instrument for a coup d'état. See Ellis, *His Excellency*, pp. 249–55.
67 Ellis notes a shift in Jefferson away from connecting the French cause with that of global liberty, quoting him as observing in 1800 that 'It is very important for ... [the American people] to be made sensible that their own character and situation are very different from the French, and that whatever may be the fate of republicanism there, we are able to preserve it inviolate here.' Ellis, *Founding Brothers*, p. 202.
68 Jefferson, 'To John Taylor,' 4 Jun 1798, in Jefferson, p. 1050. Jefferson rationalized this stance as the continuation of a long-standing wish on his part for true neutrality. His hard line against Britain, he insisted, had been aimed merely at inducing the British to accept such even-handedness. See Jefferson, 'To Elbridge Gerry', 13 May 1797, in Jefferson, pp. 1042, 1043–44.
69 Jefferson, 'To Thomas Lomax', 12 Mar 1799, in Jefferson, p. 1063.
70 The speech is remembered for the declaration that 'We are all republicans, we are all federalists'.
71 Jefferson, 'First Inaugural Address', 4 Mar 1801, in Jefferson, pp. 492, 494.
72 Jefferson, 'Third Annual Message', '17 Oct 1803, in Jefferson, p. 515.
73 Ibid., p. 516.
74 For an excellent historian's analysis of the Monroe Doctrine's conception and context, see S. F. Bemis, *John Quincy Adams and the Foundations of American Foreign Policy*, New York: Alfred A. Knopf, 1949, esp. pp. 363–408 (hereafter *JQA*).
75 The label 'Monroe Doctrine' itself was not applied until the 1850s, but I use the term here for simplicity's sake.
76 James Monroe, 'Address to Congress', 2 Dec 1823, in R. Maidment and M. Dawson (eds), *The United States in the Twentieth Century: Key Documents*, 2nd edn, London: Hodder & Stoughton Educational, 1999, pp. 301–2. Quotation p. 302.
77 Bemis, *JQA*, p. 364.
78 Ibid., p. 387.
79 In this respect the early Monroe Doctrine resembled the later 'Open Door' policy towards China, rebuked by realist thinkers such as Kennan for its universal scope and non-existent practical follow-through.
80 Adams, 'Marcellus' letter, cited in Bemis, *JQA*, p. 364.
81 Adams, Speech, 4 July 1821, ibid., pp. 364–5.
82 Adams, Instructions to Henry Middleton, minister to Russia, ibid., p. 365.
83 Adams, Special message to the House requesting appointment of ministers to Panama convention, 15 Mar 1826, ibid., pp. 554–5.
84 Jefferson, 'To Alexander von Humboldt', 6 Dec 1813, in Jefferson, p. 1312.
85 Jefferson, 'To James Monroe', 24 Oct 1823, in Jefferson, pp. 1481–8.
86 Ibid., p. 1482.
87 Hamilton died in 1804, shot in an illegal duel with Jefferson's Vice-President, Aaron Burr. This was considered only marginally less outrageous an occurrence at the time than it would be today, and Burr became a fugitive as a result.

4 Theodore Roosevelt

1 Phrase quoted in Edmund Morris, *Theodore Rex*, New York: Random House, 2001, p. 24.
2 US censuses for the relevant years at www.1930census.com/1790_census.php (accessed 2 Apr 2009).
3 Zakaria provides such an analysis, and argues that the process was well under way by the turn of the century. F. Zakaria, *From Wealth to Power: The Unusual Origins of America's World Role*, Princeton, NJ: Princeton University Press, 1998.

186 *Notes*

4 'To John Davis Long', 19 Nov 1897, in Theodore Roosevelt, *Letters and Speeches*, New York: Library of America, 2004, ed. Louis Auchincloss, pp. 122–3. Hereafter referred to as *L&S*.
5 Despite enquiries, there has never been a conclusive explanation of the *Maine*'s fate. But Roosevelt summed up the prevailing attitude of the time when he wrote: "It may be impossible to ever settle definitively whether or not the Maine was destroyed through some treachery upon the part of the Spanish. The coincidence of her destruction with her being anchored off Havana by an accident such as has never before happened, is unpleasant enough to seriously increase the many existing difficulties between ourselves and Spain." 'To John Davis Long', 14 Jan 1898, in Roosevelt, *L&S*, p. 136.
6 Quoted in M. A. Jones, *The Limits of Liberty: American History 1607–1980*, Oxford: Oxford University Press, 1983, p. 401.
7 For a survey of the world in this period see W. R. Keylor, *The Twentieth Century World: An International History*, 4th edn, Oxford: Oxford University Press, 2001, pp. 3–39.
8 Biographical information originates mainly from Morris, *Theodore Rex* and *The Rise of Theodore Roosevelt*, New York, Random House, 2001. Direct Roosevelt quotations come chiefly from *L&S*, and Theodore Roosevelt, *The Man in the Arena: Selected Writings of Theodore Roosevelt*, New York: Forge, 2003, ed. Brian M. Thomsen, hereafter referred to as *MIA*. More specific references accompany each quotation. The TR literature, like the man himself, is often gripped by the colourful story of his life and by questions of individual psychology and image projection, e.g. N. Miller, *Theodore Roosevelt: A Life*, London: Harper Perennial, 1994, or, noting and attempting to buck this trend with a more critical approach, K. Dalton, *Theodore Roosevelt: A Strenuous Life*, New York: Knopf, 2002. Specifically on his foreign policy, H. K. Beale, *Theodore Roosevelt and the Rise of America to World Power*, Baltimore: Johns Hopkins Press, 1956, was the standard work, presenting arguments regarding his assertion of the Monroe Doctrine and imperialist mindset, with which this chapter largely agrees, and arguments concerning his balance-of-power attitude to broader policy, which it seeks to qualify somewhat. Taking a thematic approach and placing significant emphasis on morality and idealism as drivers is F. W. Marks III, *Velvet on Iron: the Diplomacy of Theodore Roosevelt*, Lincoln: University of Nebraska Press, 1979. A biographical account usefully aimed at comparison and contrast with Woodrow Wilson is J. M. Cooper, *The Warrior and the Priest: Woodrow Wilson and Theodore Roosevelt*, Cambridge, MA: Harvard University Press, 1985.
9 'To Rudyard Kipling', 5 Jan 1898, in Roosevelt, *L&S*, p. 130. See also 'Orders to the Asiatic Squadron', 25 Feb 1898, ibid., p. 141.
10 'To Leonard Wood', 17 April 1901, in Roosevelt, *L&S*, p. 225.
11 Quoted in Morris, *Rex*, p. 30.
12 Adams quoted in Morris, *Rex*, p. 307, p. 82.
13 Quotation from Cecil Spring-Rice. For discussion of TR's extraordinary range of activities see Morris, *Rex*, pp. 81, 108, 246, 376, 532.
14 'Citizenship in a Republic', Address at the Sorbonne, Paris, 23 Apr 1910, in Roosevelt, *L&S*, p. 783.
15 Quoted in Morris, *Rex*, p. 420–1.
16 Ibid., p. 8.
17 'The Strenuous Life', Speech to the Hamilton Club, Chicago, 10 Apr 1899 in Roosevelt, *L&S*, pp. 755–66, quotation pp. 756–7.
18 Ibid., pp. 765–6.
19 'National Duties', Speech at the Minnesota State Fair, St Paul, 2 Sep 1901, in Roosevelt, *L&S*, p. 768.

Notes 187

20 Inaugural Address, 4 Mar 1905. Available online at www.homeofheroes.com/presidents/inaugural/26_teddy.html (accessed 3 Apr 2009). Parker had declared in the campaign that "I protest against the feeling, now far too prevalent, that by reason of the commanding position we have assumed in the world we must take part in the disputes and broils of foreign countries." Quoted in Morris, *Rex*, p. 350.
21 The word "Chinafy" is from 'To Hugo Munsterberg', in Roosevelt, *L&S*, p. 693; Longer quotation from 'The Strenuous Life', ibid., p. 757.
22 Ibid., pp. 757–8.
23 '1815: The Battle of New Orleans', in Roosevelt, *MIA*, p. 85.
24 'To Munsterberg', in Roosevelt, *L&S* p. 763.
25 Quoted in Morris, *Rex*, p. 24.
26 See Morris, *Rex*, p. 229; 'To Henry Cabot Lodge', in Roosevelt, *L&S* p. 186.
27 'The Strenuous Life', in Roosevelt, *L&S*, p. 765.
28 'Washington's Forgotten Maxim', in Roosevelt, *MIA*, pp. 315–31. This thought was hardly unique to Washington, of course, but the attribution made sense in the context of American politics.
29 Ibid., p. 315.
30 Ibid., p. 316.
31 Ibid., p. 318.
32 'To Finley Peter Dunne', 23 Nov 1904, in Roosevelt, *L&S*, p. 366.
33 'To Cecil Spring-Rice', 21 Dec 1907, in Roosevelt, *L&S*, p. 544.
34 'Washington's Forgotten Maxim', in Roosevelt, *MIA* p. 318.
35 Ibid., p. 316.
36 'To Cecil Spring-Rice', 21 Dec 1907, in Roosevelt, *L&S*, p. 544.
37 'To Granville Stanley Hall', 29 Nov 1899, in Roosevelt, *L&S*, p. 183; 'To Elihu Root', 16 Feb 1904, ibid., p. 315; 'Washington's Forgotten Maxim', in Roosevelt, *MIA*, p. 329.
38 Ibid., p. 318.
39 'To Edwin Kirby Whitehead', 13 Jan 1899, in Roosevelt, *L&S*, p. 163.
40 Quoted in Morris, *Rex*, p. 215.
41 Ibid., p. 185. He may have had the German Kaiser in mind as he made this observation; Germany's manner in international dealings in this period was widely perceived as dangerously abrasive.
42 Ibid., p. 210.
43 Henry Kissinger, *Diplomacy*, New York: Touchstone, 1995, pp. 39, 39–40, 40, 41. Beale, *Theodore Roosevelt*, also gives credence to the idea of TR as a follower of balance-of-power thinking, albeit with the greater subtlety made possible by extended treatment of the topic.
44 Morris, *Rex*, pp. 272–306.
45 Quoted in Morris, *Rex*, p. 275.
46 See the relevant section below.
47 Morris, *Rex*, pp. 177–91.
48 He was aided by Britain's lack of enthusiasm for supporting the German position.
49 'To Theodore Roosevelt Jr', 16 Feb 1904, in Roosevelt, *L&S*, p. 313.
50 Quoted in Morris, *Rex*, p. 356.
51 For an account of the Portsmouth peace talks, see Morris, *Rex*, pp. 402–14.
52 Kissinger, pp. 41–2.
53 Quoted in Morris, *Rex*, p. 414.
54 Morris, *Rex*, pp. 432–3; 440–2. The 'Open Door' meant equal commercial rights for all powers; it was a term coined by Secretary of State John Hay to apply to China.
55 'To Cecil Spring-Rice', 13 Aug 1897, in Roosevelt, *L&S*, pp. 108–9.
56 Kissinger, pp. 39–40.

Notes

57 'The Roosevelt Corollary', speech to Congress, 6 Dec 1904, available online at www.historywiz.com/primarysources/rooseveltcorollary.htm (accessed 6 Apr 2009).
58 'Citizenship in a Republic', 23 Apr 1910, in Roosevelt, *L&S*, p. 797.
59 'The Roosevelt Corollary', op. cit.
60 Inaugural Address, op. cit.
61 'To Theodore Elijah Burton', 23 Feb 1904, in Roosevelt, *L&S*, p. 318.
62 'The Roosevelt Corollary', op. cit.
63 'To Kermit Roosevelt', 28 Aug 1915, in Roosevelt, *L&S*, p. 698.
64 See 'To Henry Cabot Lodge', 20 Feb 1917, in Roosevelt, *L&S*, pp. 7, 18–19.
65 Quoted in Morris, *Rex*, p. 528.
66 'The Roosevelt Corollary', op. cit.
67 Ibid.
68 'Quasi' because it was based on hegemonic domination but not formal territorial conquest.
69 'The Roosevelt Corollary', op. cit.
70 The unspoken fourth option of displacement or extermination of the natives – a strategy pursued with great success against the Native American Indians – was no longer considered morally or politically acceptable by this period.
71 On the imperialist ideology of Roosevelt and his supporters, both in the heat of 1898 and later, see Beale, pp. 14–80.
72 'National Duties', in Roosevelt, *L&S*, p. 775.
73 Ibid., p. 776.
74 Morris, *Rex*, p. 24.
75 Quoted in Morris, *Rex*, p. 110; 'To Rudyard Kipling', 1 Nov 1904, in Roosevelt, *L&S*, p. 357.
76 On Roosevelt's China policy see Beale, pp. 172–252.
77 Quoted in Morris, *Rex*, p. 456.
78 Ibid., p. 319.
79 'To Rafael Reyes' [President of Colombia], 20 Feb 1905, in Roosevelt, *L&S*, p. 384.
80 'To Theodore Roosevelt Jr', 10 Feb 1904, in Roosevelt, *L&S*, p. 312.
81 Quoted in Morris, *Rex*, p. 176.
82 'To Stanwood Menken', 10 Jan 1917, in Roosevelt, *L&S*, p. 713.
83 'To Arthur Hamilton Lee', 22 Aug 1914, in Roosevelt, *L&S*, p. 685. This is an odd criticism for Roosevelt to have levelled, of course, if we are to take him as a pure realist. What other motive should Germany have had regard for?
84 Quoted in E. H. Buehrig, *Woodrow Wilson and the Balance of Power*, Bloomington: Indiana University Press, 1955, p. 158.
85 Ibid., p. 160.
86 'To Hugo Munsterberg', 3 Oct 1914, in Roosevelt, *L&S*, pp. 691.
87 Quoted in Buehrig, p. 154.
88 Ibid., p. 152.
89 'To Cecil Spring-Rice', 3 Oct 1914, in Roosevelt, *L&S*, pp. 689–90.
90 'To Arthur Hamilton Lee', 19 Nov 1918, in Roosevelt, *L&S*, pp. 745–6.
91 Ibid.
92 'To Hugo Munsterberg', 3 Oct 1914, in Roosevelt, *L&S*, pp. 693.
93 For deeper discussion of TR's desired post-war order see S. Ricard, 'Anti-Wilsonian Internationalism: Theodore Roosevelt in the Kansas City Star', in D. Rossini (ed.), *From Theodore Roosevelt to FDR: Internationalism and Isolationism in American Foreign Policy*, Keele: Ryburn Publishing, Keele University Press, 1995.
94 'The Peace of Righteousness', in Roosevelt, *MIA*, p. 342.
95 Ibid., p. 341.
96 Speech in Pittsburgh, July 1917, quoted in Buehrig, p. 162.
97 'To Carl Schurz', 8 Sep 1905, in Roosevelt, *L&S*, pp. 405–6.
98 'To Andrew Carnegie', 6 Aug 1906, in Roosevelt, *L&S*, p. 489.

99 'To Carl Schurz', 8 Sep 1905, in Roosevelt, *L&S*, p. 405.
100 'The Roosevelt Corollary', op. cit.
101 'To Cleveland Dodge', 11 May 1918, in Roosevelt, *L&S* p. 736.
102 'To Henry Cabot Lodge', 24 Oct 1918, in Roosevelt, *L&S*, p. 744.
103 'To Cecil Spring-Rice', 13 Jun 1904, in Roosevelt, *L&S*, p. 334.
104 'To Hugo Munsterberg', 3 Oct 1914, in Roosevelt, *L&S*, p. 693.

5 Woodrow Wilson

1 Woodrow Wilson, Speech at Omaha, Nebraska, 8 Sep 1919, WP2 p. 42 (see note 3).
2 For detailed analysis of the First World War, its causes and context see D. Stevenson, *1914–1918: The History of the First World War*, London: Penguin, 2005.
3 My chief primary source in conveying Wilson's thinking on foreign affairs is Woodrow Wilson, *War and Peace: Presidential Messages, Addresses and Public Papers*, Volumes I and II, eds R. S. Baker and W. E. Dodd, Honolulu, Hawaii: University Press of the Pacific, 2002, reprinted from 1927, hereafter referenced as *WP1* and *WP2*. My chief secondary sources providing the basis for analysis of his biography, policies and thought are: L. E. Ambrosius, *Wilsonianism: Woodrow Wilson and his Legacy in American Foreign Relations*, New York: Palgrave Macmillan, 2002; Ambrosius, *Woodrow Wilson and the American Diplomatic Tradition: The Treaty Fight in Perspective*, Cambridge: Cambridge University Press, 1987; E. H. Buehrig, *Woodrow Wilson and the Balance of Power*, Bloomington: Indiana University Press, 1955; Buehrig (ed.), *Wilson's Foreign Policy in Perspective*, Bloomington: Indiana University Press, 1957; A. R. Pierce, *Woodrow Wilson and Harry Truman: Mission and Power in American Foreign Policy*, Westport, CT and London: Praeger, 2003; H. Notter, *The Origins of the Foreign Policy of Woodrow Wilson*, Baltimore: Johns Hopkins Press, 1937; A. S. Link, *The Higher Realism of Woodrow Wilson and Other Essays*, Nashville: Vanderbilt University Press, 1971; K. A. Clements, *The Presidency of Woodrow Wilson*, Lawrence, KS: University Press of Kansas, 1992; S. Bell, *Righteous Conquest: Woodrow Wilson and the Evolution of the New Diplomacy*, Port Washington, NY: National University Publications, Kennikat Press, 1972; A. Dawley, *Changing the World: American Progressives in War and Revolution*, Princeton and Oxford: Princeton University Press, 2003; R. W. Tucker, *Woodrow Wilson and the Great War: Reconsidering America's Neutrality, 1914–1917*, Charlottesville: University of Virginia Press, 2007. These authors, naturally, vary in their emphasis. Bell, especially, looks to economic matters, albeit with some attention to relevant ideological superstructure. Others such as Ambrosius and Dawley concentrate on social and political thought. Tucker emphasizes Wilson's regard for international law. There is also divergence between authors, such as Link, who on the whole sympathize with Wilson's ideas and a majority who see his goals as inherently unachievable and his approach to politics as fatally rigid. My own argument here does not set out to resolve many of these disputes. The purpose of this chapter is only to support the point that Wilson fashioned a new American internationalism that was predicated on the abolition of the balance-of-power system and the pursuit of liberal universalism. The wisdom of his fashioning such a worldview is an argument for another place.
4 Quoted in Notter, p. 217. This remark notwithstanding, Notter makes a convincing case that it would be misleading to classify the Wilson of 1913 as a complete foreign policy novice.
5 For comparison and contrast see J. M. Cooper, *The Warrior and the Priest: Woodrow Wilson and Theodore Roosevelt*, Cambridge, MA: Harvard University Press, 1985; and H. Kissinger, *Diplomacy*, New York: Touchstone, 1995, ch. 2, pp. 29–55.
6 Quoted in Notter, p. 132.
7 See Notter, pp. 122–32.

8. Link, *Higher Realism*, p. 129.
9. Wilson, Telegram to Madame Bressovsky, 18 Oct 1917, *WP1*, p. 107.
10. Wilson, Address to Congress, 2 April 1917, *WP1*, p. 11; see also Address at Mount Vernon, 4 July 1918, *WP1*, p. 234.
11. Dawley, pp. 76, 79. Ambrosius draws similar links between Progressivism and Wilsonianism.
12. Quoted in Notter, p. 75.
13. Wilson, Los Angeles, California, 20 Sep 1919, *WP2*, p. 323.
14. Clements, pp.xii–xiii.
15. Wilson, Washington, 5 June 1917, *WP1*, p. 56.
16. Quoted in Clements, p. 93.
17. Quoted in Notter, pp. 194, 197.
18. Ibid., pp. 234, 270, 543.
19. Bell, pp. 36, 38.
20. Wilson, Turin, 6 Jan 1919, *WP1*, p. 383.
21. Quoted in Clements, p. 93.
22. See Wilson, Des Moines, Iowa, 6 Sep 1919, *WP2*, p. 20; Wilson, Bismarck, N. Dakota, 10 Sep 1919, *WP2*, p. 93; Wilson, Opera House, Helena, Montana, 11 Sep 1919, *WP2*, p. 127.
23. Wilson, State Legislature, St Paul, Minnesota, 9 Sep 1919, *WP2*, p. 63.
24. Wilson, Armory, Tacoma, Washington, 13 Sep 1919, *WP2*, p. 176.
25. Quoted in Notter, p. 275.
26. Quoted in Notter, pp. 291–2.
27. Quoted in Notter, p. 419.
28. Bell, p. 98.
29. Quoted in Notter, p. 257.
30. Bell, p. 71.
31. Quoted in Notter, pp. 292, 293.
32. Bell, p. 190.
33. Bell, p. 8.
34. Occupation came to be 'the least of the evils in sight in this very perplexing situation', Wilson noted in the case of the Dominican Republic. Quoted in Notter, p. 536.
35. Quoted in Notter, pp. 458–9.
36. Clements, p. 106.
37. Quoted in Notter, p. 274.
38. Bell, p. 81.
39. Wilson, Address to a Party of Mexican Editors, White House, 7 June 1918, *WP1*, pp. 226, 227.
40. For discussion of the Pan-American Pact, see S. F. Bemis, 'Woodrow Wilson and Latin America', in Buehrig (ed.), *Wilson's Foreign Policy*.
41. Quoted in Notter, p. 224.
42. Quoted in Ambrosius, *Wilsonianism*, p. 37.
43. Wilson, Address to the Senate, 19 July 1919, *WP1*, pp. 550–1.
44. Quoted in Notter, p. 452.
45. Bell, p. 114.
46. See Wilson, Speech to Pan-American Peace Delegation, Paris, 27 May 1919, *WP1*, pp. 499, 499–500.
47. Wilson, Reno, Nevada, 22 Sep 1919, *WP2*, p. 331.
48. Quoted in Ambrosius, *Wilsonianism*, p. 41.
49. Quoted in Notter, pp. 371, 325.
50. Ibid., p. 328.
51. Quoted in Notter, p. 404.
52. Wilson, Second Inaugural Address, 5 Mar 1917, *WP1*, p. 2.

53 The years of neutrality are best discussed by Tucker, *Woodrow Wilson and the Great War*.
54 Wilson, Flag Day Address, 14 June 1917, *WP1*, p. 65.
55 Ibid., p. 66–7.
56 Wilson, Turin, 6 Jan 1919, *WP1*, p. 380.
57 'Presenting the Treaty for Ratification', Address to the Senate, 19 July 1919, WP1, p. 551.
58 Quoted in Pierce, p. 44. See Pierce's interpretation of the transition of national identity which Wilson was attempting, pp. 118–19.
59 Ibid.
60 Quoted in Ambrosius, *Wilsonianism*, p. 27.
61 Wilson, To Congress, 11 Feb 1918, *WP1*, p. 179, pp. 182–3.
62 Wilson, Labor Day Message, 2 Sep 1918, *WP1*, p. 247.
63 Quoted in Pierce, p. 34.
64 Quoted in Ambrosius, *Wilsonianism*, p. 45.
65 Pierce, p. 28.
66 Pierce, p. 36.
67 Wilson, London, 28 Dec 1918, *WP1*, pp. 342–3.
68 The League was in fact an Anglo-American brainchild, but by 1918–19 Wilson was the figure most associated with it.
69 Wilson, New York City, 27 Sep 1919, *WP1*, p. 258.
70 Wilson, New York City, 4 Mar 1919, *WP1*, p. 452.
71 Wilson, Los Angeles, California, 20 Sep 1919, *WP2*, p. 309.
72 See Ambrosius on the role of the ideal of the League in bridging tensions in Wilson's thinking. *Wilson*, p. 290.
73 Wilson, San Diego, California, 19 Sep 1919, *WP2* p. 294.
74 Wilson, Italian Parliament, 3 Jan 1919, *WP1*, pp. 363–4.
75 Ibid., p. 364.
76 Pierce, p. 18. Similar thinking led Wilson's most comprehensive and sympathetic biographer, Link, to laud him for a 'higher realism'.
77 Wilson, Minneapolis, Minnesota, 9 Sep 1919, *WP2*, pp. 67, 68, 69.
78 Wilson, St Louis, Missouri, 5 Sep 1919, *WP1*, pp. 622, 623.
79 Wilson, Manchester, 30 Dec 1918, *WP1*, p. 353.
80 Wilson, Paris, 25 Jan 1919, *WP1*, p. 397.
81 See Ambrosius, *Wilson*, pp. 9, 50, 123–4, 244, 250; Pierce, p. 64.
82 Ibid., pp. 233, 292.
83 Wilson, New York City, 27 Sep 1919, *WP1*, p. 257.
84 Ibid., p. 259. See also Wilson, To Congress, 11 Nov 1918, *WP1*, p. 300.
85 Wilson, Paris, 26 June 1919, *WP1*, p. 521.
86 Quoted in Pierce, p. 101.
87 Wilson, New York City, 4 Mar 1919, *WP1*, pp. 452, 450.
88 Wilson, San Francisco, California, 17 Sep 1919, *WP2*, p. 234.
89 Wilson, To Congress, 2 April 1917, *WP1*, p. 11.
90 Ibid., p. 13.
91 Ibid., p. 14.
92 Wilson, Flag Day Address, 14 June 1917, *WP1*, p. 66.
93 Wilson, Boston, 24 Feb 1919, *WP1*, p. 439.
94 For a critique of this and of Wilson's general tendency to conflate US interests with those of others, see Ambrosius, *Wilson*, p. 51 and *Wilsonianism*, p. 33.
95 Lansing, 'Three Cablegrams on the Adriatic Question', in Wilson, *WP2*, p. 465.
96 Pierce notes convincingly that: 'There is a premonition of the Cold War in Wilsonian tactics. The idea that the domestic political structure, in this case the German autocracy, is implicated when there is external aggression would recur in the 1940s.' Pierce, p. 55.

192 Notes

97 Wilson, To Congress, 2 Apr 1917, *WP1*, p. 12.
98 Quoted in Notter, p. 569.
99 Wilson, Buffalo, NY, 12 Nov 1917, *WP1*, p. 119.
100 Quoted in Notter, pp. 581, 460.
101 Wilson, Labor Day Message to the American People, 2 Sep 1918, *WP1*, p. 247.
102 Wilson, To Socialist Delegation, Paris, 16 Dec 1918, *WP1*, p. 326; University of Paris, 21 Dec 1918, *WP1*, p. 329.
103 Wilson, Columbus, Ohio, 4 Sep 1919, WP1, pp. 595–96.
104 Wilson, Kansas City, Missouri, 6 Sep 1919, *WP2*, p. 5.
105 Wilson, Minneapolis, Minnesota, 9 Sep 1919, *WP2*, p. 70.
106 Wilson, Auditorium, St Paul, Minnesota, 9 Sep 1919, *WP2*, p. 84.
107 Wilson, Announcement of Signing of Armistice, 11 Nov 1918, *WP1*, p. 293.
108 Quoted in Pierce, p. 42.
109 Wilson, Reno, Nevada, 22 Sep 1919, *WP2*, pp. 328, 329.
110 Wilson, Sioux Falls, S. Dakota, 8 Sep 1919, *WP2*, p. 44.
111 Wilson, Address to Soldiers and Sailors on the After Hatch of the USS 'George Washington', 4 July 1919, *WP1*, p. 531.
112 Wilson, Coliseum, St Louis, Missouri, 5 Sep 1919, *WP1*, p. 640.
113 Wilson, Cheyenne, Wyoming, 24 Sep 1919, *WP2*, p. 374.
114 Wilson, To Fifteen Pro-League Republicans, 27 Oct 1920, *WP2*, p. 510.
115 Critics of Wilson in the literature have picked up on his vulnerability to the charge of unspoken but intense nationalism. See Bell, p. 41; Dawley, p. 24.
116 Wilson, St Louis, Missouri, 5 Sep 1919, *WP1*, p. 621.
117 Wilson, Des Moines, Iowa, 6 Sep 1919, *WP2*, p. 26; Sioux Falls, S. Dakota, 8 Sep 1919, *WP2*, p. 52.
118 Ambrosius, *Wilson*, p. 57; see also p. 79.
119 Ibid., p. 57.
120 Wilson, Billings, Montana, 11 Sep 1919, *WP2*, pp. 113–14.
121 Wilson, Couer D'Alene, Idaho, 12 Sep 1919, *WP2*, p. 147.
122 Ibid., p. 157.
123 Wilson, Des Moines, Iowa, 6 Sep 1919, *WP2*, pp. 18–19.
124 Wilson, Reno, Nevada, 22 Sep 1919, *WP2*, p. 344.
125 Wilson, St Paul, Minnesota, 9 Sep 1919, *WP2*, p. 89.
126 Wilson, Senate, 19 July 1919, *WP1*, pp. 551–2.
127 Wilson, Baltimore, Maryland, 6 Apr 1918, *WP1*, p. 202.
128 Wilson, Buckingham Palace, 27 Dec 1918, *WP1*, p. 338.
129 Wilson, Carlisle, 29 Dec 1918, *WP1*, pp. 347–8.
130 Wilson, Peace Conference, 14 Feb 1919, *WP1*, pp. 425–6.
131 Wilson, Columbus, Ohio, 4 Sep 1919, *WP1*, p. 597; Sioux Falls, S. Dakota, 8 Sep 1919, *WP2*, p. 54; Richmond, Indiana, 4 Sep 1919, *WP1*, p. 612.
132 Wilson, Salt Lake City, Utah, 23 Sep 1919, *WP2*, p. 363.
133 Quoted in Ambrosius, *Wilsonianism*, p. 58.
134 Wilson, Sioux Falls, S. Dakota, 8 Sep 1919, *WP2*, pp. 54–5.
135 Wilson, Paris, 3 Feb 1919, *WP1*, p. 408; Sioux Falls, S. Dakota, 8 Sep 1919, *WP2*, p. 51.
136 See his use of this argument at Bismarck Hill, N. Dakota, 10 Sep 1919, *WP2*, p. 98; Spokane, Washington, 12 Sep 1919, *WP2*, p. 155; Seattle, Washington, 13 Sep 1919, *WP2*, p. 191; Portland, Oregon, 15 Sep 1919, *WP2*, pp. 203–4; San Diego, California, 19 Sep 1919, *WP2*, pp. 282–3; Pueblo, Colorado, 25 Sep 1919, *WP2*, pp. 410–11.
137 Wilson, To Foreign Relations Committee, 19 Aug 1919, *WP1*, p. 579.
138 Wilson, Sioux Falls, S. Dakota, 8 Sep 1919, *WP2*, p. 47.
139 Wilson, Omaha, Nebraska, 8 Sep 1919, *WP2*, p. 42.
140 Wilson, San Francisco, California, 17 Sep 1919, *WP2*, p. 235.

141 Quoted in Ambrosius, *Wilson*, p. 150.
142 Wilson, Message for Jackson Day Celebration, 8 Jan 1920, *WP2*, p. 455.
143 Quoted in Clements p. 223.

6 The Truman administration

1 NSC-68, p. 11. See note 71.
2 For a detailed account of FDR's creeping insertion of the US into the conflict through verbal and material support for the Allies, see Conrad Black, *Franklin Delano Roosevelt*, London: Weidenfeld and Nicolson, 2003, pp. 455–680.
3 D. J. Macdonald, 'Formal Ideologies in the Cold War: Toward a Framework for Empirical Analysis', in O. A. Westad, *Reviewing the Cold War: Approaches, Interpretations, Theory*, London: Frank Cass, 2000, pp. 180–204. Quotation p. 182.
4 The best-known 'isolationist' of the immediate post-war period was Senator Robert Taft of Ohio, who espoused historically familiar concerns regarding overseas commitments and their corresponding requirement for a national security state antithetical to constitutional liberty at home. See J. Moser, 'Principles Without Program: Senator Robert A. Taft and American Foreign Policy', *Ohio History*, 108, 1999, pp. 177–92.
5 For a general survey of the historiography of the Cold War, see 'America and the Cold War: Containment of Hegemony?' in F. G. Couvares et al., *Interpretations of American History: Patterns and Perspectives*, 7th edn, New York: Free Press, 2000, Chapter 8. See also M. P. Leffler and D. S. Painter, *Origins of the Cold War*, New York: Routledge, 1994; Westad, *Reviewing the Cold War*. The founding division in the field is that between 'orthodoxy', which chiefly blames the Soviet Union for the conflict, and 'revisionism', which points to the political and economic ambitions of the United States as a cause. This initial split was followed by increasingly subtle and sophisticated divergences between post-revisionism, neo-orthodoxy and neo-revisionism. This second stage of debate has been more sympathetic on all sides to the role of ideology in the construction of US perceptions of national interest, even as authors have continued to disagree on the extent to which this allows 'blame' for the Cold War's outbreak to be distributed. For the 'orthodox' argument, see George Kennan's 'X' article and NSC-68, discussed in more detail later. For revisionism see W. Lippmann, *The Cold War: A Study in US Foreign Policy*, New York: Harper & Row, 1972, 1st edn 1947. Later, more radical, revisionist critiques include most notably W. A. Williams, *The Tragedy of American Diplomacy*, New York: Dell, 1972; W. LaFeber, *America, Russia, and the Cold War, 1945–2000*, 9th edn, London: McGraw-Hill, 2002. Most radical of all is the revisionism of the 'New Left', for which see G. Kolko, *The Politics of War: Allied Diplomacy and the World Crisis of 1943–45*, London: Weidenfeld & Nicolson, 1969; N. Chomsky, *Deterring Democracy*, London: Vintage, 1992. Post-revisionism and neo-orthodoxy are both represented best – at different stages of his career – by Gaddis; see J. L. Gaddis, 'The Emerging Post-Revisionist Thesis on the Origins of the Cold War', *Diplomatic History*, 7, Summer 1983, pp. 171–90; *The United States and the Origins of the Cold War*, New York: Columbia University Press, 1972; *Strategies of Containment: a Critical Appraisal of Postwar American National Security Policy*, Oxford: Oxford University Press, 1982; *We Now Know: Rethinking Cold War History*, Oxford: Oxford University Press, 1997. The best representative of subtle neo-revisionism is M. P. Leffler, 'The American Conception of National Security and the Beginnings of the Cold War', *American Historical Review*, 89, Apr 1984, pp. 346–81. This chapter's argument is broadly sympathetic to the neo-revisionist approach, which places emphasis on the importance of America's ideological definition of its interests and the threats facing them, but does not seek particularly to condemn

the US as the 'guilty party' in the Cold War's emergence, as much early revisionism does seek to do.
6 David McCullough, *Truman*, New York: Simon & Schuster, 1992, pp. 339, 355.
7 For an example of a standard survey account emphasizing Truman's inexperience and bluntness, see W. H. Chafe, *The Unfinished Journey: America Since World War II*, Oxford: Oxford University Press, 1999, pp. 54–78.
8 My three chief sources for insight into US policy under FDR are: T. Hoopes and D. Brinkley, *FDR and the Creation of the UN*, New Haven: Yale University Press, 1997; Gaddis, *United States and the Origins of the Cold War*; Black, *Franklin Delano Roosevelt*.
9 A. R. Pierce, *Woodrow Wilson and Harry Truman: Mission and Power in American Foreign Policy*, Westport, CT and London: Praeger, 2003, p. 153.
10 See Gaddis, *United States*, pp. 157–73.
11 Quoted in Hoopes and Brinkley, pp. 74, 64.
12 Ibid., pp. 46, 28. This latter concern cannot have been eased by the famous (or infamous) meeting of Churchill and Stalin where explicit 'percentages' of Soviet and US/UK influence in the states of liberated Europe were discussed and agreed. See p. 171.
13 Gaddis, *United States*, pp. 30–1.
14 Quoted in Pierce, p. 127. Willkie was the Republican presidential candidate of 1940, and had gone on to write a popular book promoting internationalism under the title 'One World'.
15 Ibid., pp. 127, 123.
16 Pierce, p. 129.
17 Quoted in McCullough, p. 445.
18 In what follows, my chief sources are the major histories of the early Cold War cited earlier, supplemented by primary and secondary sources specifically focused on the Truman administration. Most notable among the latter are: McCullough, *Truman*; Pierce, *Woodrow Wilson and Harry Truman*; R. L. Beisner, *Dean Acheson: A Life in the Cold War* Oxford: Oxford University Press, 2006; H. S. Truman, *Memoirs, Volume One: Year of Decisions*, Great Britain: Hodder & Stoughton, 1955; *Memoirs, Volume Two: 1946–52 Years of Trial and Hope*, New York: Smithmark, 1996; D. Acheson, *Present at the Creation: My Years in the State Department*, New York: W.W. Norton & Co., 1987. Also of importance were the papers available at the Truman library. Available online at www.trumanlibrary.org/photos/av-photo.htm (accessed 7 Apr 2009), especially the sub-collection of documents entitled 'Ideological Foundations of the Cold War', and public papers available via www.presidency.ucsb.edu/ws (accessed 7 Apr 2009). Specific sources are cited for specific quotations throughout the text.
19 'Rooseveltianism' referring here to Theodore, not Franklin.
20 Pierce, p. 150.
21 Address to Congress, 12 Mar 1947. Available online at http://avalon.law.yale.edu/20th_century/trudoc.asp (accessed 7 Apr 2009).
22 Ibid. The same principle was advanced in parallel by Secretary of State George Marshall in announcing the 'Marshall Plan' of economic aid to Europe. 'Its purpose', he said of the plan, 'should be the revival of a working economy in the world so as to permit the emergence of political and social conditions in which free institutions can exist.' Marshall Plan Speech, 5 June 1947. Available online at www.nato.int/docu/speech/1947/s470605a_e.htm (accessed 7 Apr 2009).
23 Address to Congress, 12 Mar 1947. Available online at http://avalon.law.yale.edu/20th_century/trudoc.asp (accessed 7 Apr 2009).
24 Radio Address to the American People on the Special Session of Congress, 24 Oct 1947. Available online at www.presidency.ucsb.edu/ws/index.php?pid=12779 (accessed 7 Apr 2009).
25 Quoted in McCullough, p. 628.

Notes 195

26 Address in Chicago Before the Imperial Council Session of the Shrine of North America, 19 July 1949. Available online at www.presidency.ucsb.edu/ws/index.php?pid=13248 (accessed 7 Apr 2009).
27 Ibid.
28 Farewell Address, 15 Jan 1953. Available online at www.trumanlibrary.org/calendar/viewpapers.php?pid=2059 (accessed 7 Apr 2009).
29 Quoted in McCullough, p. 472.
30 Quoted in Pierce, p. 131.
31 Pierce, p. 156.
32 27 Oct 1945, quoted in Pierce, p. 166.
33 Address to Congress, 12 Mar 1947. Available online at http://avalon.law.yale.edu/20th_century/trudoc.asp (accessed 7 Apr 2009).
34 Inaugural Address, 20 Jan 1949. Available online at www.trumanlibrary.org/whistlestop/50yr_archive/inagural20jan1949.htm (accessed 7 Apr 2009).
35 Pierce, p. 135.
36 Address on Foreign Policy at the George Washington National Masonic Memorial, 22 Feb 1950. Available online at www.presidency.ucsb.edu/ws/print.php?pid=13713 (accessed 7 Apr 2009).
37 Annual Message to the Congress on the State of the Union, 9 Jan 1952. Available online at www.presidency.ucsb.edu/ws/print.php?pid=14418 (accessed 7 Apr 2009).
38 Quoted in McCullough, p. 628.
39 Address Broadcast from the Voice of America floating Radio Transmitter Courier, 4 Mar 1952. Available online at www.presidency.ucsb.edu/ws/index.php?pid=14423 (accessed 7 Apr 2009).
40 Quoted in McCullough, p. 138.
41 Truman, *Memoirs Vol. 2*, p. 102.
42 President Truman's Message To Congress Recommending Army-Navy Merger, 19 Dec 1945. Available online at www.ibiblio.org/pha/policy/post-war/451219a.html (accessed 7 Apr 2009).
43 Address in Chicago on Army Day, 6 Apr 1946. Available online at www.presidency.ucsb.edu/ws/index.php?pid=12625 (accessed 7 Apr 2009).
44 Quoted in McCullough, p. 474.
45 Ibid., p. 480.
46 Quoted in McCullough, p. 517.
47 Telegram, George Kennan to George Marshall ['Long Telegram'], 22 Feb 1946. Available online at www.trumanlibrary.org/whistlestop/study_collections/coldwar/documents/index.php?documentdate=1946-02-22&documentid=6-6&studycollectionid=&pagenumber=1 (accessed 7 Apr 2009).
48 'X' [George Kennan], 'The Sources of Soviet Conduct', *Foreign Affairs*, 25:1/4, 1946/47 (hereafter 'Sources'), pp. 566–82.
49 See George F. Kennan, *American Diplomacy*, expanded edition, Chicago: University of Chicago Press, 1984; *Memoirs 1925–1950*, (New York: Pantheon, 1983).
50 Kennan, 'Long Telegram' (hereafter 'LT'), p. 1.
51 Kennan, 'LT', p. 4.
52 Kennan, 'Sources', p. 569.
53 Kennan, 'LT', pp. 5–6.
54 Kennan, 'LT', p. 6.
55 Kennan, 'Sources', p. 569.
56 Kennan, 'LT' p. 6.
57 Kennan, 'LT', pp. 6, 7.
58 Kennan, 'Sources', p. 570.
59 Kennan, 'LT', p. 8.
60 Kennan, 'Sources', p. 573.
61 Kennan, 'LT', p. 15.

62 Kennan, 'Sources', p. 574.
63 Kennan, 'Sources', pp. 576, 575.
64 Kennan, 'Sources', p. 581.
65 Kennan, 'LT', pp. 15–16.
66 Kennan, 'LT', p. 4.
67 Kennan, 'Sources', p. 582.
68 Kennan, 'LT' p. 17.
69 Kennan, 'Sources', p. 582.
70 Report, 'American Relations with the Soviet Union' by Clark Clifford, 24 Sep 1946, hereafter 'CER'. Available online at www.trumanlibrary.org/whistlestop/study_collections/coldwar/documents/pdf/4–1.pdf#zoom=100 (accessed 7 Apr 2009).
71 'A Report to the National Security Council – NSC 68', 12 Apr 1950, hereafter NSC-68. Available online at www.trumanlibrary.org/whistlestop/study_collections/coldwar/documents/pdf/10–11.pdf#zoom=100 (accessed 7 Apr 2009).
72 McCullough, pp. 545, 772.
73 Acheson, *Present*, pp. 374, 375.
74 CER, p. 3.
75 Ibid., p. 4.
76 Ibid., p. 8.
77 Ibid., pp. 16, 18, 21.
78 Ibid., p. 27.
79 Ibid., p. 10.
80 Ibid., p. 28.
81 Ibid., p. 4.
82 Ibid., p. 59.
83 Ibid., p. 71.
84 Ibid., p. 79.
85 Ibid., p. 72.
86 Ibid., p. 73.
87 Ibid., p. 75.
88 Ibid., pp. 74, 75.
89 Ibid., p. 4.
90 Ibid., p. 5.
91 Ibid., p. 6.
92 Ibid., p. 8.
93 Ibid., p. 7.
94 Ibid., p. 8.
95 Ibid., pp. 52, 53.
96 The leftist critic Noam Chomsky sarcastically describes the document as possessing 'the child-like simplicity of a fairy tale'. Chomsky, *Deterring Democracy*, p. 10.
97 NSC-68, p. 10.
98 Ibid., p. 21.
99 Ibid., p. 9.
100 Ibid., p. 10.
101 Ibid., p. 12.
102 Ibid., p. 64.
103 Ibid., p. 56.
104 Ibid., p. 12.
105 Ibid., p. 12.
106 Ibid., p. 10.
107 Ibid., p. 24.
108 Ibid., pp. 15, 16.

109 Ibid., p. 24. For the full checklist of the report's recommendations, involving increased spending in a range of areas relating to the military, intelligence and foreign aid, see pp. 56–7.
110 Ibid., p. 31.
111 Ibid., p. 49.
112 Ibid., p. 36.
113 Ibid., p. 17.
114 Quoted in McCullough, p. 549.

7 The George W. Bush administration

1 I. H. Daalder and J. M. Lindsay, *America Unbound: The Bush Revolution in Foreign Policy*, Washington, DC: Brookings Institution Press, 2003. See also J. Mann, *Rise of the Vulcans: The History of Bush's War Cabinet*, London: Penguin, 2004, for detailed discussion of the views held by those who came into office with Bush.
2 For discussion of relative American power and reach, see A. Bacevich, *American Empire: The Realities and Consequences of US Diplomacy*, Cambridge, MA: Harvard University Press, 2002.
3 See J. S. Nye, *The Paradox of American Power: Why the World's Only Superpower Can't Go It Alone*, New York: Oxford University Press, 2002.
4 White House, 'The National Security Strategy of the United States of America' (hereafter cited as 'NSS'), Sep 2002. Available online at http://georgewbush-whitehouse.archives.gov/nsc/nss.pdf (accessed 9 Apr 2009).
5 NSS, p. 15.
6 Its prominence in media coverage was in no small part thanks to unnamed administration sources briefing in advance on the adoption of pre-emption as policy in the NSS. This ensured that the press went looking for it when the document itself was published. See T. E. Ricks and V. Loeb, 'Bush Developing Military Policy of Striking First: New Doctrine Addresses Terrorism', *Washington Post*, 10 Jun 2002.
7 C. Rice, 'A Balance of Power that Favors Freedom', 2002 Wriston Lecture, delivered to the Manhattan Institute, New York City, 1 Oct 2002. Available online at www.manhattan-institute.org/html/wl2002.htm (accessed 9 Apr 2009). C. L. Powell, 'A Strategy of Partnerships', *Foreign Affairs*, 83:1, Jan/Feb 2004.
8 C. Rice, 'Promoting the National Interest', *Foreign Affairs*, 79:1, Jan/Feb 2000, pp. 45–62.
9 These themes correspond roughly with sections V, II and VIII of the document, but each runs through the whole document.
10 Some of the secondary literature consulted on the Bush administration in the course of formulating the arguments made below is cited below in the section 'Critiques of Bush'. In addition, the author engaged in extensive reading of the speeches and public pronouncements of President Bush, as well as certain key statements and writings on the part of Powell and Rice. All specific quotations are referenced in detail, though many communicate ideas for which multiple further citations could be produced if space were unlimited. For context on the decision making and ideas of the administration, useful texts include Daalder and Lindsay, *America Unbound*; Mann, *Rise of the Vulcans*; B. Woodward, *Bush at War*, London: Simon & Schuster, 2003; *Plan of Attack*, London: Simon & Schuster 2004; *State of Denial*, London: Simon & Schuster 2006; D. Frum, *The Right Man: An Inside Account of the Surprise Presidency of George W. Bush*, New York: Weidenfeld and Nicolson, 2003; T. E. Ricks, *Fiasco: The American Military Adventure in Iraq*, London: Allen Lane, 2006; R. Draper, *Dead Certain: The Presidency of George W. Bush*, London: Simon & Schuster, 2007.

198 *Notes*

11 NSS, foreword.
12 G. Bush, Inaugural address. 20 Jan 2001. Available online at http://georgewbush-whitehouse.archives.gov/news/inaugural-address.html (accessed 9 Apr 2009).
13 Bush, State of the Union, 29 Jan 2002. Available online at http://georgewbush-whitehouse.archives.gov/news/releases/2002/01/20020129-11.html (accessed 9 Apr 2009).
14 Bush, 'President Bush Calls for New Palestinian Leadership', 24 Jun 2002. Available online at http://georgewbush-whitehouse.archives.gov/news/releases/2002/06/20020624-3.html (accessed 9 Apr 2009).
15 Bush, State of the Union, 28 Jan 2003. Available online at http://georgewbush-whitehouse.archives.gov/news/releases/2003/01/20030128-19.html (accessed 9 Apr 2009).
16 Bush, Graduation Speech at West Point, 1 Jun 2002. Available online at http://georgewbush-whitehouse.archives.gov/news/releases/2002/06/20020601-3.html (accessed 9 Apr 2009).
17 Bush, 'Operation Iraqi Freedom', Radio Address, 12 Apr 2003. Available online at http://georgewbush-whitehouse.archives.gov/news/releases/2003/04/20030412.html (accessed 9 Apr 2009).
18 Bush, 'President Discusses the Future of Iraq', 28 Apr 2003. Available online at http://georgewbush-whitehouse.archives.gov/news/releases/2003/04/20030428-3.html (accessed 9 Apr 2009).
19 Bush, 'President Bush Welcomes Canadian Prime Minister Martin to White House', 30 Apr 2004. Available online at http://georgewbush-whitehouse.archives.gov/news/releases/2004/04/20040430-32.html (accessed 9 Apr 2009).
20 Bush, 'President Bush Discusses Freedom in Iraq and Middle East', 6 Nov 2003. Available online at http://georgewbush-whitehouse.archives.gov/news/releases/2003/11/20031106-2.html (accessed 9 Apr 2009).
21 Bush, Second Inaugural Address, 20 Jan 2005. Available online at http://georgewbush-whitehouse.archives.gov/news/releases/2005/01/20050120-21.html (accessed 9 Apr 2009).
22 Bush 'Freedom in Iraq', op. cit.
23 Bush, State of the Union 2002, op. cit.
24 Bush, 'West Point', op. cit.
25 Bush, 'President Bush Outlines Iraq Threat', 7 Oct 2002. Available online at http://georgewbush-whitehouse.archives.gov/news/releases/2002/10/20021007-8.html (accessed 9 Apr 2009).
26 Bush, 'President Discusses the Future of Iraq', 26 Feb 2003. Available online at http://georgewbush-whitehouse.archives.gov/news/releases/2003/02/20030226-11.html (accessed 9 Apr 2009).
27 Ibid.
28 Bush, 'President Bush Outlines Progress in Operation Iraqi Freedom', 16 Apr 2003. Available online at http://georgewbush-whitehouse.archives.gov/news/releases/2003/04/20030416-19.html (accessed 9 Apr 2009).
29 Bush, 'President Bush Announces Major Combat Operations in Iraq Have Ended', 1 May 2003. Available online at http://georgewbush-whitehouse.archives.gov/news/releases/2003/05/20030501-15.html (accessed 9 Apr 2009).
30 Rice, At Los AngelesTown Hall, 12 Jun 2003. Available online at http://georgewbush-whitehouse.archives.gov/news/releases/2003/06/20030612-12.html (accessed 9 Apr 2009).
31 Bush, 'Freedom in Iraq', op. cit.
32 Bush, 'President Bush Discusses Iraq Policy at Whitehall Palace in London', 19 Nov 2003. Available online at http://georgewbush-whitehouse.archives.gov/news/releases/2003/11/20031119-1.html (accessed 9 Apr 2009).

Notes 199

33 Bush, 'President Speaks to the American Israel Public Affairs Committee', 18 May 2004. Available online at http://georgewbush-whitehouse.archives.gov/news/releases/2004/05/20040518-1.html (accessed 9 Apr 2009).
34 Bush, 'Second Inaugural', op. cit.
35 Ibid.
36 Rice, 'The Promise of Democratic Peace: Why Promoting Freedom Is the Only Realistic Path to Security', *Washington Post*, 11 Dec 2005, p. B07.
37 See esp. section VIII, pp. 25–8.
38 Rice, 'A Balance of Power', p. 3; Powell, 'A Strategy of Partnerships'. Of pre-emption, Powell declared: 'As to being central, it isn't. The discussion of pre-emption in the NSS takes up just two sentences in one of the document's eight sections.'
39 Rice, p. 5.
40 Powell, 'A Strategy of Partnerships'.
41 Bush, 'West Point', op. cit.
42 Ibid.
43 Ibid.
44 Woodward, *Bush at War*, p. 327.
45 Bush, 'Remarks by the President', 12 Sep 2001. Available online at http://georgewbush-whitehouse.archives.gov/news/releases/2001/09/20010912-14.html (accessed 9 Apr 2009).
46 Bush, 'Address to a Joint Session of Congress and the American People', 20 Sep 2001. Available online at http://georgewbush-whitehouse.archives.gov/news/releases/2001/09/20010920-28.html (accessed 9 Apr 2009). An exhaustive list of examples of Bush's use of this sort of terminology would be of inordinate length. Some other examples may be found in: Bush, 'Address to the Nation', 8 Nov 2001. Available online at http://georgewbush-whitehouse.archives.gov/news/releases/2001/11/20011108-13.html (accessed 9 Apr 2009), 'Remarks on The USS Enterprise', 7 Dec 2001. Available online at http://georgewbush-whitehouse.archives.gov/news/releases/2001/12/20011207.html (accessed 9 Apr 2009).
47 Rice, 'Town Hall, LA', op. cit.
48 Bush, 'President, House Leadership Agree on Iraq Resolution', 2 Oct 2002. Available online at http://georgewbush-whitehouse.archives.gov/news/releases/2002/10/20021002-7.html (accessed 9 Apr 2009).
49 Bush, 'President Bush Outlines Iraqi Threat', 7 Oct 2002. Available online at http://georgewbush-whitehouse.archives.gov/news/releases/2002/10/20021007-8.html (accessed 9 Apr 2009).
50 Ibid.
51 Bush, 'Operation Iraqi Freedom', Radio Address, 12 Apr 2003. Available online at http://georgewbush-whitehouse.archives.gov/news/releases/2003/04/20030412.html (accessed 9 Apr 2009).
52 Rice, 'Town Hall, LA', op. cit.
53 Bush, 'Second Inaugural', op. cit.
54 Ibid.
55 Bush, 'To Congress and the American People', op. cit.
56 Bush, 'President Bush Speaks to United Nations', 10 Nov 2001. Available online at http://georgewbush-whitehouse.archives.gov/news/releases/2001/11/20011110-13.html (accessed 9 Apr 2009).
57 Bush, 'Remarks on USS Enterprise', op. cit.
58 Bush, 'President Bush Discusses Freedom in Iraq and Middle East', 6 Nov 2003. Available online at http://georgewbush-whitehouse.archives.gov/news/releases/2003/11/20031106-2.html (accessed 19 Jun 2008).
59 Ibid.
60 Bush, 'Second Inaugural', op. cit.

61 Bush, 'Inaugural Address', op. cit.
62 Rice, 'A Balance of Power'.
63 Department of Defense, Quadrennial Defense Review Reports. Available online at www.defenselink.mil/pubs/pdfs/qdr2001.pdf (2001); www.defenselink.mil/pubs/pdfs/QDR20060203.pdf (2006) (accessed 9 Apr 2009). It should be noted in the spirit of bipartisanship that planning for unchallengeable American military superiority was likewise a cornerstone of the Clinton administration's thinking, and defence spending had actually begun to climb again during Clinton's second term, after a post-Cold War dip. Figures from Center for Defense Information. Available online at www.infoplease.com/ipa/A0904490.html (accessed 9 Apr 2009).
64 Bush, At West Point, op. cit.
65 J. J. Mearsheimer and S. M. Walt, 'An Unnecessary War', *Foreign Policy*, Jan/Feb 2003, 134, pp. 51–61. A question mark hovered over structural realists' anti-war policy advocacy as to where the room for choice existed, given its usually mechanistic account of international behaviour.
66 D. K. Simes, 'End the Crusade', *The National Interest*, 87, Jan/Feb 2007, pp. 4–11.
67 For realist analyses of and responses to the policy dilemmas arising from the Bush administration's problems, see A. Lieven and J. Hulsman, *Ethical Realism*, New York: Pantheon, 2007; A. Etzioni, *Security First*, New Haven and London: Yale University Press, 2007; C. Dueck, *Reluctant Crusaders*, p. 3; C. Layne, *The Peace of Illusions: American Grand Strategy from 1940 to the Present*, Ithaca and London: Cornell University Press, 2006. For contemporary analysis of Bush's actions with a generally realist standpoint, see R. K. Betts 'The Political Support System for American Primacy', *International Affairs*, Jan 2005, 81:1, pp. 1–14; 'Suicide From Fear of Death?', *Foreign Affairs*, Jan/Feb 2003, 82:1, pp. 34–43; 'Striking First: a History of Thankfully Lost Opportunities', *Ethics and International Affairs*, 17:1, 2003, pp. 17–24.
68 F. Zakaria, 'The Arrogant Empire', *Newsweek*, 24 Mar 2003, US edition, p. 18.
69 The so-called 'Baker Report' of 2006, widely regarded as a realist push-back against Bush's policy, implicitly made this criticism, calling for a new engagement with such powers as Iran and Syria in order to rescue the strategic situation in Iraq. Report of the Iraq Study Group. Available online at www.usip.org/isg/iraq_study_group_report/report/1206/iraq_study_group_report.pdf (accessed 9 Apr 2009).
70 See J. Monten, 'The Roots of the Bush Doctrine: Power, Nationalism and Democracy Promotion in US Strategy', *International Security*, 29:4, Spring 2005, pp. 112–56; R. Jervis, 'Understanding the Bush Doctrine', *Political Science Quarterly*, 118:3, 2003, pp. 365–88.
71 For examples of liberal criticism of Bush along these lines, see: S. Hoffmann, 'America Goes Backward', *New York Review of Books*, 50:10, 12 June 2003; T. G. Ash, 'The War After War With Iraq', *Washington Post*, 20 Mar 2003; J. L. Gaddis, 'A Grand Strategy of Transformation', *Foreign Policy*, Nov/Dec 2002; R. W. Tucker and D. C. Hendrickson, 'The Sources of American Legitimacy', *Foreign Affairs*, Nov/Dec 2004, 83:6, pp. 18–32; G. Soros, *The Bubble of American Supremacy: Correcting the misuse of American power*, London: Weidenfeld and Nicolson, 2004; M. Hirsh, *At War with Ourselves: Why America is squandering its chance to build a better world*, Oxford: Oxford University Press, 2003; M. K. Albright, 'Bombs, Bridges, or Bluster', *Foreign Affairs*, Sep/Oct 2003; J. P. Rubin, 'Stumbling into War', *Foreign Affairs*, Sep/Oct 2003, 82:5, pp. 46–66.
72 A. Bacevich, *American Empire: The Realities & Consequences of US Diplomacy*, Cambridge, MA: Harvard University Press; 2002; D. K. Simes, 'America's Imperial Dilemma', *Foreign Affairs*, Nov/Dec 2003, 82:6, pp. 91–102; C. Prestowitz, *Rogue Nation: American Unilateralism and the Failure of Good Intentions*, New York: Basic, 2003. Robert Jervis has written about the matter from a theoretically universalizing perspective, attributing American imperial impulses to the

'mission creep' which affects all nations granted unrivalled power: R. Jervis, 'The Compulsive Empire', *Foreign Policy*, 137, 2003 Jul/Aug, pp. 82–7.
73 G. J. Ikenberry, 'America's Imperial Ambition', *Foreign Affairs*, Sep/Oct 2002, 81:5, pp. 44–60; 'Liberalism and empire: logics of order in the American unipolar age', *Review of International Studies*, 30:4, 2004, pp. 609–30; E. Rhodes, 'The Imperial Logic of Bush's Liberal Agenda', *Survival*. 45:1, Spring 2003, pp. 131–53.
74 R. Jackson, *Writing the War on Terrorism: Language, Politics and Counter-terrorism*, Manchester: Manchester University Press, 2005.
75 Frum, *The Right Man*; D. Frum and Richard Perle, *An End To Evil: How to Win the War on Terror*, New York: Random House, 2003. Some neoconservatives have since changed their mind. See Francis Fukuyama, *After the Neocons: America at the Crossroads*, London: Profile, 2006. It should also be noted that even those neoconservatives one might have thought of as the hard core have proven in the end to be less than unstinting in their defence of Bush. See D. Millbank, 'Prince of Darkness Denies Own Existence', *Washington Post*, 2 Feb 2009, p. A03.
76 For example Christopher Hitchens., 'Taking Sides', *The Nation*, 26 Sep 2002. Available online at www.thenation.com/doc/20021014/hitchens (accessed 9 Apr 2009), 'The End of Fukuyama: Why his Latest Pronouncements Miss the Mark', *Slate*, 1 Mar 2006. Available online at www.slate.com/id/2137134/ (accessed 9 Apr 2009). Even the liberal Daalder and Lindsay, *America Unbound*, seem somewhat admiring of Bush's boldness.
77 See Timothy J. Lynch, and Robert S. Singh, *After Bush: The Case for Continuity in American Foreign Policy*, Cambridge: Cambridge University Press, 2008.
78 For another, shorter argument for continuity see John Lewis Gaddis, *Surprise, Security and the American Experience*, London: Harvard University Press, 2004.
79 Regarding the spectrum of ideology from fundamentalism to pragmatism, see D. J. Macdonald, 'Formal Ideologies in the Cold War: Toward a Framework for Empirical Analysis', in O. A. Westad, *Reviewing the Cold War: Approaches, Interpretations, Theory*, London: Frank Cass, 2000, pp. 180–204.

Bibliography

Primary sources

I have defined 'primary sources' as including articles by government officials, even if they appeared in a journal or newspaper. This is because they are direct communications of policy by policymakers. I have also included memoirs.

Acheson, Dean, *Present at the Creation: My Years in the State Department*, New York: W.W. Norton & Co., 1987.
Bush, George, Inaugural Address, 20 Jan 2001. Available online at http://georgewbush-whitehouse.archives.gov/news/inaugural-address.html (accessed 9 Apr 2009).
—— 'Remarks by the President', 12 Sep 2001. Available online at http://georgewbush-whitehouse.archives.gov/news/releases/2001/09/20010912-14.html (accessed 9 Apr 2009).
—— 'Address to a Joint Session of Congress and the American People', 20 Sep 2001. Available online at http://georgewbush-whitehouse.archives.gov/news/releases/2001/09/20010920-28.html (accessed 9 Apr 2009).
—— Address to the Nation, 8 Nov 2001. Available online at http://georgewbush-whitehouse.archives.gov/news/releases/2001/11/20011108-13.html (accessed 9 Apr 2009).
—— 'President Bush Speaks to United Nations', 10 Nov 2001. Available online at http://georgewbush-whitehouse.archives.gov/news/releases/2001/11/20011110-13.html (accessed 9 Apr 2009).
—— 'Remarks on The USS Enterprise', 7 Dec 2001. Available online at http://georgewbush-whitehouse.archives.gov/news/releases/2001/12/20011207.html (accessed 9 Apr 2009).
—— State of the Union Address, 29 Jan 2002. Available online at http://georgewbush-whitehouse.archives.gov/news/releases/2002/01/20020129-11.html (accessed 9 Apr 2009).
—— Graduation Speech at West Point, 1 Jun 2002. Available online at http://georgewbush-whitehouse.archives.gov/news/releases/2002/06/20020601-3.html (accessed 9 Apr 2009).
—— 'President, House Leadership Agree on Iraq Resolution', 2 Oct 2002. Available online at http://georgewbush-whitehouse.archives.gov/news/releases/2002/10/20021002-7.html (accessed 9 Apr 2009).
—— 'President Bush Calls for New Palestinian Leadership', 24 June 2002. Available online at http://georgewbush-whitehouse.archives.gov/news/releases/2002/06/20020624-3.html (accessed 9 Apr 2009).

—— 'Remarks by the President on Iraq', 7 Oct 2002. Available online at http://georgewbush-whitehouse.archives.gov/news/releases/2002/10/20021007-8.html (accessed 9 Apr 2009).
—— State of the Union, 28 Jan 2003. Available online at http://georgewbush-whitehouse.archives.gov/news/releases/2003/01/20030128-19.html (accessed 9 Apr 2009).
—— 'President Discusses the Future of Iraq', 26 Feb 2003. Available online at http://georgewbush-whitehouse.archives.gov/news/releases/2003/02/20030226-11.html (accessed 9 Apr 2009).
—— 'Operation Iraqi Freedom', Radio Address, 12 Apr 2003. Available online at http://georgewbush-whitehouse.archives.gov/news/releases/2003/04/20030412.html (accessed 9 Apr 2009).
—— 'President Bush Outlines Progress in Operation Iraqi Freedom', 16 Apr 2003. Available online at http://georgewbush-whitehouse.archives.gov/news/releases/2003/04/20030416-19.html (accessed 9 Apr 2009).
—— 'President Discusses the Future of Iraq', 28 Apr 2003. Available online at http://georgewbush-whitehouse.archives.gov/news/releases/2003/04/20030428-3.html (accessed 9 Apr 2009).
—— 'Remarks from USS Abraham Lincoln', 1 May 2003. Available online at http://georgewbush-whitehouse.archives.gov/news/releases/2003/05/20030501-15.html (accessed 9 Apr 2009).
—— 'President Bush Discusses Freedom in Iraq and Middle East', 6 Nov 2003. Available online at http://georgewbush-whitehouse.archives.gov/news/releases/2003/11/20031106-2.html (accessed 9 Apr 2009).
—— 'President Bush Discusses Iraq Policy at Whitehall Palace in London', 19 Nov 2003. Available online at http://georgewbush-whitehouse.archives.gov/news/releases/2003/11/20031119-1.html (accessed 9 Apr 2009).
—— 'President Bush Welcomes Canadian Prime Minister Martin to White House', 20 Apr 2004. Available online at http://georgewbush-whitehouse.archives.gov/news/releases/2004/04/20040430-32.html (accessed 9 Apr 2009).
—— 'President Speaks to the American Israel Public Affairs Committee', 18 May 2004. Available online at http://georgewbush-whitehouse.archives.gov/news/releases/2004/05/20040518-1.html (accessed 9 Apr 2009).
—— 'Second Inaugural Address', 20 Jan 2005. Available online at http://georgewbush-whitehouse.archives.gov/news/releases/2005/01/20050120-21.html (accessed 9 Apr 2009).
Clifford, Clark, 'American Relations with the Soviet Union' [Clifford–Elsey Report], 24 Sep 1946. Available online at www.trumanlibrary.org/whistlestop/study_collections/coldwar/documents/pdf/4-1.pdf#zoom=100 (accessed 9 Apr 2009).
Department of Defense, Quadrennial Defence Review 2001. Available online at www.defenselink.mil/pubs/pdfs/qdr2001.pdf (accessed 9 Apr 2009).
—— Quadrennial Defence Review 2006. Available online at www.defenselink.mil/pubs/qdr2001.pdfwww.defenselink.mil/pubs/pdfs/QDR20060203.pdf (accessed 9 Apr 2009).
Hamilton, Alexander, *Writings*, New York: Library of America, 2001.
Jefferson, Thomas, *Writings*, New York: Library of America, 1984.
Kennan, George, Telegram to George Marshall ['Long Telegram'], 22 Feb 1946. Available online at www.trumanlibrary.org/whistlestop/study_collections/coldwar/documents/index.php?documentdate=1946-02-22&documentid=6-6&studycollectionid=&pagenumber=1 (accessed 9 Apr 2009).
—— ['X'], 'The Sources of Soviet Conduct', *Foreign Affairs*, 25:1/4, 1946/47, pp. 566–82.

—— *Memoirs 1925–1950*, New York: Pantheon, 1983.

Madison, James, *Writings*, New York: Library of America, 1999.

Maidment, R. and Dawson, M. (eds), *The United States in the Twentieth Century: Key Documents*, 2nd edn, London: Hodder & Stoughton Educational, 1999.

Marshall, George, Marshall Plan Speech, 5 Jun 1947. Available online at www.nato.int/docu/speech/1947/s470605a_e.htm (accessed 9 Apr 2009).

Powell, Colin L., 'A Strategy of Partnerships', *Foreign Affairs*, 83:1, Jan/Feb 2004.

Report of the Iraq Study Group. Available online at www.usip.org/isg/iraq_study_group_report/report/1206/iraq_study_group_report.pdf (accessed 9 Apr 2009).

Rice, Condoleezza 'Promoting the National Interest', *Foreign Affairs*, 79:1, Jan/Feb 2000, pp. 45–62.

—— 'A Balance of Power that Favors Freedom' 2002 Wriston Lecture, delivered to the Manhattan Institute, New York City, 1 Oct 2002. Available online at www.manhattan-institute.org/html/wl2002.htm (accessed 9 Apr 2009).

—— At Los Angeles Town Hall, 12 June 2003. Available online at http://georgewbush-whitehouse.archives.gov/news/releases/2003/06/20030612-12.html (accessed 9 Apr 2009).

—— 'The Promise of Democratic Peace: Why Promoting Freedom Is the Only Realistic Path to Security', *Washington Post*, 11 Dec 2005, p. B07.

Roosevelt, Theodore, *The Man in the Arena: Selected Writings of Theodore Roosevelt*, New York: Forge, 2003, ed. Brian M. Thomsen.

—— *Letters and Speeches*, New York: Library of America, 2004, ed. Louis Auchincloss.

—— 'Inaugural Address'. Available online at www.homeofheroes.com/presidents/inaugural/26_teddy.html (accessed 9 Apr 2009).

—— 'The Roosevelt Corollary', Speech to Congress, 6 Dec 1904. Available online at www.historywiz.com/primarysources/rooseveltcorollary.htm (accessed 9 Apr 2009).

Truman, Harry S., *Memoirs, Volume One: Year of Decisions*, Great Britain: Hodder & Stoughton, 1955.

—— *Memoirs Volume Two: 1946–52 Years of Trial and Hope*, New York: Smithmark, 1996.

—— President Truman's Message To Congress Recommending Army-Navy Merger, 19 Dec 1945. Available online at www.ibiblio.org/pha/policy/post-war/451219a.html (accessed 9 Apr 2009).

—— State of the Union Address, 14 Jan 1946. Available online at www.usa-presidents.info/union/truman-1.html (accessed 9 Apr 2009).

—— Address in Chicago on Army Day, 6 Apr 1946. Available online at www.presidency.ucsb.edu/ws/index.php?pid=12625 (accessed 9 Apr 2009).

—— Address to Congress, 12 Mar 1947. Available online at www.yale.edu/lawweb/avalon/trudoc.htm (accessed 9 Apr 2009).

—— Radio Address to the American People on the Special Session of Congress, 24 Oct 1947. Available online at www.presidency.ucsb.edu/ws/index.php?pid=12779 (accessed 9 Apr 2009).

—— Inaugural Address, 20 Jan 1949. Available online at www.trumanlibrary.org/whistlestop/50yr_archive/inagural20jan1949.htm (accessed 9 Apr 2009).

—— Address in Chicago Before the Imperial Council Session of the Shrine of North America, 19 Jul 1949. Available online at www.presidency.ucsb.edu/ws/index.php?pid=13248 (accessed 9 Apr 2009).

—— Address on Foreign Policy at the George Washington National Masonic Memorial, 22 Feb 1950. Available online at www.presidency.ucsb.edu/ws/print.php?pid=13713 (accessed 9 Apr 2009).

—— Annual Message to the Congress on the State of the Union, 9 Jan 1952. Available online at www.presidency.ucsb.edu/ws/print.php?pid=14418 (accessed 9 Apr 2009).
—— Address Broadcast from the Voice of America Floating Radio Transmitter Courier, 4 Mar 1952. Available online at www.presidency.ucsb.edu/ws/index.php?pid=14423 (accessed 9 Apr 2009).
—— Farewell Address, 15 Jan 1953. Available online at www.trumanlibrary.org/calendar/viewpapers.php?pid=2059 (accessed 9 Apr 2009).
Washington, George, 'The Farewell Address', 19 Sep 1796, George Washington papers. Available online at http://gwpapers.virginia.edu/documents/farewell/transcript.html (accessed 9 Apr 2009).
White House, 'A Digest of Three Articles by Brooks Atkinson' 7, 8, 9 Jul 1946. Available online at www.trumanlibrary.org/whistlestop/study_collections/coldwar/documents/index.php?documentdate=1946-07-09&documentid=8–3&studycollectionid=&pagenumber=1 (accessed 9 Apr 2009).
White House, 'A Report to the National Security Council – NSC 68', 12 Apr 1950. Available online at www.trumanlibrary.org/whistlestop/study_collections/coldwar/documents/pdf/10-11.pdf#zoom=100 (accessed 9 Apr 2009).
White House, 'The National Security Strategy of the United States of America', Sep 2002. Available online at http://georgewbush-whitehouse.archives.gov/nsc/nss.pdf (accessed 9 Apr 2009).
Wilson, Woodrow, *War and Peace: Presidential Messages, Addresses and Public Papers*, Volumes I and II, Honolulu, Hawaii: University Press of the Pacific, 2002, ed. Ray Stannard Baker and William E. Dodd; reprinted from 1927.

Secondary sources

Albright, Madeleine K., 'Bombs, Bridges, or Bluster', *Foreign Affairs*, Sep/Oct 2003.
—— 'A Realistic Idealism', *Washington Post*, 8 May 2006, p. A19.
Ambrosius, Lloyd E., *Woodrow Wilson and the American Diplomatic Tradition: The Treaty Fight in Perspective*, Cambridge: Cambridge University Press, 1987.
—— *Wilsonianism: Woodrow Wilson and his Legacy in American Foreign Relations*, New York: Palgrave Macmillan, 2002.
Ash, Timothy Garton, 'The War After War With Iraq', *Washington Post*, 20 Mar 2003.
Bacevich, Andrew, *American Empire: The Realities and Consequences of US Diplomacy*, Cambridge, MA: Harvard University Press, 2002.
Beale, Howard K., *Theodore Roosevelt and the Rise of America to World Power*, Baltimore: Johns Hopkins Press, 1956.
Beard, Charles A., *An Economic Interpretation of the Constitution of the United States*, New York: Macmillan, 1913.
—— *The Idea of National Interest: An Analytical Study in American Foreign Policy*, New York: Macmillan, 1934.
Beisner, Robert L., *Dean Acheson: A Life in the Cold War*, Oxford: Oxford University Press, 2006.
Bell, Sidney, *Righteous Conquest: Woodrow Wilson and the Evolution of the New Diplomacy*, Port Washington, NY: National University Publications, Kennikat Press, 1972.
Bemis, Samuel Flagg, *John Quincy Adams and the Foundations of American Foreign Policy*, New York: Alfred A. Knopf, 1949.

Bibliography

—— *Jay's Treaty: A Study in Commerce and Diplomacy*, New Haven: Yale University Press, 1962.
—— *A Diplomatic History of the United States*, 5th edn, New York: Holt, Rinehart and Winston, 1965.
Betts, Richard K., 'Suicide From Fear of Death?', *Foreign Affairs*, Jan/Feb 2003, 82:1, pp. 34–43.
—— 'Striking First: a History of Thankfully Lost Opportunities', *Ethics and International Affairs*, 17:1, 2003, pp. 17–24.
—— 'The Political Support System for American Primacy', *International Affairs*, Jan 2005, 81:1, pp. 1–14.
Black, Conrad, *Franklin Delano Roosevelt*, London: Weidenfeld and Nicolson, 2003.
Boot, Max, 'The Case for American Empire', *Weekly Standard*, 15 Oct 2001.
Bowers, Claude G., *Jefferson and Hamilton: the Struggle for Democracy in America*, Cambridge, MA: Riverside Press, 1925.
Boyd, Julian, *Number 7: Alexander Hamilton's Secret Efforts to Control American Foreign Policy*, Princeton: Princeton University Press, 1964.
Brands, H.W., *What America Owes the World*, Cambridge: Cambridge University Press, 1998.
Brant, Irving, *The Fourth President: A Life of James Madison*, London: Eyre and Spottiswood, 1970.
Brooks, Stephen G. and Wohlforth, William C., 'American Primacy in Perspective', *Foreign Affairs*, Jul/Aug 2002, 81:4, pp. 20–33.
Buehrig, Edward H., *Woodrow Wilson and the Balance of Power*, Bloomington: Indiana University Press, 1955.
—— (ed.), *Wilson's Foreign Policy in Perspective*, Bloomington: Indiana University Press, 1957.
Bull, Hedley, *The Anarchical Society: A Study of Order in World Politics*, 3rd edn, New York: Columbia University Press, 1977.
Campbell, Charles S., *From Revolution to Rapprochement: The United States and Great Britain, 1783–1900*, New York: John Wiley & Sons, 1974.
Campbell, David, *Writing Security: United States Foreign Policy and the Politics of Identity*, Manchester: Manchester University Press, 1998.
Chafe, William H., *The Unfinished Journey: America Since World War II*, Oxford: Oxford University Press, 1999.
Chernow, Ron, *Alexander Hamilton*, New York: Penguin Press, 2004.
Chomsky, Noam, *Deterring Democracy*, London: Vintage, 1992.
—— *The New Military Humanism: Lessons from Kosovo*, London: Pluto Press, 1999.
—— *A New Generation Draws the Line: Kosovo, East Timor and the Standards of the West*, London: Verso, 2000.
—— *Hegemony or Survival: America's Quest for Global Dominance*, London: Penguin, 2004.
Clements, Kendrick A., *The Presidency of Woodrow Wilson*, Lawrence, KS: University Press of Kansas, 1992.
Combs, Jerald A., *The Jay Treaty: Battleground of the Founding Fathers*, Berkeley: University of California Press, 1970.
Cooper, John Milton, *The Warrior and the Priest: Woodrow Wilson and Theodore Roosevelt*, Cambridge, MA: Harvard University Press, 1985.
Couvares, Francis G., Saxton, Martha, Grob, Gerald N., and Billias, George Athan, *Interpretations of American History*, 7th edn, New York: The Free Press, 2000, Vols. 1 and 2.

Cox, Michael, 'The Empire's Back in Town: Or America's Imperial Temptation – Again', *Millennium*, 32:1, 2003, pp. 1–29.
—— 'Empire, Imperialism and the Bush doctrine', *Review of International Studies*, 30:4, 2004, pp. 585–608.
—— 'Empire by denial: the strange case of the United States', *International Affairs*, 81:1, Jan 2005, pp. 15–30.
Daalder, Ivo H. and Lindsay, James M., *America Unbound: The Bush Revolution in Foreign Policy*, Washington, DC: Brookings Institution Press, 2003.
Dalton, Kathleen, *Theodore Roosevelt: A Strenuous Life*, New York: Knopf, 2002.
Dawley, Alan, *Changing the World: American Progressives in War and Revolution*, Princeton and Oxford: Princeton University Press, 2003.
DeConde, Alexander, *A History of American Foreign Policy* New York: Scribner, 1963.
DePorte, A. W., *Europe Between the Superpowers*, Chelsea: Yale University Press 1979.
De Tocqueville, Alexis, *Democracy in America*, New York: Library of America, 2004.
Doyle, Michael W., 'Kant, liberal legacies, and foreign affairs', *Philosophy and Public Affairs*, 12:3, Summer 1983, pp. 205–35.
—— 'A more perfect union? The liberal peace and the challenge of globalization', *Review of International Studies*, 26 (Suppl.), Dec 2000, pp. 81–94.
—— 'Three Pillars of the Liberal Peace', *American Political Science Review*, 99:3, August 2005, pp. 463–66.
Draper, Robert, *Dead Certain: The Presidency of George W. Bush*, London: Simon & Schuster, 2007.
Dueck, Colin, *Reluctant Crusaders: Power, Culture and Change in American Grand Strategy*, Princeton: Princeton University Press, 2006.
Ellis, Joseph J., *American Sphinx:* New York: Vintage, 1998.
—— *Founding Brothers: The Revolutionary Generation*, New York: Vintage, 2002.
—— *His Excellency: George Washington*, New York: Alfred A. Knopf, 2004.
Etzioni, Amitai, *Security First*, New Haven and London: Yale University Press, 2007.
Ferguson, Niall, *Colossus: The Rise and Fall of the American Empire*, London: Allen Lane, 2004.
Frum, David, *The Right Man: An Inside Account of the Surprise Presidency of George W. Bush*, New York: Weidenfeld and Nicolson, 2003.
Frum, David and Perle, Richard, *An End To Evil: How to Win the War on Terror*, New York: Random House, 2003.
Flexner, James Thomas, *Washington: The Indispensable Man*, London: Purnell Book Services, 1976.
Fukuyama, Francis, *The End of History and the Last Man*, London: Penguin, 1993.
—— *After the Neocons: America at the Crossroads*, London: Profile, 2006.
Gaddis, John Lewis, *Strategies of Containment: a Critical Appraisal of Postwar American National Security Policy*, Oxford: Oxford University Press, 1982.
—— 'The Emerging Post-Revisionist Thesis on the Origins of the Cold War', *Diplomatic History*, 7, Summer 1983, pp. 171–90.
—— *We Now Know: Rethinking Cold War History*, Oxford: Oxford University Press, 1997.
—— *The United States and the Origins of the Cold War*, New York: Columbia University Press, 2000.
—— 'A Grand Strategy of Transformation', *Foreign Policy*, November/December 2002.

—— *Surprise, Security and the American Experience*, London: Harvard University Press, 2004.
Giddens, Anthony, *The Constitution of Society: Outline of the Theory of Structuration*, Cambridge: Polity Press, 1986.
Gilbert, Felix, *To the Farewell Address: Ideas of Early American Foreign Policy*, Princeton: Princeton University Press, 1961.
Goldstein, Judith and Keohane, Robert O. (eds), *Ideas and Foreign Policy: Beliefs, Institutions and Political Change*, Ithaca, NY: Cornell University Press, 1993.
Harper, John Lamberton, *American Machiavelli: Alexander Hamilton and the Origins of U.S. Foreign Policy*, Cambridge: Cambridge University Press, 2004.
Hecht, Marie B., *Odd Destiny: The Life of Alexander Hamilton*, New York: Macmillan, 1982.
Herman, Edward S. and Chomsky, Noam, *Manufacturing Consent: The Political Economy of the Mass Media*, London: Vintage, 1994.
Hirsh, Michael, *At War with Ourselves: Why America is Squandering its Chance to Build a Better World*, Oxford: Oxford University Press, 2003.
Hoffmann, Stanley, 'America Goes Backward', *New York Review of Books*, 50:10, June 2003.
Hollis, Martin and Smith, Steve, *Explaining and Understanding International Relations*, Oxford: Clarendon, 1991.
Hoopes, Townsend and Brinkley, Douglas, *FDR and the Creation of the UN*, New Haven: Yale University Press, 1997.
Hunt, Michael H., *Ideology and US Foreign Policy*, New Haven: Yale University Press, 1987.
Ignatieff, Michael, *Empire Lite: Nation-Building in Bosnia, Kosovo and Afghanistan*, London: Vintage, 2003.
Ikenberry, G. John, *After Victory: Institutions, Strategic Restraint and the Rebuilding of Order after Major Wars*, Princeton: Princeton University Press, 2001.
—— (ed.), *America Unrivaled: The Future of the Balance of Power*, New York: Cornell University Press, 2002.
—— 'Democracy, Institutions and Strategic Restraint', in Ikenberry, *America Unrivaled*, pp. 213–38.
—— 'America's Imperial Ambition', *Foreign Affairs*, 81:5, Sep/Oct 2002, pp. 44–60.
—— 'Liberalism and empire: logics of order in the American unipolar age', *Review of International Studies*, 30:4, 2004, p. 609.
Jackson, R., *Writing the War on Terrorism: Language, Politics and Counter-terrorism*, Manchester: Manchester University Press, 2005.
Jervis, Robert, 'Understanding the Bush Doctrine', *Political Science Quarterly*, 118:3, 2003, pp. 365–88.
—— 'The Compulsive Empire', *Foreign Policy*, 137, Jul–Aug 2003, pp. 82–7.
Jones, Maldwyn A., *The Limits of Liberty: American History 1607–1980*, Oxford: Oxford University Press, 1983.
Kagan, Robert, 'Power and Weakness', *Policy Review*, 113, Jun/Jul 2002, pp. 3–28.
—— *Paradise and Power: America and Europe in the New World Order*, London: Atlantic, 2003.
—— *Dangerous Nation: America's Place in the World from its Earliest Days to the Dawn of the Twentieth Century*, New York: Alfred A. Knopf, 2006.
—— 'Our "Messianic Impulse"', *Washington Post*, 10 Dec 2006, p. B07.
Kaplan, Lawrence S., *Jefferson and France: An Essay on Politics and Political Ideas*, New Haven: Yale University Press, 1967.

Kennan, George F., *American Diplomacy*, expanded edition, Chicago: University of Chicago Press, 1984.
Kennedy, Paul *The Rise and Fall of the Great Powers*, London: Vintage, 1989.
Keohane, R. (ed.), *Neorealism and Its Critics*, New York: Columbia University Press, 1986.
Keohane, R. and Nye, Joseph S., *Power and Interdependence: World Politics in Transition*, Boston, MA: Little, Brown & Co., 1977.
Keylor, William R., *The Twentieth Century World: An International History*, 4th edn, Oxford: Oxford University Press, 2001.
Kissinger, Henry, *Diplomacy*, New York: Touchstone, 1995.
Klingberg, Frank L., *Cyclical Trends in American Foreign Policy Moods: The Unfolding of America's World Role*, London: University Press of America, 1983.
Kolko, Gabriel, *The Politics of War: Allied Diplomacy and the World Crisis of 1943–45*, London: Weidenfeld & Nicolson, 1969.
—— *Confronting the Third World: United States Foreign Policy, 1945–1980*, New York: Pantheon Books, 1988.
—— *Another Century of War*, New York: The New Press, 2002.
Kolko, Joyce and Kolko, Gabriel, *The Limits of Power: the World and United States Foreign Policy*, New York: Harper & Row, 1972.
LaFeber, Walter, *The New Empire: An Interpretation of American Expansionism 1860–1898*, London: Cornell University Press, 1963.
—— *Inevitable Revolutions: The United States in Central America*, New York: W.W. Norton, 1993.
—— *America, Russia, and the Cold War, 1945–2000*, 9th edn, London: McGraw-Hill, 2002.
Layne, Christopher, *The Peace of Illusions: American Grand Strategy from 1940 to the Present*, Ithaca and London: Cornell University Press, 2006.
Leffler, Melvyn P., 'The American Conception of National Security and the Beginnings of the Cold War', *American Historical Review*, 89, April 1984, pp. 346–81.
—— 'Bringing it Together: The Parts and the Whole', in Westad, *Reviewing the Cold War*, pp. 43–63.
Leffler, Melvyn P. and Painter, David S., *Origins of the Cold War*, New York: Routledge, 1994.
Lerner, Max, *Thomas Jefferson: America's Philosopher-King*, New Brunswick, NJ: Transaction Publishers, 1996.
Lieven, Anatol, *America Right or Wrong: an Anatomy of American Nationalism*, London: HarperCollins, 2004.
Lieven, Anatol and Hulsman, John, *Ethical Realism*, New York: Pantheon, 2007.
Lind, Michael, *The American Way of Strategy*, Oxford: Oxford University Press, 2006.
—— 'Dangerous History', *Prospect*, 140, Nov 2007.
Link, Arthur S., *The Higher Realism of Woodrow Wilson and Other Essays*, Nashville, TN: Vanderbilt University Press, 1971.
Lippmann, Walter, *The Cold War*, New York: Harper & Row, 1972, 1st edn 1947.
Lipset, Seymour Martin, *American Exceptionalism: A Double-Edged Sword*, New York: W.W. Norton & Co., 1996.
Little, Richard, 'The Balance of Power in Politics Among Nations', in Michael C. Williams, *Realism Reconsidered: The Legacy of Hans J. Morgethau in International Relations*, Oxford: Oxford University Press, 2007.
Lundestad, Geir, 'How Not to Study the Origins of the Cold War', in Westad, *Reviewing the Cold War*, pp. 64–80.

Bibliography

Lycan, Gilbert, *Alexander Hamilton & American Foreign Policy*, Norman: University of Oklahoma Press, 1970.

Lynch, Timothy J. and Singh, Robert S., *After Bush: The Case for Continuity in American Foreign Policy*, Cambridge: Cambridge University Press, 2008.

Macdonald, Douglas J., 'Formal Ideologies in the Cold War: Toward a Framework for Empirical Analysis', in Westad, *Reviewing the Cold War*, pp. 180–204.

Mallaby, Sebastian, 'The Reluctant Imperialist', *Foreign Affairs*, 81:2, Mar/Apr 2002, pp. 2–7.

Mann, James, *Rise of the Vulcans: The History of Bush's War Cabinet*, London: Penguin, 2004.

Mann, Michael, *Incoherent Empire*, London: Verso, 2003.

—— 'The First Failed Empire of the 21st Century', *Review of International Studies*, 30:4, 2004, p. 631.

Marks, Frederick W. III, *Velvet on Iron: The Diplomacy of Theodore Roosevelt*, Lincoln: University of Nebraska Press, 1979.

McCullough, David, *Truman*, New York: Simon & Schuster, 1992.

McDougall, Walter A., *Promised Land, Crusader State: The American Encounter with the World since 1776*, Boston, MA: Mariner Books, 1997.

Mead, Walter Russell, *Special Providence: American Foreign Policy and How it Changed the World*, New York; Routledge, 2002.

Mearsheimer, John J., 'The Future of the American Pacifier', *Foreign Affairs*, 80:5, Sep/Oct 2001, pp. 46–61.

—— *The Tragedy of Great Power Politics*, New York: W.W. Norton & Co., 2001.

Mearsheimer, John J. and Walt, Stephen M., 'An Unnecessary War', *Foreign Policy*, 134, Jan/Feb 2003, pp. 51–61.

—— *The Israel Lobby and US Foreign Policy*, London: Penguin, 2008.

Micklethwaite, John and Woolridge, A., *The Right Nation: Why America is Different*, London: Allen Lane, 2004.

Millbank, D. 'Prince of Darkness Denies Own Existence', *Washington Post*, 2 Feb 2009, p. A03.

Miller, Nathan, *Theodore Roosevelt: A Life*, London: Harper Perennial, 1994.

Mitchell, Broadus, *Alexander Hamilton: A Concise Biography*, New York: Oxford University Press, 1976.

Monten, Jonathan 'The Roots of the Bush Doctrine: Power, Nationalism and Democracy Promotion in US Strategy', *International Security*, 29:4, Spring 2005, pp. 112–56.

Morgenthau, Hans J., *American Foreign Policy: A Critical Examination*, London: Methuen & Co., 1952.

—— *Politics Among Nations: The Struggle for Power and Peace*, 6th edn, rev. Kenneth W. Thompson, New York: McGraw Hill, 1985.

Morris, Edmund, *The Rise of Theodore Roosevelt*, New York: Random House, 2001.

—— *Theodore Rex*, New York: Random House, 2001.

Moser, John, 'Principles Without Program: Senator Robert A. Taft and American Foreign Policy', *Ohio History*, 108, 1999, pp. 177–92.

Newhouse, John, *Imperial America: The Bush Assault on the World Order*, New York: Alfred A. Knopf, 2003.

Notter, Harley, *The Origins of the Foreign Policy of Woodrow Wilson*, Baltimore: Johns Hopkins Press, 1937.

Nye, Joseph, *The Paradox of American Power: Why the World's Only Superpower Can't Go It Alone*, New York: Oxford University Press, 2002.

—— 'The American national interest and global public goods', *International Affairs*, 78:2, Apr 2002, pp. 233–44.
Osgood, Robert Endicott, *Ideals and Self-Interest in American Foreign Relations*, Chicago: University of Chicago Press, 1953.
Owen, John M., 'How Liberalism Produces Democratic Peace', *International Security*, 19:2, Fall 1994, pp. 87–125.
—— 'Democratic Peace Research: Whence and Whither', *International Politics*, 41:4, December 2004, pp. 605–17.
—— 'Transnational Liberalism and American Primacy', in Ikenberry, *America Unrivaled*, pp. 239–59.
Peterson, Merrill D., *Thomas Jefferson and the New Nation*, New York: Oxford University Press, 1970.
Pfaff, William, 'Manifest Destiny: A New Direction for America', *New York Review*, 54:2, Feb 2007, pp. 54–9.
Pierce, Anne R., *Woodrow Wilson and Harry Truman: Mission and Power in American Foreign Policy*, Westport, CT and London: Praeger, 2003.
Prestowitz, Clyde, *Rogue Nation: American Unilateralism and the Failure of Good Intentions*, New York: Basic Books, 2003.
Rhodes, Edward, 'The Imperial Logic of Bush's Liberal Agenda', *Survival*, 45:1, Spring 2003, pp. 131–53.
Ricard, Serge, 'Anti-Wilsonian Internationalism: Theodore Roosevelt in the *Kansas City Star*', in Rossini, ed., *From Theodore Roosevelt to FDR*, pp. 25–44.
Ricks, Thomas E., *Fiasco: The American Military Adventure in Iraq*, London: Allen Lane, 2006.
Ricks, Thomas E. and Loeb, Vernon, 'Bush Developing Military Policy of Striking First: New Doctrine Addresses Terrorism', *Washington Post*, 10 Jun 2002.
Risse, Thomas, 'US Power in a Liberal Security Community', in Ikenberry, *America Unrivaled*, pp. 260–83.
Rossini, Daniela (ed.), *From Theodore Roosevelt to FDR: Internationalism and Isolationism in American Foreign Policy*, Keele: Ryburn Publishing, Keele University Press, 1995.
Rubin, James P., 'Stumbling into War', *Foreign Affairs*, Sep/Oct 2003, 82:5, pp. 46–66.
Simes, Dimitri K., 'America's Imperial Dilemma', *Foreign Affairs*, 82:6, Nov/Dec 2003, pp. 91–102.
—— 'End the Crusade', *The National Interest*, 87, Jan/Feb 2007, pp. 4–11.
Soros, George, *The Bubble of American Supremacy: Correcting the Misuse of American Power*, London: Weidenfeld and Nicolson, 2004.
Stephanson, Anders, 'Liberty or Death: The Cold War as US Ideology', in Westad, *Reviewing the Cold War*, pp. 81–100.
Stevenson, David, *1914–1918: The History of the First World War*, London: Penguin, 2005.
Trubowitz, Peter, *Defining the National Interest: Conflict and Change in American Foreign Policy*, Chicago: Chicago University Press, 1998.
Tucker, Robert W. *Woodrow Wilson and the Great War: Reconsidering America's Neutrality, 1914–1917*, Charlottesville: University of Virginia Press, 2007.
Tucker, Robert W. and Hendrickson, David C., 'The Sources of American Legitimacy', *Foreign Affairs*, 83:6, Nov/Dec 2004, pp. 18–32.
Tully, James, *Meaning and Context: Quentin Skinner and His Critics*, Princeton, NJ: Princeton University Press, 1988.

Turner, Frederick Jackson, *The Frontier in American History*, New York: Henry Holt & Co., 1920.

Waltz, Kenneth, *Theory of International Politics*, Reading, MA: Addison-Wesley, 1979.

—— 'Reflections on *Theory of International Politics*: A Response to my Critics', in Keohane (ed.), *Neorealism and Its Critics*, pp. 322–45.

—— , 'Structural Realism after the Cold War', in Ikenberry, *America Unrivaled*, New York: Cornell University Press, 2002, pp. 29–67.

Wendt, Alexander, *Social Theory of International Politics*, Cambridge: Cambridge University Press, 1999.

Westad, Odd Arne *Reviewing the Cold War: Approaches, Interpretations, Theory*, London: Frank Cass, 2000.

Williams, Michael C., *Realism Reconsidered: The Legacy of Hans J. Morgethau in International Relations*, Oxford: Oxford University Press, 2007.

Williams, William Appleman, *The Tragedy of American Diplomacy*, New York: Dell, 1972.

—— *The Contours of American History*, New York: W.W. Norton, 1989.

Winik, Jay, *The Great Upheaval: America and the Birth of the Modern World, 1788–1800*, New York: Harper, 2007.

Wohlforth, William C., 'The Stability of a Unipolar World', *International Security*, 29:1, Summer 1999, pp. 5–41.

—— 'US Strategy in a Unipolar World', in Ikenberry, *America Unrivaled*, pp. 98–118.

Woodward, Bob, *Bush at War*, London: Simon & Schuster, 2003.

—— *Plan of Attack*, London: Simon & Schuster, 2004.

—— *State of Denial*, London: Simon & Schuster, 2006.

Zakaria, Fareed, *From Wealth to Power: The Unusual Origins of America's World Role*, Princeton, NJ: Princeton University Press, 1998.

—— 'The Arrogant Empire', *Newsweek*, 24 Mar 2003, US edition, p. 18.

Index

Acheson, Dean 131
Adams, Henry 65
Adams, John Quincy 45, 52–53, 55, 56, 57, 57–58
Afghanistan 142, 153
Africa 140
Algeciras Conference 71
alliances 51, 54, 98, 114, 119
al-Qaeda 142
American primacy 105–8, 155
American system 58, 60, 75, 92
Americanism 104
Articles of Confederacy, the 34–35, 36–37, 39
Austria 33
Autobiography (Jefferson) 45
autocracy 103–4
axis of evil 144

Baker Report 200n69
balance of power 2, 3, 8, 9, 19, 24, 30, 32, 52, 59, 60, 62, 70, 87, 164, 166–67; abolition of 96–100, 102; Cold War 115, 122, 138, 172; Constructivism and 20; and empire 18; European system 6, 34, 56, 167–68; favouring freedom 142, 143, 173; and the First World War 79–80; liberal school conception of 14–15; realist school's conception of 10–14, 29
Bazalgette, Leon 65
Beard, C. A. 18, 178n22, 180n50
Beckwith, George 43–44
Belgium 79
Bell, Sidney 92, 94
Bemis, Samuel Flagg 56
Berlin, blockade of 119
Bill of Rights 41
Bonaparte, Napoleon 53, 55

Borah, William 109
Boxer Rebellion, the 76–77
Bryan, William Jennings 63
Bush, George W. 9, 139–65, 181n58; advance of freedom 146–49; alternative principles for 160–62, 165; background 139; and balance of power 2; context 140–41, 167; convergence of values policies 150–53; critiques of 157–59; grand objectives 158; and historical inevitability 154–56; ideological heritage 140; ideology 148, 154–56, 158–59, 159–64; internationalism 9; liberal values 143–46; Middle East policy 145, 148, 154, 155, 162; and military power 156–57, 165; and national ideology 173–75; national interest 163; NSS (2002) 141–43, 164; people/government distinction 153–54; Second Inaugural Address 148–49, 154, 156, 158; speeches 181n57; State of the Union address, 2002 144, 146–47; on successful societies 145–46; West Point address, 2002 144, 151; worldview 143, 155–56, 159–64, 166, 173–75
Bush Doctrine 159

Campbell, David 23–24
Canada 33, 80
China 4, 64, 66–67, 76–77, 87, 90, 116, 119, 140, 151, 162
Churchill, Winston S. 116, 194n12
civilization, furtherance of 72–74, 74–77, 78–79, 115, 170
Clay, Henry 58, 124
Clements, Kendrick A. 89, 93
Clifford, Clark 130–33

Index

Clifford–Elsey Report 115, 130–33, 172
Clinton, Bill 200n63
Clinton, George 40
Cold War 4, 8–9, 12, 18, 114–38, 139, 164, 166, 172, 177n12, 180n53; balance of power 115, 122, 138, 172; and the Clifford–Elsey Report 115, 130–33, 172; context 115–16, 193n5; deterioration of relations 116–19; ideology 123, 126, 133–34, 135–36, 172; Kennan's analysis of Soviet Union 126–30; militarization 133, 136; and NSC-68 115, 125, 130–31, 133–36; polarization 131–33; policy 118–19; Truman's conception of 119–26
collective security 7
Colombia 70, 77
colonialism 64, 76
Communism 120–21
Constitution, the 35
Constructivism 20–21
containment 4, 8, 115, 119, 126, 172
Continental Congress 37
cooperation, and national interests 100–102, 103
Cuba 63, 64, 76, 77, 78, 92–93, 94
cultural imperialism 145
cultural pluralism 146
Czechoslovakia 119

Daalder, Ivo H. 159
Dawley, Alan 89
Declaration on Liberated Europe 117
democracy 16, 167; universal 15, 102–5, 113
democratic faith 144
democratic peace 146–49, 164–65, 174
detachment 54
Dewey, Admiral 69
disarmament 81, 108
dollar diplomacy 89–90
Dominican Republic 77, 92–93, 190n34
dominion of right 8
Draper, Robert 181n57
Dueck, Colin 13

economic sanctions 48
economic self-interest 90
Elsey, George 130–33
empire school, the 17–19, 30
English School, the 178n17
Europe: areas under Soviet control 118; balance of power system 6, 34, 56, 167–68; colonies 56; Founders' Era 33–34, 40, 51; and the Monroe Doctrine 56–57; Roosevelt on 68
evidence, public statements as 27–29
exceptionalism 19, 19–20

Federalist Papers, The 35, 38, 39, 51
First World War 4, 7, 61, 73, 78–83, 97, 112, 169; American entry 86, 89, 112, 170–71; American neutrality 79; and the balance of power 79–80; causes 99, 103–4; justification of American war entry 94–96; outbreak 79, 87; Paris Peace Conference 83, 97, 109; Roosevelt and the 78–83; submarine warfare 95
force, use of 81–82, 108–9; *see also* military power
Foreign Affairs 126, 142, 151
foreign policy, theories of 11–12
formative influences 4
Founders' Era, the 4, 5–7, 26, 31–60, 169, 173; background 31–33; British trade 43; constitutional convention 35, 36; context 33–35, 166–67; emergence of the Union 32; establishment of the Union 36–41; and Europe 51; European attitude of superiority 40; and the French Revolution 41, 44–47; ideology 32, 59–60; import tariffs 42; international relations 41–49; national interests 32; neutral shipping rights negotiated 47–49; Proclamation of Neutrality 47; relations with Britain 31, 34–35, 36, 41, 42–44, 47, 47–49, 53, 168; relations with France 31, 52–54, 55, 168; sedition laws 53; strategic consensus 6–7; Washington's Farewell Address 49–52, 52, 54
France 31, 33, 52, 52–54, 55, 64, 115–16, 168
freedom 2, 78, 94, 117, 119, 120, 121, 134, 137, 142, 143, 144, 146–49, 154–55, 170, 172, 173
French Revolution 4, 34, 41, 44–47, 53
Frontier Thesis 179n32

Gaddis, John Lewis 12
generosity 72
Germany 1, 64, 69, 71, 74, 187n41; Cold War 119, 132; and the First World War 79–80, 95–96, 171; and the

Second World War 115; Wilson and 102, 110
Giddens, Anthony 25
Goldstein, Judith 23
government, structures of 14
Great Britain 4, 59; American wars 36; and Canada 33; empire 64; and the First World War 80; Founders' Era relations with 31, 34–35, 36, 41, 42–44, 47, 47–49, 53, 168; naval power 56, 168; restrictions on trade 34–35; and the Revolutionary War 31; and the Second World War 116
Greece 119, 120, 125

Haiti 92–93
Hamilton, Alexander 35, 36–41, 41, 42, 43–44, 44, 45–47, 48–49, 50, 53, 59, 183n29, 183n37, 184n54, 185n66, 185n87
Hanna, Mark 65
hard power 156–57
Hay, John 63
historical inevitability 154–56
history 10, 30; directionality of 8; and realism 12; relevance of 25–27
Holy Alliance, the 55
Huerta, General Victoriano 91
Hull, Cordell 118
human rights 90
Hunt, Michael H. 21, 21–22, 22, 27, 28, 180n43, 183n46

idealism 12, 15
ideology 3, 5, 20, 167; Bush administration 148, 154–56, 158–59, 159–64; Bush's heritage 140; Cold War 123, 126, 133–34, 135–36, 172; continuity and change 24–25, 25–27, 29, 164–65, 166–75; definition 22–24; development of 26–27; Founders' Era, the 32, 59–60; national 13–14, 16–17, 19, 21, 21–22, 23–24, 24–25, 25, 26, 29, 173–75; parameters set by 28–29; and policy makers 27, 28–29; source material 28; Soviet Union 126–27; Wilsonian 96, 112–13
Ikenberry, G. John 14, 159
imperialism 7, 17–18, 19, 66–67, 74–78, 157, 169–70; commercial 90; cultural 145
India 140
institutions 14
interdependence 14

international relations (IR) 10; and American history 10–22; Constructivism and 20–21; empire school 17–19; empire school, the 30; and exceptionalism 19–20; ideology studies 21–22; liberal school 14–17, 29–30; realist school 10–14, 15, 29; role of ideology 23; structuration model 25–26
internationalism 7–8, 9, 30, 62, 83, 87, 100, 110, 113, 115, 137, 166, 167–72, 173, 174–75
interventionism 7, 91–94, 137, 162, 170
inter-war years 114, 171
Iran 119
Iraq, invasion of 18, 142, 144, 144–45, 147, 152, 153, 153–54, 158
isolationism 15, 60, 110, 116, 124, 193n4
Italy 1

Japan 64, 76–77, 116
Jay, John 49, 52
Jefferson, Thomas 35, 36, 41–42, 42–43, 44–45, 46, 47, 48, 53–54, 58–59, 59, 168, 183n28, 183n29, 184n52, 184n53, 185n67, 185n68
Jeffersonian consensus 54, 55, 168, 173
Jefferson's Embargo 55
Jervis, Robert 200n72
justice 72, 80

Kagan, Robert 16
Kellogg-Briand Pact 114
Kennan, George 2, 8, 11, 12, 115, 130, 138, 172, 177n11, 178n23, 179n26; analysis of Soviet Union 126–30
Keohane, Robert O. 23
Kissinger, Henry 2, 4, 11, 12, 69–70, 71, 72, 74, 84
Klingberg, Frank L. 21
Korean War 118–19, 125, 130

Lafayette, Marquis de 45–46
LaFeber, Walter 18
Latin America 7, 55, 58, 70, 71, 74–75, 78, 84, 89, 90–94, 112, 120, 140, 168
League of Nations 94, 98, 101, 105, 106–7, 108–11, 114, 116, 117, 170
legalism 177n11
legalistic-moralistic mindset 2, 178n23
liberalism 14–17, 29–30, 76, 78, 83, 104, 167: universal validity of 143–46
liberty 45, 78, 94, 103, 122, 144, 149, 154, 181n58

Index

Lieven, Anatol 21, 28–29
Lindsay, James M. 159
Link, Arthur 149
Lippmann, Walter 138
Lipset, S. M. 179n32
Lodge, Henry Cabot 109, 111
London 148
Louisiana 33
Louisiana Purchase 55
Lusitania, sinking of the 95

Macdonald, Douglas J. 22–23, 115
McDougall, Walter A. 21, 22
McKinley, William 63, 65
Madison, James 35, 36–41, 41, 42, 43–44, 47, 48, 53
Maine, USS 63, 186n5
Mao Zedong 119
Marshall, George 194n22
Marshall Plan 119, 126, 194n22
Massachusetts 34
Mearsheimer, John J. 11, 177n4
Mexico 91–92, 93
Middle East 145, 148, 154, 155, 162
military power 81–82, 83–84; Bush administration and 156–57, 165; and the Cold War 120, 124–25, 128, 133; Roosevelt's expansion of 67–69, 73–74
monarchies 33–34
Monroe, James 52–53, 55–59
Monroe Doctrine 4, 5, 6, 32, 55–59, 62, 69, 70, 71, 74, 100, 106, 124, 157, 165, 167, 168; deepened 86; expanded 90–94, 112, 170, 171; the Roosevelt Corollary 74–76, 78, 84, 90, 169, 170
Monten, Jonathan 21
morality and moralism 71–74, 88–89, 108–9, 109–11, 169, 177n11
Morgenthau, Hans 2, 11, 14, 181n4
Morocco 71
Morris, Edmund 76
Munsterberg, Hugo 83

national character 3–4, 25
national culture 3–4
national debt 42
national greatness 66–67
national ideology 1, 10, 13–14, 16–17, 19, 21, 21–22, 23–24, 24–25, 25, 26, 29, 173–75
national interests 12, 13, 24, 32, 50, 52, 70, 84, 162–63, 167; and American primacy 106; and cooperation 100–102, 103; Jeffersonian consensus 54; restraint in pursuit of 12
national security 146, 149
National Security Strategy (NSS) (2002) 2, 9, 139, 141–43, 150–51, 156–57, 164, 173, 197n6, 199n38
nationalism 21, 105
nation-state, the, pursuit of power 11
Native American Indians 188n70
Naval War College 67–68, 69
neoclassical realists 2–3, 12, 13
neo-imperialism 18
Netherlands, the 33
neutral shipping rights, Founders' Era 47–49
neutrality 73, 79
New Left, the 18
Nicaragua 92–93
Nitze, Paul 130
Nixon, Richard M. 4
non-alignment 50, 52
non-intervention 56, 59
norms 14
North Atlantic Treaty 114, 119, 125
NSC-68 115, 125, 130–31, 133–36, 147, 172
Nye, Joseph 140

Operation Iraqi Freedom, *see* Iraq, invasion of
Osgood, Robert Endicott 21
Ottoman empire 82
overreach 12, 15

Panama 93
Panama Canal 70, 93
Paris Peace Conference 83, 97, 109
Parker, Alton 66–67
people/government distinction 101–2, 103, 123–24, 128–29, 135, 153–54
Philadelphia 35, 36, 37
Philippines, the 63, 64, 67, 76, 78
Pierce, Anne R. 117, 118, 120, 122, 123
Pitt, William, the Younger 42
Platt, Thomas C. 64
Plutarch 181n54
policy makers, and ideology 27, 28–29
political culture 25
post-structuralism 20
Potsdam Conference 118
Powell, Colin 142, 151, 199n38
power 11, 14; *see also* military power; hard 156–57; soft 140; sovereign 39
pre-emption 142, 146, 150, 199n38

public statements, as evidence 27–29
Puerto Rico 63

Quadrennial Defence Reviews 156–57

realists and realism 2, 2–3, 5, 8, 10–14, 15, 16, 20, 29, 62, 157–58, 177n12, 177n14; moralism 169; Roosevelt's 62, 69–71, 73–74, 84, 169
regime change 142, 152
Revolutionary War, the 31, 47
Rice, Condoleezza 142, 148, 150–51, 153, 153–54
righteousness 74
rogue regimes 142–43, 162
Roosevelt, Franklin 114, 116, 116–18
Roosevelt, Kermit 73
Roosevelt, Theodore 4, 7, 24–25, 61–85, 111, 157, 169–70, 174; as Assistant Secretary of the Navy 63, 64, 71; becomes president 65; comparison with Wilson 88–89, 109; context 63–64; death 83; on Europe 68; and the First World War 78–83; imperialism 66–67, 74–78, 169–70; interventionism 7; liberalism 76, 78, 83; militarism 67–69, 73–74, 81–82, 83–84, 124; moralism 71–74; Naval War College address 67–68, 69; Nobel Prize for Peace 70–71; and peace 73; personal exuberance 65; realism 62, 69–71, 73–74, 84, 169; role in Russo-Japanese War 70–71; Strenuous Life speech 66, 67; and the use of force 81–82; as vice president 64–65, 65; on war 69, 78–79
Root, Elihu 109
Russia 33, 64, 80, 82–83, 151, 162
Russo-Japanese War 70–71

Saddam Hussein 144, 147, 152, 153
Saratoga, battle of 31
Scowcroft, Brent 149
Second World War 4, 62, 113, 114, 115–16, 121, 171
security 81
self-determination 77, 103, 120, 171
self-government 145
separateness 57
September 11, 2001 terrorist attacks 141, 142, 164
Seven Years' War 31
Shays' Rebellion 34
slaves and slavery 41
soft power 140

South America 55
sovereign power 39
Soviet Union 8, 115, 137, 172; Clifford–Elsey Report analysis 131–33; collapse of 139, 180n53; deterioration of relations with 116–19; expansion 121, 128; ideology 126–27; Kennan's analysis of 126–30; leadership 128–29, 132; NSC-68 analysis 133–36; paranoia 127; and the Second World War 116; threat 119; totalitarianism 127–28; in Truman's conception of the Cold War 119–26; worldview 126–27
Spain 33, 55, 63–64
Spanish–American War (1898) 7, 63–64, 64, 186n5
spheres-of-influence 56–57, 75, 84, 91, 118, 120, 122, 135, 172
Spring-Rice, Cecil 68, 79
Stalin, Josef 116, 117, 118, 119, 194n12
state sovereignty 34–35
strategic visions 1
structuration 25

Taft, Robert 193n4
Taft, William H. 89
Taliban, the 142, 153
tariffs 42
terrorism 18, 152; September 11, 2001 attacks 141, 142, 164; threat 142
Thucydides, 11
torture 181n58
trade 42–43
tradition 1
Truman, Harry 4, 8–9, 24–25, 114–38, 139, 154, 166, 172, 174; assumes office 116–19; and the Clifford–Elsey Report 115, 130–33; and Communism 120–21; comparison with Wilson 124; conception of the Cold War 119–26; context 115–16; deterioration of relations with Soviet Union 116–19; emergence of Cold War Policy 118–19; farewell address 121–22; and FDR 116–19; and military power 124–25; and NSC-68 115, 125, 130–31, 133–36; on the Soviet Union 121–22
Truman Doctrine 119, 120, 122–23, 126, 138
Turkey 82, 119, 120, 125
Turner, Frederick Jackson 179n32

unilateralism 19
Union, the: as balance of power 32; establishment of 32, 36–41
United Nations 117–18
United States of America: achieves independence 31, 33; commercial imperialism 90; deterioration of relations with Soviet Union 116–19; empire 17–19, 30, 76; entry into First World War 86, 89, 112, 170–71; entry into the global system 100; establishment 6; external influence 18; hegemony 2, 9, 14–15, 58, 59, 70, 74, 75, 156–57, 164; justification of war entry 94–96; Kennan's role for 128–30; national destiny 107–8, 129; neutrality 79; Neutrality Acts 114; NSC-68 goals for 134–36; perception of national youth 1; political stability 27; power capabilities 14; primacy 105–8, 155; and the Second World War 116; self image 6; territorial expansion 61; universalization of values 2, 25
universal cooperation 7
universalism 19, 30, 86, 87, 104, 115, 125, 136, 172

values: convergence of 150–53; liberal 2; shared 1; universalization of American 2, 25
Venezuela 69, 70, 74
Villa, Pancho 91
Virginia plan, the 35

Wallace, Henry 125
Waltz, Kenneth 11, 176n2, 177n3, 180n51
War of Independence; *see* Revolutionary War, the
war on terror 146, 148, 152, 158
warfare 36
Washington, George 35, 41, 43, 47, 48–49, 98, 124, 182n26; Farewell Address 49–52, 52, 53, 54, 57, 168, 184n61
Washington Post 149
Waterloo, Battle of 55

weapons of mass destruction (WMD) 142, 143, 152, 153, 163
West Point Military Academy 144, 151
Westernization 145
Williams, Michael C. 18
Willkie, Wendell 118
Wilson, Woodrow 4, 7–8, 8, 24–25, 27, 29, 61, 73, 79, 83, 86–113, 118, 121, 153, 154, 157, 169, 170–71, 174, 175, 181n54; and American primacy 105–8; Armistice Day address, 1923 111; on autocracy 103–4; comparison with Roosevelt 88–89, 109; comparison with Truman 124; context 87–88; and the First World War 80–81, 86, 97, 112, 170; foundation of League of Nations 98; and Germany 102, 110; goals 100, 104; idealism 70, 89–90; ideology 96, 102, 112–13; internationalism 7–8; justification of war entry 94–96, 170–71; Latin American policy 90–94, 112; and moral force 108–9; morality and moralism 88–89, 109–11; and national interests 100–102; Pan-American Pact 93–94; Paris Peace Conference 83; rejection of the balance of power 96–100, 102; and universal democracy 102–5; universalist principles 86, 87; worldview 107, 171
Wilsonianism 7–8, 62, 75, 87, 100–102, 103, 112–13, 170, 172; *see also* Wilson, Woodrow
Woodward, Bob 152
World Trade Centre, September 11, 2001 terrorist attacks 141
worldviews 1, 5; alternative principles for Bush administration 160–62; Bush administration 143, 155–56, 159–60, 166, 173–75; and national ideology 173–75; Soviet Union 126–27; Wilson's 107, 171

XYZ affair 53, 184n65

Yalta Conference 117, 118

Zimmermann Telegram, the 102

eBooks – at www.eBookstore.tandf.co.uk

A library at your fingertips!

eBooks are electronic versions of printed books. You can store them on your PC/laptop or browse them online.

They have advantages for anyone needing rapid access to a wide variety of published, copyright information.

eBooks can help your research by enabling you to bookmark chapters, annotate text and use instant searches to find specific words or phrases. Several eBook files would fit on even a small laptop or PDA.

NEW: Save money by eSubscribing: cheap, online access to any eBook for as long as you need it.

Annual subscription packages

We now offer special low-cost bulk subscriptions to packages of eBooks in certain subject areas. These are available to libraries or to individuals.

For more information please contact webmaster.ebooks@tandf.co.uk

We're continually developing the eBook concept, so keep up to date by visiting the website.

www.eBookstore.tandf.co.uk

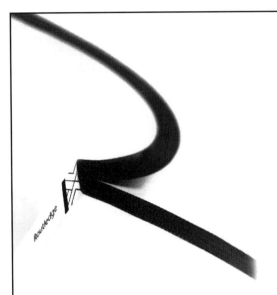

Routledge Paperbacks Direct

Bringing you the cream of our hardback publishing at paperback prices

This exciting new initiative makes the best of our hardback publishing available in paperback format for authors and individual customers.

Routledge Paperbacks Direct is an ever-evolving programme with new titles being added regularly.

To take a look at the titles available, visit our website.

www.routledgepaperbacksdirect.com

Printed in Great Britain
by Amazon.co.uk, Ltd.,
Marston Gate.